WAR CRIMES

Incinerated body of an Iraqi soldier on the "Highway of Death," a name the
press has given to the road from Mutlaa, Kuwait, to Basra, Iraq. U.S. planes
immobilized the convoy by disabling vehicles at its front and rear, then
bombing and straffing the resulting traffic jam for hours. More than 2,000
vehicles and tens of thousands of charred and dismembered bodies littered the
sixty miles of highway. The clear rapid incineration of the human being on the
cover suggests the use of napalm, phosphorous, or other incendiary bombs.
These are anti-personnel weapons outlawed under the 1977 Geneva Protocols.
This massive attack occurred after Saddam Hussein announced a complete
troop withdrawl from Kuwait in compliance with UN Resolution 660. Such a
massacre of withdrawing Iraqi soldiers violates the Geneva Convention of 1949,
common article 3, which outlaws the killing of soldiers who "are out of
combat." There are, in addition, strong indications that many of those killed
were Palestinian and Kuwaiti civilians trying to escape the impending seige of
Kuwait City and the return of Kuwaiti armed forces. No attempt was made by
U.S. military command to distinguish between military personnel and civilians
on the "highway of death." The whole intent of international law with regard
to war is to prevent just this sort of indescriminate and excessive use of force.
(Photo Credit: © 1991 Kenneth Jarecke / Contact Press Images)
    Cover: a market place in Basra after intense U.S. bombing.

War Crimes

A Report on United States War Crimes Against Iraq

Ramsey Clark

and

Others

Maisonneuve Press

Washington, D.C. 1992

Ramsey Clark and Others, *War Crimes: A Report on United States War Crimes Against Iraq.*

Copyright © 1992 by The Commission of Inquiry for the International War Crimes Tribunal
  36 East 12th Street, New York, NY 10003
  phone 212-254-5385 / fax 212-979-1583

Published by Maisonneuve Press
  P. O. Box 2980, Washington, D.C. 20013

Library of Congress Cataloging-in-Publication Data

War crimes: a report on United States war crimes against Iraq /   Ramsey Clark and others.
     p.   cm.
    Includes bibliographical notes
    Index
    1. Persian Gulf War, 1991 -- Destruction and pillage. 2. Persian Gulf War, 1991 –United States. I. Clark, Ramsey, 1927- .

DS79.736.W37 1992	91-48036
956.704'3--dc20	CIP

ISBN 0-944624-15-4 (pbk.)

Printed in the United States

Dedication

This book is dedicated to the memory of the more than 200,000 Iraqi people who were killed in an intense high-tech slaughter that was carried out in the forty-two days between January 16th and February 27th 1991.

This book is also dedicated to the ongoing international struggle against continued U.S. aggression. The shooting war may be over but the deadly character of U.S. policy continues to wreak havoc and suffering on the people of Iraq. Unless the draconian economic sanctions are lifted, tens of thousands will continue to die from malnutrition and disease.

This international effort is undertaken in the belief that millions of lives in future generations can be saved by exposing and mobilizing against the crimes of the past.

Preface

The material in this book was compiled by the Commission of Inquiry for the International War Crimes Tribunal. Most of the material in the first part of the book was originally presented at the first hearings of the Commission of Inquiry in New York City on May 11, 1991. More than 1,000 people attended the hearings held at Stuyvesant Auditorium. Since the announcement of the formation of the Commission of Inquiry, organizations world-wide have come forward to participate and to offer evidence and testimony. A few selections of this additional testimony from other Commission hearings have been included where space permits. Commissions of Inquiry have been established in fifteen countries around the world, and public hearings where new testimony was presented were held in twenty-eight cities in the U.S. Obviously a great deal of this valuable material could not be presented in the short confines of this book.

At the May 11, 1991, hearing in New York, former U.S. Attorney General Ramsey Clark outlined the 19-point indictment of the U.S. government's conduct in the Gulf War that served as the basis of the Commission's work. For seven hours eyewitnesses who had traveled to Iraq during and following the war presented evidence on the extensive and deliberate destruction of Iraq's infrastructure.

Compelling video testimony was shown. Images of destroyed neighborhoods, shrapnel and burn victims, dehydrated and undernourished children in hospitals lacking electricity and necessary drugs were displayed in a photo exhibit. Some of these photos are also included in this book.

The Commission of Inquiry for an International War Crimes Tribunal was initiated by Ramsey Clark and the Coalition to Stop U.S. Intervention in the Middle East following Mr. Clark's February trip to Iraq. Accompanied by a video filmmaker and a photographer, Mr. Clark traveled 2,000 miles through Iraq during a time when the U.S. was running up to 3,000 bombing sorties a day. He first documented the systematic destruction of the civilian infrastructure, a view later confirmed by a number of other delegations and even by the United Nation's own team of investigators.

The Commission of Inquiry was established to gather testimony and evidence on an international basis and to present the testimony in a series of public hearings. Evidence gathered at all these hearings is to be presented to an international Tribunal of Judges on February 27, 28, and 29, 1992 in New York—the one-year anniversary of the war.

This book contains in the Appendix the information detailing the extent of the destruction that Ramsey Clark originally presented in a letter to then United Nations Secretary General Javier Pérez de Cuéllar and President George Bush and released to the world press. Other eyewitness reports and passages from several of the international laws and conventions along with U.S. Representative Henry Gonzalez's Resolution of Impeachment of President Bush on the basis of violations of the U.S. Constitution, the United Nations Charter and international laws have also been included.

Acknowledgments

This book represents the combined efforts of many hundreds of people who have helped to present and publicize much of this material. The staff of the Commission consisted of Adeeb Abed, Teresa Gutierrez, Brian Becker, Gavrielle Gemma, Sara Flounders, Bill Doares, Karen Talbot, and Phil Wilayto.

Special acknowledgment should be given to the New York Research Committee which spent many hours filing reports, gathering the footnotes and checking facts. This committee was coordinated by Michelle Le Blanc and Barbara Nell Perrin and included Wallace Cheatham, Magie L. Dominic, Chris Beauchamp, Kathy Avakian, David Finklestein, Max Becher, Andrea Robbins, Pat Hockmeyer, Brian Becker, Thelma Easy, Stephan Patty, Beth Barnsley, Bonna Whitten-Stoval and Paudy Hopkins.

We want to specially acknowledge the contributions of Prof. Francis Boyle, M. A. Samad-Matias, Bob Schwartz, Yuriko Okiwara, Joan Sekler, Samori Marksman, Jan van Heurck, Hugh Stephans, Richard Becker, John Philpot, and David Jacobs.

In addition, Betsy Gimbel and Rosemary Neidenberg spent many hours transcribing tapes of talks and testimony. Help in editing this material was provided by John Catalinotto and Gary Wilson. Paddy Colligan and Greg Dunkel did the copy-editing and proof-reading.

Lal Rookh designed the cover and Kate Castle drew the cover graphic.

This book would not have been possible without the help of our publisher Maisonneuve Press. Special thanks to Robert Merrill of Maisonneuve Press who recognized the importance of establishing a permanent record of the work of the International Commission of Inquiry. His active participation and encouragement in each step and his final editing of the abundance of material made all the difference.

Contents

Preface and Acknowledgements   vii
The Tribunal's Final Judgment, February 29, 1992   1

Part One: The Charges
Initial Complaint Charging George Bush,   9
    J. Danforth Quayle, James Baker, Richard Cheney,
    William Webster, Colin Powell, Norman Schwarzkopf and
    Others to be Named with Crimes Against Peace,
    War Crimes, Crimes Against Humanity

Part Two: The Basis in International Law
Why an Inquiry / Sara Flounders   29
The Legal and Moral Basis for an International   32
    War Crimes Tribunal / Ramsey Clark
International Law and War Crimes / Michael Ratner   39
War Crimes Committed Against the People   47
    of Iraq / Francis Kelly

Part Three: Testimony and Evidence
Provoking Iraq / Gautam Biswas and Tony Murphy   63
U.S. Conspiracy to Initiate the War Against Iraq / Brian Becker 74
The Myth of Surgical Bombing in the Gulf War / Paul Walker   83
The Massacre of Withdrawing Soldiers on "The   90
    Highway of Death" / Joyce Chediac
The Effects of the War on Health Care in Iraq   94
    / David Levinson

The Impact of Sanctions on Baghdad's Children's   99
    Hospital / Ann Montgomery
The Impact of the War on Iraqi Society / Adeeb Abed   102
    and Gavrielle Gemma
Eyewitness Interviews   119
Crimes Against Egyptian and Palestinian   139
    Civilians in Iraq / Mustafa El Bakri
Waging War on Civilization / Fadwa El Guindi   146
The Attack on the Women's Peace Ship / E. Faye Williams   158
The Truth Behind Economic Sanctions: Report on the   164
    Embargo of Food and Medicines / Eric Hoskins

Part Four: The New World Order

The New World Order: What It Is and   173
    How to Fight It / Monica Moorehead
The Demonization of Saddam Hussein: A Violation of the   176
    UN Convention Against Racism / Esmeralda Brown
The Impact of the Gulf War on Women   180
    and Children / Nawal El Saadawi
The Continuing War and the Kurds / Ali Azad   184
Government Attacks and Violence Against Arab   188
    People / Neal Saad
The Gulf War: A Crime Against the Peoples of Africa   191
    and Asia / Karen Talbot
Yemen: A Victim of the Bribery and Corruption of   193
    the UN / Abdel Hameed Noaman
Expulsion of Guest Workers and the Impact   195
    on Africa / M. A. Samad-Matias
Palestine and the Gulf War / Houda Gazalwin   198
The Harsh Government Prosecution of   201
    Military Resisters / William Kunstler
The Old World Order and the Causes of the   204
    Gulf War / Tony Benn

Appendix A: International Law

Selections from the Geneva Conventions 211
Selections from the Principles of the Nuremberg Tribunals 217
Selections from the United Nations Charter 219

Appendix B: Background Documents for the Tribunal

The Announcement of the Formation of a Commission 223
of Inquiry
A Letter to Javier Pérez de Cuéllar / Ramsey Clark 227
A Letter to Claiborne Pell / Ramsey Clark 234
Selections from The Report to the Secretary General 236
on Humanitarian Needs in Kuwait
and Iraq / Martti Ahtisaari
H.Res. 86: A Motion to Impeach George 245
Bush / Henry Gonzalez
H.Res. 180: A Resolution to Lift the 248
Economic Embargo
on Iraq / Henry Gonzalez
The April Glaspie Connection 250

Appendix C: International Tribunals

Report from Belgium 259
Report from Turkey 266
Report from East Asia 274

Index 277

The Final Judgment

The International War Crimes Tribunal

The February 29, 1992, International War Crimes Tribunal was the culmination of one of the largest independent worldwide investigations into war crimes ever undertaken.

Founded a year before, the Commission of Inquiry for the International War Crimes Tribunal issued a call to the people of the entire world to hold independent peoples' investigations into the causes of the Gulf war and the conduct of its participants. The charge of war crimes against the U.S. for its conduct in the war, made by political forces in within the United States, inspired a wave of similar actions across the world. Pacifist groups, anti-imperialist groups, trade unions, mass organizations, members of parliaments, and official religious bodies joined to call Commission of Inquiry hearings in twenty countries in Europe, Africa, the Middle East, south and east Asia, and in at least twenty-four cities in North America. Thousands of people took part, representing millions more people all around the world. Many local commissions brought and substantiated charges against their own governments. Before 1,000 people in New York on May 11, 1991, Ramsey Clark charged George Bush and his lieutenants with nineteen counts of war crimes, crimes against peace, and crimes against humanity. These nineteen charges became the basis of all the other international hearings.

The fact that large and culturally diverse groups could hold internationally coordinated public scrutinies of both the United States' and their own governments' role in a "popular" war is in itself a surprising achievement. It is all the more significant that this was accomplished without support from any government or international agency. This form of grassroots political activism had not been attempted before.

At the final February 29, 1992 Tribunal, Ramsey Clark and the Commission of Inquiry research staff prepared a summary of the charges and evidence based on material gathered at Commission hearings and presented it to a panel of judges. It included testimony from witnesses such as Mohammed Khader, a Palestinian living in Baghdad during the war, who told how "smart bombs" killed hundreds of civilians at the Ameriyh shelter on February 13, 1991, including his wife and four daughters. Included also were computer print-outs of every installation hit by U.S. and allied bombs.

In addition to oral testimony and documents, the Commission made available photographic, videotape, and audio evidence.

The panel of judges included internationally known civil and human rights activists, legal scholars, and freedom fighters. Some have served in the governments of their countries, others have served time in prison for their efforts on behalf of human rights. The judges reflected a diversity of cultures, nationalities, and ideologies. After reviewing all of the evidence and testimony, the panel returned its judgment (printed below).

The aim of the Tribunal was to demand that the U.S. government be held accountable for its actions and to stop future war crimes. Its goal was to arouse and organize anger and opposition to U.S. policies which involve the use of military force against developing nations, whether through direct U.S. intervention or through the use of surrogate or covert armies. In rebuilding an organized political opposition to the war, these mass hearings played an important role. This was a public inquiry fueled by the determination that the victors would not write the history of this war. It is critical for this and future generations to learn the true history of the Gulf war.

The major U.S. media did not cover the tribunal at all. This glaring censorship is all the more apparent when contrasted to the coverage that the press from a number of other countries accorded to this unprecedented event. Delegates had come from thirty-three countries. International media focussed on the drama of a public Tribunal with 1,500 observers packing a hall in New York City to hear evidence of U.S. war crimes. The aura of U.S. invincibility was cracking. Two of Japan's three largest daily papers, Tokyo Broadcasting System, Danish National Television, newspapers throughout the Middle East and North Africa all gave major coverage. The largest Urdu and English language papers in Pakistan, although denied visas by the State Department to come to the Tribunal, published extensive reports. A number of international reporters based at the United Nations filed stories. Media throughout Europe, from Sweden to Italy, covered news conferences hosted by delegations returning from New York. Within the U.S., listener-sponsored radio stations gave detailed coverage, as did African American weekly newspapers, much of the Spanish language media, and a number of progressive news weeklies.

Despite the censorship of the major U.S. media, the information so strictly suppressed will continue to seep out. This book, now in its second printing, is a living part of a continuing struggle for truth and justice.

Seventy-five years ago those who opposed World War I, as a battle of the great imperialist powers to re-divide and carve up the world markets, were jailed and denounced as traitors. But today who would describe that war, which cost twenty million lives, as a "war to end all wars" or much less a "war to make the world safe for democracy"? The perception and understanding of the Gulf war also will change. But many thousands of people are determined not to wait a generation for the research of historians through old archives to bring out the real economic and political interests that led up to the Gulf war and determined the conduct of the aggressors. The policy must be understood and opposed now because other U.S. wars and interventions are on the agenda of the New World Order.

The panel of Tribunal Judges and the international delegates came not just to hear the evidence of a past U.S. war. They challenged the Commission staff to consider ways to continue their international collaboration and exchange of information. The first step was the founding of the new International Action Center in New York City.

Truth is a powerful weapon. Heightened cooperation between international contacts could prevent further U.S. militarism, not just respond to it. The International Action Center will help to provide continuing opposition to U.S. intervention around the world. The Center will help with organizing support on difficult international issues, such as the continuing attacks on Cuba, the CIA support of the military coup in Haiti, and the continuing Israeli occupation of Palestinian territory.

This is the challenge in the work ahead and it is the challenge in reading the testimony in this book. The world cannot be viewed in isolated, unconnected segments. Learning about these hearings and the judgment will help the reader develop a clearer understanding of the real issues behind the assault on Iraq and an appreciation of the international movement that organized a powerful struggle for truth. This the hope for the future.

Adeeb Abed
Sara Flounders

The Commission of Inquiry
for the International
War Crimes Tribunal

Final Judgment: International War Crimes Tribunal

The members of the International War Crimes Tribunal, meeting in New York, have carefully considered the Initial Complaint of the Commission of Inquiry dated May 6, 1991 against President George H. W. Bush, Vice President J. Danforth Quayle, Secretary of Defense Richard Cheney, Gen. Norman Schwarzkopf Commander of the Allied Forces in the Persian Gulf, and others named in the Complaint charging them with nineteen separate crimes against peace, war crimes, and crimes against humanity in violation of the Charter of the United Nations, the 1949 Geneva Conventions, the First Protocol thereto, and other international agreements and customary international law:

having the right and obligation as citizens of the world to sit in judgment regarding violations of international humanitarian law;

having heard the testimony from various Commissions of Inquiry hearings held within their own countries and/or elsewhere during the past year and having received reports from numerous other Commission hearings which recite the evidence there gathered;

having been provided with documentary evidence, eyewitness statements, photos, videotapes, special reports, expert analyses and summaries of evidence available to the Commission;

having access to all evidence, knowledge, and expert opinion in the Commission files or available to the Commission;

having been provided by the Commission, or elsewhere obtained, various books, articles, and other written materials on various aspects of events and conditions in the Persian Gulf and military and arms establishments;

having considered newspaper coverage, magazine and periodical reports, special publications, T.V., radio, and other media coverage and public statements by the accused, other public officials and other public materials;

having heard the presentations of the Commission of Inquiry in public hearing on February 29, 1992, the testimony and evidence there presented;

and having met, considered and deliberated with each other and with Commission staff and having considered all the evidence that is relevant to the nineteen charges of criminal conduct alleged in the Initial Complaint make the following findings.

Findings

The members of the International War Crimes Tribunal finds each of the named accused Guilty on the basis of the evidence against them and that each of the nineteen crimes alleged in the Initial Complaint, attached hereto, has been established to have been committed beyond a reasonable doubt.

The members believe that it is imperative if there is ever to be peace that power be accountable for its criminal acts and we condemn in the strongest possible terms those found guilty of the charges herein. We urge the Commission of Inquiry and all people to act on recommendations developed by the Commission to hold power accountable and to secure social justice on which lasting peace must be based.

Recommendations

The Members urge the immediate revocation of all embargoes, sanctions and penalties against Iraq because they constitute a continuing crime against humanity.

The Members urge public action to prevent new aggressions by the United States threatened against Iraq, Libya, Cuba, Haiti, North Korea, Pakistan and other countries and the Palestine people; fullest condemnation of any threat or use of military technology against life, both civilian and military, as was used by the United States against the people of Iraq.

The Members urge that the power of the United Nations Security Council, which was blatantly manipulated by the U.S. to authorize illegal military action and sanctions, be vested in the General Assembly; that all permanent members be removed and that the right of veto be eliminated as undemocratic and contrary to the basic principles of the U.N. Charter.

The Members urge the Commission to provide for the permanent preservation of the reports, evidence, and materials gathered to make them available to others, and to seek ways to provide the widest possible distribution of the truth about the U.S. assault on Iraq.

Charges of Other Countries

In accordance with the last paragraph of the Initial Complaint designated Scope of Inquiry, the Commission has gatherd substantial evidence of criminal acts by governments and individual officials in addition to those formally presented here. Formal charges have been drafted by some Commissions of Inquiry against other governments in addition to the United States. Those charges have not been acted upon here. The Commission of Inquiry or any of its national components may choose to pursue such other charges at some future time. The Members urge all involved to exert their utmost effort to prevent recurrences of violations by other governments that were not considered here.

Done in New York this 29th day of February, 1992.

(signed)

Olga Mejia, Panama
President of the National Human
Rights Commission in Panama, a non-
governmental body representing
peasants' organizations, urban trade
unions, women's groups and others.

Sheik Mohamed Rashid, Pakistan
Former deputy prime minister. Long-
term political prisoner during the
struggle against British colonialism and
activist for workers' and peasants' rights.

Dr. Haluk Gerger, Turkey
Founding member of Turkish Human Rights Association and professor of political science. Dismissed from Ankara University by military government.

Susumu Ozaki, Japan
Former judge and pro-labor attorney imprisoned 1934-1938 for violating Security Law under militarist government for opposing Japan's invasion of China.

Bassam Haddadin, Jordan
Member of Parliament, Second Secretary for the Jordanian Democratic Peoples Party. Member of Parliamentary Committee on Palestine.

Dr. Sherif Hetata, Egypt
Medical Doctor, author, member of the Central Committee of the Arab Progressive Unionist Party. Political prisoner 14 years in 1950s and 1960s.

Deborah Jackson, USA
First vice president of the American Association of Jurists, former director of National Conference of Black Lawyers.

Opato Matamah, Menominee Nation of North America
Involved in defense of human rights of indigenous peoples since 1981. Represented the International Indian Treaty Council at the Commission of Human Rights at the U.N.

Laura Albizu, Campos Meneses, Puerto Rico
Past President of the Puerto Rican Nationalist Party and current Secretary for Foreign Relations. Honorary president of Peace Council.

Aisha Nyerere, Tanzania
Resident Magistrate of the High Court in Arusha, Tanzania. Researched the impact of the Gulf war on East Africa.

Peter Leibovtich, Canada
President of United Steel Workers of America, USWA, Local 8782 and of the Executive Council of the Ontario Federation of Labor.

John Philpot, Quebec
Attorney, member of Board of Directors of Quebec Movement for Sovereignty. Organizing Secretary for the American Association of Jurist in Canada.

Lord Tony Gifford, Britain
Human rights lawyer practicing in England and Jamaica. Investigated human rights abuses in British-occupied Ireland.

John Jones, USA
Community leader in the state of New Jersey. Vietnam veteran who became leader of movement against U.S. attack on Iraq.

Gloria La Riva, USA
Founding member of the Farmworkers Emergency Relief Committee and Emergency Committee to Stop the U.S. War in the Middle East in San Francisco.

Key Martin, USA
Member of Executive Committee of Local 3 of the Newspaper Guild in New York. Jailed in 1967 for taking message of Bertrand Russell Tribunal on Vietnam to active duty GIs.

Dr. Alfred Mechtersheimer, Germany
Former member of the Bundestag from the Green Party. Former Lieutenant Colonel in the Bundeswher; current peace researcher.

Michael Ratner, USA
Attorney, former director of the Center for Constitutional Rights, past president of the National Lawyers Guild.

Abderrazak Kilani, Tunisia
Tunisian Bar Association. Former President, Association of Young Lawyers; founding member, National Committee to Lift the Embargo from Iraq.

René Dumont, France
Agronomist, ecologist, specialist in agriculture of developing countries, author. His 45th book, *This War Dishonors Us*, appears in 1992.

Tan Sri Ahmad Noordin bin Zakaria, Malaysia
Former Auditor General of Malaysia. Known throughout his country for battling corruption in government.

P. S. Poti, India
Former Chief Justice of the Gujarat High Court. In 1989 elected president of the All-India Lawyers Union.

Part One:

The Charges

The civilian infrastructure was directly targeted. This photo shows the Al Jisser al Mualaq suspension bridge in Baghdad. Three Baghdad bridges were destroyed. They are vital arteries straddling the Tigris River and linking a city of three million people. Sixty-one bridges were bombed throughout Iraq, most of them several times. Bridges are essential for transporting supplies to the civilian population. (Photo: Commission of Inquiry for the International War Crimes Tribunal, April 1991)

Initial Complaint

Charging

George Bush, J. Danforth Quayle, James Baker,
Richard Cheney, William Webster, Colin Powell,
Norman Schwarzkopf and Others to be named

With

Crimes Against Peace, War Crimes, Crimes Against
Humanity and Other Criminal Acts and High Crimes in
Violation of the Charter of the United Nations,
International Law, the Constitution of the United States
and Laws made in Pursuance Thereof.

Preliminary Statement

These charges have been prepared prior to the first hearing of the Commission of Inquiry by its staff. They are based on direct and circumstantial evidence from public and private documents; official statements and admissions by the persons charged and others; eyewitness accounts; Commission investigations and witness interviews in Iraq, the Middle East and elsewhere during and after the bombing; photographs and video tape; expert analyses; commentary and interviews; media coverage, published reports and accounts gathered between December 1990 and May 1991. Commission of Inquiry hearings will be held in key cities where evidence is available supporting, expanding, adding, contradicting, disproving or explaining these, or similar charges against the accused and others of whatever nationality. When evidence sufficient to sustain convictions of the accused or others is obtained and after demanding the production of documents from the U.S. government, and others, and requesting testimony from the accused, offering them a full opportunity to present any defense personally, or by counsel, the evidence will be presented to an International War Crimes Tribunal. The Tribunal will consider the evidence gathered, seek and examine whatever additional evidence it chooses and render its judgment on the charges, the evidence, and the law.

Background

Since World War I, the United Kingdom, France, and the United States have dominated the Arabian Peninsula and Gulf region and its oil resources. This has been accomplished by military conquest and coercion, economic control and exploitation, and through surrogate governments and their military forces. Thus, from 1953 to 1979 in the post World War II era, control over the region was exercised primarily through U.S. influence and control over the Gulf sheikdoms of Saudi Arabia and through the Shah of Iran. From 1953 to 1979 the Shah of Iran acted as a Pentagon/CIA surrogate to police the region. After the fall of the Shah and the seizure of U.S. Embassy hostages in Teheran, the U.S. provided military aid and assistance to Iraq, as did the USSR, Saudi Arabia, Kuwait and most of the Emirates, in its war with Iran. U.S. policy during that tragic eight year war, 1980 – 1988, is probably best summed up by the phrase, "we hope they kill each other."

Throughout the seventy-five year period from Britain's invasion of Iraq early in World War I to the destruction of Iraq in 1991 by U.S. air power, the United States and the United Kingdom demonstrated no concern for democratic values, human rights, social justice, or political and cultural integrity in the region, nor for stopping military aggression there. The U.S. supported the Shah of Iran for 25 years, selling him more than $20 billion of advanced military equipment between 1972 and 1978 alone. Throughout this period the Shah and his brutal secret police called SAVAK had one of the worst human rights records in the world. Then in the 1980s, the U.S. supported Iraq in its wrongful aggression against Iran, ignoring Iraq's own poor human rights record.[1]

When the Iraqi government nationalized the Iraqi Petroleum Company in 1972, the Nixon Administration embarked on a campaign to destabilize the Iraqi government. It was in the 1970s that the U.S. first armed and then abandoned the Kurdish people, costing tens of thousands of Kurdish lives. The U.S. manipulated the Kurds through CIA and other agencies to attack Iraq, intending to harass Iraq while maintaining Iranian supremacy at the cost of Kurdish lives without intending any benefit to the Kurdish people or an autonomous Kurdistan.[2]

The U.S. with close oil and other economic ties to Saudi Arabia and Kuwait has fully supported both governments despite the total absence of democratic institutions, their pervasive human rights violations and the infliction of cruel, inhuman and degrading punishments such as stoning to death for adultery and amputation of a hand for property offenses.

The U.S., sometimes alone among nations, supported Israel when it defied scores of UN resolutions concerning Palestinian rights, when it invaded Lebanon in a war which took tens of thousands of lives, and during its continuing occupation of southern Lebanon, the Golan Heights, the West Bank and Gaza.

The United States itself engaged in recent aggressions in violation of international law by invading Grenada in 1983, bombing Tripoli and Benghazi in Libya in 1986, financing the *contra* in Nicaragua, UNITA in southern Africa and supporting military dictatorships in Liberia, Chile, El Salvador, Guatemala, the Philippines, and many other places.

The U.S. invasion of Panama in December 1989 involved the same and additional violations of international law that apply to Iraq's invasion of Kuwait. The U.S. invasion took between 1,000 and 4,000 Panamanian lives. The United States government is still covering up the death toll. U.S. aggression caused massive property destruction throughout Panama.[3] According to U.S. and international human rights organization estimates, Kuwait's casualties from Iraq's invasion and the ensuing months of occupation were in the "hundreds"—between 300 and 600.[4] Reports from Kuwait list 628 Palestinians killed by Kuwaiti death squads since the Sabah royal family regained control over Kuwait.

The United States changed its military plans for protecting its control over oil and other interests in the Arabian Peninsula in the late 1980s when it became clear that economic problems in the USSR were debilitating its military capacity and Soviet forces withdrew from Afghanistan. Thereafter, direct military domination within the region became the U.S. strategy.

With the decline in U.S. oil production through 1989, experts predicted U.S. oil imports from the Gulf would rise from 10% that year to 25% by the year 2000. Japanese and European dependency is much greater.[5]

The Charges

1. The United States engaged in a pattern of conduct beginning in or before 1989 intended to lead Iraq into provocations justifying U.S. military action against Iraq and permanent U.S. military domination of the Gulf.

In 1989, General Colin Powell, Chairman of the Joint Chiefs of Staff, and General Norman Schwarzkopf, Commander in Chief of the Central Command, completely revised U.S. military operations and plans for the Persian Gulf to prepare to intervene in a regional conflict against Iraq. The CIA assisted and directed Kuwait in its actions. At the time, Kuwait was violating OPEC oil production agreements, extracting excessive amounts of oil from pools shared with Iraq and demanding repayment of loans it made to Iraq during the Iran-Iraq war. Kuwait broke off negotiations with Iraq over these disputes. The U.S. intended to provoke Iraq into actions against Kuwait that would justify U.S. intervention.

In 1989, CIA Director William Webster testified before the Congress about the alarming increase in U.S. importation of Gulf oil, citing U.S. rise in use from 5% in 1973 to 10% in 1989 and predicting 25% of all U.S. oil consumption would come from the region by 2000.[6] In early 1990, General Schwarzkopf informed the Senate Armed Services Committee of the new military strategy in the Gulf designed to protect U.S. access to and control over Gulf oil in the event of regional conflicts.

In July 1990, General Schwarzkopf and his staff ran elaborate, computerized war games pitting about 100,000 U.S. troops against Iraqi armored divisions.

The U.S. showed no opposition to Iraq's increasing threats against Kuwait. U.S. companies sought major contracts in Iraq. The Congress approved agricultural loan subsidies to Iraq of hundreds of millions of dollars to benefit U.S. farmers. However, loans for food deliveries of rice, corn, wheat and other essentials bought almost exclusively from the U.S. were cut off in the spring of 1990 to cause shortages. Arms were sold to Iraq by U.S. manufacturers. When Saddam Hussein requested U.S. Ambassador April Glaspie to explain State Department testimony in Congress about Iraq's threats against Kuwait, she assured him the U.S. considered the dispute a regional concern, and it would not intervene. By these acts, the U.S. intended to lead Iraq into a provocation justifying war.

On August 2, 1990, Iraq occupied Kuwait without significant resistance.

On August 3, 1990, without any evidence of a threat to Saudi Arabia, and King Fahd believed Iraq had no intention of invading his country, President Bush vowed to defend Saudi Arabia. He sent Secretary Cheney, General Powell, and General Schwarzkopf almost immediately to Saudi Arabia where on August 6, General Schwarzkopf told King Fahd the U.S. thought Saddam Hussein could attack Saudi Arabia in as little as 48 hours. The efforts toward an Arab solution of the crisis were destroyed. Iraq never attacked Saudi Arabia and waited over five months while the U.S. slowly built a force of more than 500,000 soldiers and began the systematic destruction by aircraft and missiles of Iraq and its military, both defenseless against U.S. and coalition technology. In October 1990, General Powell referred to the new military plan developed in 1989. After the war, General Schwarzkopf referred to eighteen months of planning for the campaign.

The U.S. retains troops in Iraq as of May 1991 and throughout the region and has announced its intention to maintain a permanent military presence.

This course of conduct constitutes a crime against peace.

2. President Bush from August 2, 1990, intended and acted to prevent any interference with his plan to destroy Iraq economically and militarily.

Without consultation or communication with Congress, President Bush ordered 40,000 U.S. military personnel to advance the U.S. buildup in Saudi Arabia in the first week of August 1990. He exacted a request from Saudi Arabia for U.S. military assistance and on August 8, 1990, assured the world his acts were "wholly defensive." He waited until after the November 1990 elections to announce his earlier order sending more than 200,000 additional military personnel, clearly an assault force, again without advising Congress. As late as January 9, 1991, he insisted he had the constitutional authority to attack Iraq without Congressional approval.

While concealing his intention, President Bush continued the military build up of U.S. forces unabated from August into January 1991, intending to attack and destroy Iraq. He pressed the military to expedite preparation and to commence the assault before military considerations were optimum. When Air Force Chief of Staff General Michael J. Dugan mentioned plans to destroy the Iraqi civilian economy to the press on September 16, 1990, he was removed from office.[7]

President Bush coerced the United Nations Security Council into an unprecedented series of resolutions, finally securing authority for any nation in its absolute discretion by all necessary means to enforce the resolutions. To secure votes the U.S. paid multi-billion dollar bribes, offered arms for regional wars, threatened and carried out economic retaliation, forgave multi-billion dollar loans (including a $7 billion loan to Egypt for arms), offered diplomatic relations despite human rights violations and in other ways corruptly exacted votes, creating the appearance of near universal international approval of U.S. policies toward Iraq. A country which opposed the U.S., as Yemen did, lost millions of dollars in aid, as promised, the costliest vote it ever cast.

President Bush consistently rejected and ridiculed Iraq's efforts to negotiate a peaceful resolution, beginning with Iraq's August 12, 1990, proposal, largely ignored, and ending with its mid-February 1991 peace offer which he called a "cruel hoax." For his part, President Bush consistently insisted there would be no negotiation, no compromise, no face saving, no reward for aggression. Simultaneously, he accused Saddam Hussein of rejecting diplomatic solutions.

President Bush led a sophisticated campaign to demonize Saddam Hussein, calling him a Hitler, repeatedly citing reports—which he knew were false—of the murder of hundreds of incubator babies, accusing Iraq of using chemical weapons on his own people and on the Iranians knowing U.S. intelligence believed the reports untrue.

After subverting every effort for peace, President Bush began the destruction of Iraq answering his own question, "Why not wait? . . . The world could wait no longer."

The course of conduct constitutes a crime against peace.

3. President Bush ordered the destruction of facilities essential to civilian life and economic productivity throughout Iraq.

Systematic aerial and missile bombardment of Iraq was ordered to begin at 6:30 p.m. EST January 16, 1991, eighteen and one-half hours after the deadline set on the insistence of President Bush, in order to be reported on television evening news in the U.S. The bombing continued for forty-two days. It met no resistance from Iraqi aircraft and no effective anti-aircraft or anti-missile ground fire. Iraq was defenseless.

The United States reports it flew 110,000 air sorties against Iraq, dropping 88,000 tons of bombs, nearly seven times the equivalent of the atomic bomb that destroyed Hiroshima. 93% of the bombs were free falling bombs, most dropped from higher than 30,000 feet. Of the remaining 7% of the bombs with electronically guided systems, more than 25% missed their targets, nearly all caused damage primarily beyond any identifiable target. Most of the targets were civilian facilities.

The intention and effort of the bombing of civilian life and facilities was to systematically destroy Iraq's infrastructure leaving it in a preindustrial condition. Iraq's civilian population was dependent on industrial capacities. The U.S. assault left Iraq in a near apocalyptic condition as reported by the first United Nations observers after the war.[8] Among the facilities targeted and destroyed were:

- electric power generation, relay and transmission;
- water treatment, pumping and distribution systems and reservoirs;
- telephone and radio exchanges, relay stations, towers and transmission facilities;
- food processing, storage and distribution facilities and markets, infant milk formula and beverage plants, animal vaccination facilities and irrigation sites;
- railroad transportation facilities, bus depots, bridges, highway overpasses, highways, highway repair stations, trains, buses and other public transportation vehicles, commercial and private vehicles;
- oil wells and pumps, pipelines, refineries, oil storage tanks, gasoline filling stations and fuel delivery tank cars and trucks, and kerosene storage tanks;
- sewage treatment and disposal systems;
- factories engaged in civilian production, e.g., textile and automobile assembly; and
- historical markers and ancient sites.

As a direct, intentional and foreseeable result of this destruction, tens of thousands of people have died from dehydration, dysentery and diseases caused by impure water, inability to obtain effective medical assistance and debilitation from hunger, shock, cold and stress. More will die until potable water, sanitary living conditions, adequate food supplies and other necessities are provided. There is a high risk of epidemics of cholera, typhoid, hepatitis and other diseases as well as starvation and malnutrition through the summer of 1991 and until food supplies are adequate and essential services are restored.

Only the United States could have carried out this destruction of Iraq, and the war was conducted almost exclusively by the United States. This conduct violated the UN Charter, the Hague and Geneva Conventions, the Nuremberg Charter, and the laws of armed conflict.

4. The United States intentionally bombed and destroyed civilian life, commercial and business districts, schools, hospitals, mosques, churches, shelters, residential areas, historical sites, private vehicles and civilian government offices.

The destruction of civilian facilities left the entire civilian population without heat, cooking fuel, refrigeration, potable water, telephones, power for radio or TV reception, public transportation and fuel for private automobiles. It also limited food supplies, closed schools, created massive unemployment, severely limited economic activity and caused hospitals and medical services to shut down. In addition, residential areas of every major city and most towns and villages were targeted and destroyed. Isolated Bedouin camps were attacked by U.S. aircraft. In addition to deaths and injuries, the aerial assault destroyed 10 – 20,000 homes, apartments and other dwellings. Commercial centers with shops, retail stores, offices, hotels, restaurants and other public accommodations were targeted and thousands were destroyed. Scores of schools, hospitals, mosques and churches were damaged or destroyed. Thousands of civilian vehicles on highways, roads and parked on streets and in garages were targeted and destroyed. These included public buses, private vans and mini-buses, trucks, tractor trailers, lorries, taxi cabs and private cars. The purpose of this bombing was to terrorize the entire country, kill people, destroy property, prevent movement, demoralize the people and force the overthrow of the government.

As a result of the bombing of facilities essential to civilian life, residential and other civilian buildings and areas, at least 125,000 men, women and children were killed. The Red Crescent Society of Jordan estimated 113,000 civilian dead, 60% children, the week before the end of the war.

The conduct violated the UN Charter, the Hague and Geneva Conventions, the Nuremberg Charter, and the laws of armed conflict.

5. The United States intentionally bombed indiscriminately throughout Iraq.

In aerial attacks, including strafing, over cities, towns, the countryside and highways, U.S. aircraft bombed and strafed indiscriminately. In every city and town bombs fell by chance far from any conceivable target, whether a civilian facility, military installation or military target. In the countryside random attacks were made on travelers, villagers, even Bedouins. The purpose of the attacks was to destroy life, property and terrorize the civilian population. On the highways, civilian vehicles including public buses, taxicabs and passenger cars were bombed and strafed at random to frighten civilians from flight, from seeking food or medical care, finding relatives or other uses of highways. The effect was summary execution and corporal punishment indiscriminately of men, women and children, young and old, rich and poor, all nationalities including the large immigrant populations, even Americans, all ethnic groups, including many Kurds and Assyrians, all religions including Shia and Sunni Moslems, Chaldeans and other Christians, and Jews. U.S. deliberate indifference to civilian and military casualties in Iraq, or their nature, is exemplified by General Colin Powell's response to a press inquiry about the number dead from the air and ground campaigns: "It's really not a number I'm terribly interested in."[9]

The conduct violates Protocol I Additional, Article 51.4 to the Geneva Conventions of 1977.

6. The United States intentionally bombed and destroyed Iraqi military personnel, used excessive force, killed soldiers seeking to surrender and in disorganized individual flight, often unarmed and far from any combat zones and randomly and wantonly killed Iraqi soldiers and destroyed materiel after the cease fire.

In the first hours of the aerial and missile bombardment, the United States destroyed most military communications and began the systematic killing of soldiers who were incapable of defense or escape and the destruction of military equipment. Over a period of forty-two days, U.S. bombing killed tens of thousands of defenseless soldiers, cut off most of their food, water and other supplies and left them in desperate and helpless disarray. Without significant risk to its own personnel, the U.S. led in the killing of at least 100,000 Iraqi soldiers at a cost of 148 U.S. combat casualties, according to the U.S. government. When it was determined that the civilian economy and the military were sufficiently destroyed, the U.S. ground forces moved into Kuwait and Iraq attacking disoriented, disorganized, fleeing Iraqi forces wherever they could be found, killing thousands more and destroying any equipment found. The slaughter continued after the cease fire. For example, on March 2, 1991, U.S. 24th Division

Forces engaged in a four-hour assault against Iraqis just west of Basra. More than 750 vehicles were destroyed, thousands were killed without U.S. casualties. A U.S. commander said, "We really waxed them." It was called a "Turkey Shoot." One Apache helicopter crew member yelled "Say hello to Allah" as he launched a laser-guided Hellfire missile.[10]

The intention was not to remove Iraq's presence from Kuwait. It was to destroy Iraq. In the process there was great destruction of property in Kuwait. The disproportion in death and destruction inflicted on a defenseless enemy exceeded 1,000 to one.

General Thomas Kelly commented on February 23, 1991, that by the time the ground war begins "there won't be many of them left." General Norman Schwarzkopf placed Iraqi military casualties at over 100,000. The intention was to destroy all military facilities and equipment wherever located and to so decimate the military age male population that Iraq could not raise a substantial force for half a generation.

The conduct violated the Charter of the United Nations, the Hague and Geneva Conventions, the Nuremberg Charter, and the laws of armed conflict.

7. The United States used prohibited weapons capable of mass destruction and inflicting indiscriminate death and unnecessary suffering against both military and civilian targets.

Among the known illegal weapons and illegal uses of weapons employed by the United States are the following:
- fuel air explosives capable of widespread incineration and death;
- napalm;
- cluster and anti-personnel fragmentation bombs; and
- "superbombs," 2.5 ton devices, intended for assassination of government leaders.

Fuel air explosives were used against troops-in-place, civilian areas, oil fields and fleeing civilians and soldiers on two stretches of highway between Kuwait and Iraq. Included in fuel air weapons used was the BLU-82, a 15,000-pound device capable of incinerating everything within hundreds of yards.

One seven mile stretch called the "Highway of Death" was littered with hundreds of vehicles and thousands of dead. All were fleeing to Iraq for their lives. Thousands were civilians of all ages, including Kuwaitis, Iraqis, Palestinians, Jordanians and other nationalities. Another 60-mile stretch of road to the east was strewn with the remnants of tanks, armored cars, trucks, ambulances and thousands of bodies following an attack on convoys on the night of February 25, 1991. The press reported that no survivors are known or likely. One flatbed truck contained nine bodies, their hair and clothes were burned off, skin incinerated by heat so intense it melted the windshield onto the dashboard.

Napalm was used against civilians, military personnel and to start fires. Oil well fires in both Iraq and Kuwait were intentionally started by U.S. aircraft dropping napalm and other heat intensive devices.

Cluster and anti-personnel fragmentation bombs were used in Basra and other cities, and towns, against the convoys described above and against military units. The CBU-75 carries 1,800 bomblets called Sadeyes. One type of Sadeyes can explode before hitting the ground, on impact, or be timed to explode at different times after impact. Each bomblet contains 600 razor sharp steel fragments lethal up to 40 feet. The 1,800 bomblets from one CBU-75 can cover an area equal to 157 football fields with deadly shrapnel.

"Superbombs" were dropped on hardened shelters, at least two in the last days of the assault, with the intention of assassinating President Saddam Hussein. One was misdirected. It was not the first time the Pentagon targeted a head of state. In April 1986, the U.S. attempted to assassinate Col. Muammar Qaddafi by laser directed bombs in its attack on Tripoli, Libya.

Illegal weapons killed thousands of civilians and soldiers.

The conduct violated the Hague and Geneva Conventions, the Nuremberg Charter and the laws of armed conflict.

8. The United States intentionally attacked installations in Iraq containing dangerous substances and forces.

Despite the fact that Iraq used no nuclear or chemical weapons and in the face of UN resolutions limiting the authorized means of removing Iraqi forces from Kuwait, the U.S. intentionally bombed alleged nuclear sites, chemical plants, dams and other dangerous forces. The U.S. knew such attacks could cause the release of dangerous forces from such installations and consequent severe losses among the civilian population. While some civilians were killed in such attacks, there are no reported cases of consequent severe losses presumably because lethal nuclear materials and dangerous chemical and biological warfare substances were not present at the sites bombed.

The conduct violates Protocol I Additional, Article 56, to the Geneva Convention, 1977.

9. President Bush ordered U.S. forces to invade Panama, resulting in the deaths of 1,000 to 4,000 Panamanians and the destruction of thousands of private dwellings, public buildings, and commercial structures.

On December 20, 1989, President Bush ordered a military assault on Panama using aircraft, artillery, helicopter gunships and experimenting with new weapons, including the Stealth bomber. The attack was a surprise assault targeting civilian and non-combatant government structures. In the El Chorillo district of Panama City alone, hundreds of civilians were killed and between 15,000 and 30,000 made homeless. U.S. soldiers buried dead Panamanians in mass graves, often without identification. The head of state, Mañuel Noriega, who was systematically demonized by the U.S. government and press, ultimately surrendered to U.S. forces and was brought to Miami, Florida, on extra-territorial U.S. criminal charges.

The U.S. invasion of Panama violated all the international laws Iraq violated when it invaded Kuwait and more. Many more Panamanians were killed by U.S. forces than Iraq killed Kuwaitis.

President Bush violated the Charter of the United Nations, the Hague and Geneva Conventions, committed crimes against peace, war crimes and violated the U.S. Constitution and numerous U.S. criminal statutes in ordering and directing the assault on Panama.

10. President Bush obstructed justice and corrupted United Nations functions as a means of securing power to commit crimes against peace and war crimes.

President Bush caused the United Nations to completely bypass Chapter VI provisions of its Charter for the Pacific Settlement of Disputes. This was done in order to obtain Security Council resolutions authorizing the use of all necessary means, in the absolute discretion of any nation, to fulfill UN resolutions directed against Iraq and which were used to destroy Iraq. To obtain Security Council votes, the U.S. corruptly paid member nations billions of dollars, provided them arms to conduct regional wars, forgave billions in debts, withdrew opposition to a World Bank loan, agreed to diplomatic relations despite human rights violations and threatened economic and political reprisals. A nation which voted against the United States, Yemen, was immediately punished by the loss of millions of dollars in aid. The U.S. paid the UN $187 million to reduce the amount of dues it owed to the UN to avoid criticism of its coercive activities. The United Nations, created to end the scourge of war, became an instrument of war and condoned war crimes.

The conduct violates the Charter of the United Nations and the Constitution and laws of the United States.

11. President Bush usurped the Constitutional power of Congress as a means of securing power to commit crimes against peace, war crimes, and other high crimes.

President Bush intentionally usurped Congressional power, ignored its authority, and failed and refused to consult with the Congress. He deliberately misled, deceived, concealed and made false representations to the Congress to prevent its free deliberation and informed exercise of legislature power. President Bush individually ordered a naval blockade against Iraq, itself an act of war. He switched U.S. forces from a wholly defensive position and capability to an offensive capacity for aggression against Iraq without consultation with and contrary to assurances given to the Congress. He secured legislation approving enforcement of UN resolutions vesting absolute discretion in any nation, providing no guidelines and requiring no reporting to the UN, knowing he intended to destroy the armed forces and civilian economy of Iraq. Those acts were undertaken to enable him to commit crimes against peace and war crimes.

The conduct violates the Constitution and laws of the United States, all committed to engage in the other impeachable offenses set forth in this Complaint.

12. The United States waged war on the environment.

Pollution from the detonation of 88,000 tons of bombs, innumerable missiles, rockets, artillery and small arms with the combustion and fires they caused and by 110,000 air sorties at a rate of nearly two per minute for six weeks has caused enormous injury to life and the ecology. Attacks by U.S. aircraft caused much if not all of the worst oil spills in the Gulf. Aircraft and helicopters dropping napalm and fuel-air explosives on oil wells, storage tanks and refineries caused oil fires throughout Iraq and many, if not most, of the oil well fires in Iraq and Kuwait. The intentional destruction of municipal water systems, waste material treatment and sewage disposal systems constitutes a direct and continuing assault on life and health throughout Iraq.

The conduct violated the UN Charter, the Hague and Geneva Conventions, the laws of armed conflict and constituted war crimes and crimes against humanity.

13. President Bush encouraged and aided Shiite Muslims and Kurds to rebel against the government of Iraq causing fratricidal violence, emigration, exposure, hunger and sickness and thousands of deaths. After the rebellion failed, the U.S. invaded and occupied parts of Iraq without authority in order to increase division and hostility within Iraq.

Without authority from the Congress or the UN, President Bush continued his imperious military actions after the cease fire. He encouraged and aided rebellion against Iraq, failed to protect the warring parties, encouraged migration of whole populations, placing them in jeopardy from the elements, hunger, and disease. After much suffering and many deaths, President Bush then without authority used U.S. military forces to distribute aid at and near the Turkish border, ignoring the often greater suffering among refugees in Iran. He then arbitrarily set up bantustan-like settlements for Kurds in Iraq and demanded Iraq pay for U.S. costs. When Kurds chose to return to their homes in Iraq, he moved U.S. troops further into northern Iraq against the will of the government and without authority.

The conduct violated the Charter of the United Nations, international law, the Constitution and laws of the United States, and the laws of Iraq.

14. President Bush intentionally deprived the Iraqi people of essential medicines, potable water, food, and other necessities.

A major component of the assault on Iraq was the systematic deprivation of essential human needs and services. To break the will of the people, destroy their economic capability, reduce their numbers and weaken their health, the United States:

- imposed and enforced embargoes preventing the shipment of needed medicines, water purifiers, infant milk formula, food and other supplies;
- individually, without congressional authority, ordered a U.S. naval blockade of Iraq, an act of war, to deprive the Iraqi people of needed supplies;
- froze funds of Iraq and forced other nations to do so, depriving Iraq of the ability to purchase needed medicines, food and other supplies;
- controlled information about the urgent need for such supplies to prevent sickness, death and threatened epidemic, endangering the whole society;
- prevented international organizations, governments and relief agencies from providing needed supplies and obtaining information concerning needs;
- failed to assist or meet urgent needs of huge refugee populations including Egyptians, Indians, Pakistanis, Yemenis, Sudanese, Jordanians, Palestinians, Sri Lankans, Filipinos, and interfered with efforts of others to do so;
- consistently diverted attention from health and epidemic threats within Iraq caused by the U.S. even after advertising the plight of Kurdish people on the Turkish border;
- deliberately bombed the electrical grids causing the closure of hospitals and laboratories, loss of medicine and essential fluids and blood; and
- deliberately bombed food storage, fertilizer, and seed storage facilities.

As a result of these acts, thousands of people died, many more suffered illness and permanent injury. As a single illustration, Iraq consumed infant milk formula at a rate of 2,500 tons per month during the first seven months of 1990. From November 1, 1990, to February 7, 1991, Iraq was able to import only 17 tons. Its own productive capacity was destroyed. Many Iraqis believed that President Bush intended that their infants die because he targeted their food supply. The Red Crescent Society of Iraq estimated 3,000 infant deaths as of February 7, 1991, resulting from infant milk formula and infant medication shortages.

This conduct violates the Hague and Geneva Conventions, the Universal Declaration of Human Rights and other covenants and constitutes a crime against humanity.

15. The United States continued its assault on Iraq after the cease fire, invading and occupying areas at will.

The United States has acted with dictatorial authority over Iraq and its external relations since the end of the military conflict. It has shot and killed Iraqi military personnel, destroyed aircraft and materiel at will, occupied vast areas of Iraq in the north and south and consistently threatened use of force against Iraq.

This conduct violates the sovereignty of a nation, exceeds authority in UN resolutions, is unauthorized by the Constitution and laws of the United States, and constitutes war crimes.

16. The United States has violated and condoned violations of human rights, civil liberties and the U.S. Bill of Rights in the United States, in Kuwait, Saudi Arabia and elsewhere to achieve its purpose of military domination.

Among the many violations committed or condoned by the U.S. government are the following:

- illegal surveillance, arrest, interrogation and harassment of Arab-American, Iraqi-American, and U.S. resident Arabs;
- illegal detention, interrogation and treatment of Iraqi prisoners of war;
- aiding and condoning Kuwaiti summary executions, assaults, torture and illegal detention of Palestinians and other residents in Kuwait after the U.S. occupation; and
- unwarranted, discriminatory, and excessive prosecution and punishment of U.S. military personnel who refused to serve in the Gulf, sought conscientious objector status or protested U.S. policies.

Persons were killed, assaulted, tortured, illegally detained and prosecuted, harassed and humiliated as a result of these policies.

The conduct violates the Charter of the United Nations, the Universal Declaration of Human Rights, the Hague and Geneva Conventions and the Constitution and laws of the United States.

17. The United States, having destroyed Iraq's economic base,

demands reparations which will permanently impoverish Iraq and threaten its people with famine and epidemic.

Having destroyed lives, property and essential civilian facilities in Iraq which the U.S. concedes will require $50 billion to replace (estimated at $200 billion by Iraq), killed at least 125,000 people by bombing and many thousands more by sickness and hunger, the U.S. now seeks to control Iraq economically even as its people face famine and epidemic.[12] Damages, including casualties in Iraq, systematically inflicted by the U.S. exceed all damages, casualties and costs of all other parties to the conflict combined many times over. Reparations under these conditions are an exaction of tribute for the conqueror from a desperately needy country. The United States seeks to force Iraq to pay for damage to Kuwait largely caused by the U.S. and even to pay U.S. costs for its violations of Iraqi sovereignty in occupying northern Iraq to further manipulate the Kurdish population there. Such reparations are a neocolonial means of expropriating Iraq's oil, natural resources, and human labor.

The conduct violates the Charter of the United Nations and the Constitution and laws of the United States.

18. President Bush systematically manipulated, controlled, directed, misinformed and restricted press and media coverage to obtain constant support in the media for his military and political goals.

The Bush Administration achieved a five-month-long commercial for militarism and individual weapons systems. The American people were seduced into the celebration of a slaughter by controlled propaganda demonizing Iraq, assuring the world no harm would come to Iraqi civilians, deliberately spreading false stories of atrocities including chemical warfare threats, deaths of incubator babies and threats to the entire region by a new Hitler.

The press received virtually all its information from or by permission of the Pentagon. Efforts were made to prevent any adverse information or opposition views from being heard. CNN's limited presence in Baghdad was described as Iraqi propaganda. Independent observers, eyewitnesses' photos, and video tapes with information about the effects of the U.S. bombing were excluded from the media. Television network ownership, advertizers, newspaper ownership, elite columnists and commentators intimidated and instructed reporters and selected interviewees. They formed a near-single voice of praise for U.S. militarism, often exceeding the Pentagon in bellicosity.

The American people and their democratic institutions were deprived of information essential to sound judgment and were regimented, despite profound concern, to support a major neocolonial intervention and war of aggression. The principal purpose of the First Amendment to the United States was to assure the press and the people the right to criticize their government with impunity. This purpose has been effectively destroyed in relation to U.S. military aggression since the press was denied access to assaults on Grenada, Libya, Panama and, now on a much greater scale, against Iraq.

This conduct violates the First Amendment to the Constitution of the United States and is part of a pattern of conduct intended to create support for conduct constituting crimes against peace and war crimes.

19. The United States has by force secured a permanent military presence in the Gulf, the control of its oil resources and geopolitical domination of the Arabian Peninsula and Gulf region.

The U.S. has committed the acts described in this complaint to create a permanent U.S. military presence in the Persian Gulf, to dominate its oil resources until depleted and to maintain geopolitical domination over the region.

The conduct violates the Charter of the United Nations, international law, and the Constitution and laws of the United States.

Scope of the Inquiry

The Commission of Inquiry will focus on U.S. criminal conduct because of its destruction of Iraq, killing at least 125,000 persons directly by its bombing while proclaiming its own combat losses as 148, because it destroyed the economic base of Iraq and because its acts are still inflicting consequential deaths that may reach hundreds of thousands. The Commission of Inquiry will seek and accept evidence of criminal acts by any person or government, related to the Gulf conflict, because it believes international law must be applied uniformly. It believes that "victors' justice" is not law, but the extension of war by force of the prevailing party. The U.S. Senate, European Community foreign ministers, and the western press, even former Nuremberg prosecutors, have overwhelmingly called for war crimes trials for Saddam Hussein and the Iraqi leadership alone. Even Mrs. Barbara Bush has said she would like to see Saddam Hussein hanged, albeit without mentioning a trial. Comprehensive efforts to gather and evaluate evidence, objectively judge all the conduct that constitutes crimes against peace and war crimes and to present these facts for judgment to the court of world opinion requires that at least one major effort focus on the United States. The Commission of Inquiry believes its focus on U.S. criminal acts is important, proper, and the only way to bring the whole truth, a balanced perspective and impartiality in application of legal process to this great human tragedy.

Ramsey Clark
May 9, 1991

Notes

1. *Covert Operations: The Persian Gulf and the New World Order* (Washington, DC: Christic Institute, 1991).

2. Rhodri Jeffreys-Jones, *The CIA and American Democracy* (New Haven: Yale University Press, 1989), p. 206.

3. Independent Commission of Inquiry on the U.S. Invasion of Panama, *The U.S. Invasion of Panama: The Truth Behind Operation Just Cause* (Boston: South End Press, 1990).

4. *Amnesty International Reports*, 1991, pp. 122-124.

5. *Congressional Record*, June 12, 1990, S8605.

6. "Saddam's Oil Plot." *London Observer*, October 21, 1990.

7. Rick Atkinson, "U.S. to Rely on Air Strikes if War Erupts," *Washington Post*, September 16, 1990: A1+. Eric Schmitt, "Ousted General Gets A Break," *New York Times*, November 7, 1991: A19.

8. *Joint WHO / UNICEF Team Report: A Visit to Iraq* (New York: United Nations, 1991). A report to the Secretary General, dated March 20, 1991 by representatives of the U.N. Secretariat, UNICEF, UNDP, UNDRO, UNHCR, FAO and WHO. *Reprinted in Appendix B, below.*

9. Patrick E. Tyler, "Powell Says U.S. Will Stay In Iraq," *New York Times*, March 23, 1991: A1+.

10. Patrick J. Sloyan, "Massive Battle After Cease Fire," *New York Newsday*, May 8, 1991: A4+.

11. "U.S. Prepares UN Draft on Claims Against Iraq," *New York Times*, November 1, 1990.

Nowhere to Hide

At the height of the allied bombing of Iraq in early 1991, Jon Alpert, a long-time contributor to NBC News, shot the only footage of the war's impact not censored by either Iraq or the U.S. Traveling with former U.S. Attorney General Ramsey Clark, Alpert captured on camera what it was like to be on the ground during the allied bombing. In an often harrowing journey, they witnessed widespread civilian casualties and extensive damage to homes, villages and markets, sometimes minutes after it occurred. In dramatic and often graphic scenes, **NOWHERE TO HIDE** shows a far different reality than what most Americans saw on the nightly news.

Produced by Jon Alpert   28 Minutes ● 1991 ● VHS
Distributed by
Commission of Inquiry for the International War Crimes Tribunal
36 East 12th Street, 6th Floor, NY, NY 10003   212-254-5385
All orders must be prepaid $25 Video/ $3 shipping and handling

Speakers are available upon request

"Horrifying glimpses at the civilian devastation inflicted by allied bombing (of Iraq)."
— San Jose Mercury News

VIDEO

Part Two:

The Basis in
International Law

(Above) New York Commission of Inquiry, May 11, 1991. (Below) Egyptian Commission Hearing, August 8, 1991, held at the Hall of the Arab Progressive Unionist Party, Egypt's main opposition party. (Photos: Commission of Inquiry for the International War Crimes Tribunal)

Why an Inquiry

Sara Flounders

We are beginning a worldwide series of public forums to uncover, to expose, to examine that which has been hidden, suppressed and censored. This is the first in a series of public hearings on evidence of U.S. and allied war crimes that will be held all across the U.S. and the world, from New York City to Cairo, from London to Manila, from Rome to New Delhi, from Toronto to San Francisco.

Why is this so important? Since the days of the earliest societies, murder has always been considered a crime, in every society on the face of the earth, in every age. Long before there was any international order, any parliaments, any states, murder was considered a crime, and especially repugnant has been murder when the victim is defenseless.

What do we do? We are witness to a collective crime against a portion of humanity. Life has the same value in Iraq as it does for all of us living in the United States. We have witnessed an unprovoked and cynical slaughter, a use of the most extreme form of terror against a community. Never in the history of the human race has so massive a concentration of military, economic and political power focused on one small portion of the earth's surface. In the essays which follow, there will be detailed accounts of this destruction that was wreaked on one country; there will also be provided material and evidence on its impact on the entire region and the rippling disruption through the developing countries of Africa and Asia.

But perhaps the most important aspect of this crime that we all publicly witnessed is that it was done in contravention of the very laws of each nation that participated in the invasion. It's a crime not alone of the supreme military world power, the U.S. It was done collectively by the leading industrial powers. These leading industrial powers in their foreign and economic policy are regarded by the oppressed and exploited people of the world as imperialist powers. This was a crime done under the mantle of the UN Security Council, and there will be material presented on the United States' use of bribery and coercion to gain these votes and on the resolution of the UN Security Council and its use of military force. But despite all the countries involved, it was a decision of generals and rulers, corporate and industrial leaders, and not a democratic decision of the people, even in its form. This decision, momentous as it was, was not ratified nor ever even discussed in the UN General Assembly to this very day. Among the principal powers who participated, none of their parliamentary institutions were asked to decide. They were only given the opportunity to ratify a decision for destruction. This happened in the U.S., and it happened in every country.

The papers presented here will begin to carry forward new material and new evidence, which grows every day. Some of it is even beginning to be recognized in the mass media. On May 8, 1991, an article appeared in *New York Newsday* by Patrick Sloyan, based on actual army footage of what he described as the largest battle of the war. The catch was that the battle occurred two days after Bush had ordered the final cease-fire, and eight days after Iraq had announced its full withdrawal, and fighting had ceased. It was a violation even of the cease-fire guidelines. A division of the Republican Guard withdrawing on a long, unprotected causeway, high above a swamp, on Highway 8, was attacked. General Schwarzkopf himself ordered this attack, claiming that a single infantryman had fired a round at a U.S. patrol. We'll never know if Schwarzkopf told the truth. But the footage tells us what happened: the U.S. assembled attack helicopters, tanks, artillery, and opened fire with laser-guided weapons. The footage shows, and the commander describes: "We went right up the column like a turkey shoot, we really waxed them." That's on tape! Thousands of Iraqi soldiers were killed; not one U.S. soldier died.[1]

The New World Order proposed by President Bush embodies the wish of the U.S., Britain, and France to return the world to the time a century ago, the 1890s, when they could sit down and carve up the entire world, when they could draw the lines through Africa and Asia. This is what the New World Order is all about. It's a restoring of the old colonial world order, and the colonial wars that they fought in the 19th Century. The great Battle of Omdurman in 1898 sounds a lot like the Iraq war. Tens of thousands of Sudanese troops were mowed down by waves of machine gun fire: 11,000 Sudanese killed, 49 Europeans.

The U.S. press which during the Gulf War so demonized Saddam Hussein, did the same a little more than 100 years ago to Sitting Bull. Then the real issue was the gold in the Black Hills of South Dakota, and it led to one of many slaughters of the Native people. Today it's the oil in the Gulf. But the press coverage is the same. The government treaties, international agreements, and the conventions signed are treated with the same cynicism as the treaties signed with the Native people.

These imperial forces have built a coalition, and we need a coalition for truth. There is a crying need for truth on a worldwide scale, and a crying need to mobilize the anger. Millions worldwide are suffering and struggling against this New World Order, and we hope that this commission will accomplish a serious, factual presentation. But also that it will provide a basis for a coalition of the many forces scattered—to join forces in a common effort to prepare for the continuing wars, to connect the great crimes that have been committed to the war crimes here in the U.S. The budget cuts are a war crime against every city of the U.S. The 10,000 people who died here in the U.S. of AIDS during the six months of this war should also be considered casualties of the Gulf War.

The public hearings conducted by the Commission of Inquiry will connect these crimes against peace, war crimes, crimes against humanity, and will record and broadcast nationally and internationally the acts of the New World Order. The many representatives from the mass media who attend these Commission meetings have really a special and unique responsibility to the world movement to disseminate this material as widely as possible. They have a real role and a contribution that they can make.

There's a great deal of material already in and a great deal of information that we don't yet have. To obtain it will take a powerful movement—to release Bush's battle plans, the decisions, and all that's been suppressed. We have filed Freedom of Information requests, but it takes a large struggle to force out into the open and to free up a great deal of this material. It takes a movement to encourage many of the troops who witnessed or even committed atrocities and others who have information and material to come forward. It takes a movement to encourage the media, to embolden them to release that which they already know. It will take a movement to embolden a whole layer of society that has been gagged and silenced. These Commission Reports are a first step in a long struggle.

Notes

1. Patrick J. Sloyan, "Massive Battle After Cease Fire," *New York Newsday*, May 8, 1991: A4. Also, "Pullback A Bloody Mismatch: Rout of Iraqi Became Savage 'Turkey Shoot,'" *New York Newsday*, March 31, 1991.

Sara Flounders is a member of the Executive Staff of the Commission of Inquiry for the International War Crimes Tribunal.

The Legal and Moral Basis for an International War Crimes Tribunal

Ramsey Clark

I'm a lawyer, and therefore, according to Franz Kafka, never very far from evil. I don't happen to share his philosophy of evil. I do recognize that nearly all lawyers are involved in misery, and that human rights lawyers are involved constantly in human tragedy.

This Commission is involved in the greatest tragedy that afflicts our species: war. It seeks to do something that has never been done before, but that is imperative to survival of life on the planet, and that is to hold governments that wage wars of conquest against others accountable to the people for their conduct. All governments—now and forever hereafter.

If the citizens of Greece had had the vision and the courage and the compassion to do it after the destruction of Milos, where all the men were killed, and all the elderly and women and children were sold in slavery, Athens could have prevailed. They pursued a policy, described by Thucydides, as one in which the powerful do as they will, and the weak suffer as they must. That is a policy that is impermissible by all human standards.

Had the people of Rome demanded that their legions not ravage major parts of Europe and North Africa and the Middle East, there might have been peace at the time. Had the Mongolians contained the Khans so that they could graze in their own pastures, hundreds of thousands of people who met death at their hands could have raised their children in peace. If the Spanish Conquistadors had been contained by their own people, the peers of Cervantes, if they just heard the voice of one man, Bartolome de las Casas—whom, and we should never forget, said the Indians are human beings as worthy as any Spanish child and must be accorded full human rights—then the tens of millions—because that's the number—that died in this hemisphere as a result of conquest and disease would have been spared. Had the imperial forces of England, France, and others respected the rights of the people in Africa and Asia and elsewhere on the planet, rather than reaping wealth from the sweat of slave labor's brow, if their peoples had demanded accountability by their governments, if they had recognized that they too were victims, not just those who were conquered, all of this long human history of war and violence might have ended.

Now we see new threats to life, the use of technology against life, and we come to a moment when it is absolutely imperative that the peoples of this planet hold accountable the great powers using technology against life on the planet, who destroyed Iraq and threatened every poor nation that exists today.

It is for this reason that these Commission hearings, engaging in one of the largest investigations of criminal conduct in history, a process that will take many months and thousands and thousands of people on six separate continents, and hundreds of organizations from scores of nations, to examine a single complaint. It's a complaint charging George Bush, Dan Quayle, James Baker, Dick Cheney, William Webster, Colin Powell, Norman Schwarzkopf, and others to be named, with crimes against peace, with war crimes, crimes against humanity and other criminal acts and high crimes, in violation of the Charter of the United Nations, international law, the Constitution of the United States, and laws made in pursuance thereof.

These Commissions can and must be historic meetings. It's probably worth observing that the historic importance of any meeting doesn't occur in the meeting but thereafter. Independence Hall would have been soon forgotten if the British had won, wouldn't it? The imperative need is that we recognize our role in history from this moment, to establish the facts set forth in this charge, and bring the transgressors to justice.

The charge is initial, because the investigation, the Commission of Inquiry, is a process, as all quests for truth are, in a sense never ending. But we've allotted ourselves six months, and more if it becomes necessary, to find the essential facts supporting what at this moment are nineteen charges of the highest crimes that can be committed against humanity. There may be more charges as the evidence comes in. There may be alterations and modifications of some of the existing charges, but each of us as a citizen of this planet has an obligation to take this complaint, to master its substance, to see what the evidence that is needed is, and make sure that it is provided in hearings going on all over the world during the next six months.

Let me describe the charges briefly. It's what any prosecutor does in beginning a grand jury inquiry or the *voir dire* for a petty jury in a criminal trial. I won't deal with each of the nineteen charges because they will be taken up in particular papers throughout this volume and in Commission meetings held all over the world. But we must never lose our focus on the charges. The first two have to do with the most tragic crime of all, the crime against peace, the causing of war. There are no war crimes until there is war, and in that sense, a preamble to every war crime is a crime against peace. We charge, and we have substantial evidence, and we're seeking more evidence, that George Bush and others, beginning sometime in 1988 or before, deliberately began a course of conduct intending to provoke actions by Iraq in the Persian Gulf that would justify a military attack and the destruction of the military of Iraq and its civilian economic support system. We charge that between August 2nd 1990 and January 17th 1991, George Bush and others systematically and in concert engaged in activity intended to bring the conflict to a violent conclusion by destroying Iraq. There was never during that period, according to the evidence that we have and the evidence that we expect to accumulate, any intent of negotiation, any intent toward peace, any intent of compromise or face-saving. As the president said so many times, there will be no reward for aggression (I might note that Panamanians ought to pay attention).

The charges three to eight deal with the heart of the violence that was inflicted upon Iraq. It's awfully important that its nature and its many aspects be clearly understood. This was not really a war. This was the use of technological war materiel to destroy a defenseless country. We can talk about the billions of dollars of arms that the United States and others sold to Iraq, but it takes only the most casual investigation of what happened over there to see that none of them afforded that nation any chance to really defend itself. It was destroyed from afar, systematically, without any capability of protecting the lives of its citizens, civilian or military.

All you have to do to recognize this is look at the casualties. The United States is responsible for the deaths of at least 125,000, perhaps more than 300,000 by now, human beings living in Iraq between August and March of these past years. It claims to have lost 148 military people in combat, but in the type of war that it waged, it needn't have lost any, because it was destroying by aircraft, missile, and other devices the civilian infrastructure.

We identify eight essential elements of urban and rural life in a partially industrialized and largely agricultural and poor nation, eight specific systemic parts of the economy that were destroyed throughout the nation. There was no running water, as we know. There was no electric power, and that means no heat and no refrigeration. There were no communications by any means other than voice and couriers carrying documents that could be read. There was no transportation other than that of a few vehicles, because systematically instruments of power, electric generation plants, oil wells, refineries, pipelines, storage tanks, down to the filling stations, were destroyed.

The nation was rendered powerless even to function. It all came together in the hospitals, where there was no water to wash your hands with; there was no water to give to dehydrated people who were suffering from nausea and diarrhea. There was no heat, and it was winter, and even in the war, the temperature would be 50 degrees Fahrenheit or less. There was no light. Maybe two candles in a ward of twenty people.

There was no anesthesia for an 11-year-old girl whose leg had to be amputated near the hip, and who was still delirious a few hours later when you talked to her. There was no anesthesia for a man who had to be held down by four people while you watched as radical surgery was performed on an arm. There was no pain killer to relieve the throbbing, aching pain of wounds from shrapnel. There weren't doctors who had equipment and hands that were clean that could heal the sick.

There was a systematic destruction as well of civilian life itself. But we had found a new technique of war. You can cut off everything that people in the city need, and let them die on their own. You don't have to carpet bomb any more, although the U.S. military did a fair share of that, too. Our planes came in with bombs that destroyed residential areas in every city, every major town, and most villages. We destroyed the infrastructure there, and we destroyed residential areas, schools, hospitals, transportation centers, mosques and all the rest. Even most of their military.

U.S.-led Coalition forces destroyed the capacity of the Iraqi military to function before they were ever engaged. We have to remember what we're told, because the context isn't clear at the time. General Kelly, when the so-called ground war began, said, "There aren't many left alive to fight." Those that were left alive, those that hadn't been killed in their bunkers and elsewhere by planes that came in the night primarily, but often in the day, planes that they couldn't see, they couldn't hit, that they couldn't defend themselves from, that they couldn't even flee from. How do you surrender in the middle of the night to a B-52 at 40,000 feet?

But those who had survived the bombing had no communications, had been deprived of food and water, of essential supplies, had no organization or command structure left, were completely disoriented, largely in bad health, sick if you will, and we rolled over them. Many, as the U.S. military now admits, were simply buried alive by tanks specially modified with bulldozer blades. And this was not something that came up in the heat of battle. U.S. soldiers practiced for months techniques for burying alive Iraqi soldiers. There is no indication that any Iraqis attempted to fight back. They were simply buried.

The Bush-Schwarzkopf plan called for a whole variety of illegal weapons. It used fuel air explosives, which can incinerate hundreds, even thousands of people at once. We used super-bombs, trying to assassinate leaders. That information has only recently come out, and we'll find a lot more. At least three super-bombs were dropped, trying to assassinate leaders in Iraq in violation of international law and the laws of the United States.

The military used napalm against civilians. It used napalm and other heat-intensive explosives to start oil well fires, to start fires in anything that was highly inflammable. We used anti-personnel devices, mother-bombs with 800 or more bomblets, each bomblet in some configurations containing 6,000 razor-sharp pieces of shrapnel. One mother bomb dropped from one plane is capable of covering the equivalent of more than 150 football fields with razor-sharp shrapnel flying everywhere, fatal within 50 feet of each bomblet to anybody that it hits.

Our military violated all the laws of war. These laws are intended to restrain the excessive use of force against civilians and the military. These laws principally include indiscriminate bombing, including the destruction of plants and facilities, including dams, nuclear-viable materials, chemicals known to threaten civilian populations if released into the atmosphere. These are a violation necessarily of law.

Our military intended to destroy not only the military capacity of Iraq, but to kill sufficient numbers of its civilian population and so destroy its civilian economic capacity that it would be at least half a generation and perhaps longer before Iraq could struggle to a standard of living that is acceptable by any humane criteria. And we did it, and we did it without risk because of our technology.

By the time what was called the ground war started, there was no effective capacity to resist, and there was no ground war, and we never stopped after that. Look at that 60-mile long roadway on the eastern side of the highway from Kuwait City to Basra, 60 miles long, strewn with human bodies and trucks and tanks and armored cars and all the rest. Look at the so-called Highway of Death, seven miles on the super-highway that a lot of the press saw because that's where they could travel. Look at what we continue to do in the north.

The United States subverted the integrity of the United Nations in its quest for war. The United Nations was created in the aftermath of the greatest mass destructiveness in human history, World War II, to end the scourge of war. By bribery, coercion, corruption and unlawful means of many other types, the United States deliberately bought votes, forced votes and caused the United Nations to become an instrumentality of war.

An imperial president violated the Constitution of the United States, usurping all the powers of the legislature over war and peace, lying to the public, lying to the Congress, refusing to consult, and proclaiming as late as January 9, 1991, that he individually had plenary power to engage in a war of aggression against Iraq without talking to anybody. What military dictatorship in history ever claimed greater power than that?

If we want integrity in the Constitution of the United States, these war crimes that have been described must be considered here as a domestic matter, because each constitutes a high crime under the Constitution, and an impeachable offense. It's been very rare in history that the people who lose a war don't suffer terribly, but it's never happened in history that a nation that has won a war has been held accountable. We intend to make this one different.

There are more than a dozen additional charges. I can't get through them all, but they include various types of human rights violations here in the United States against Palestinians and other peoples in Kuwait, the people in north and south Iraq and elsewhere that were either caused or condoned by the United States government and its military forces. They include the terrible suffering that arose directly from embargoes, from blockades, illegal naval blockades, acts of war themselves, from demand for reparations from people who had already been destroyed beyond the capacity to support themselves, in effect taxing their wealth and oil revenues for future generations, for the benefit of conquering nations. These have caused tens of thousands of deaths already, for lack of food, for lack of medicine, for lack of shelter. Just think of the refugees.

After six months, when all the evidence that we seek has been accumulated and organized, it will be presented to an International War Crimes Tribunal, probably in February of 1992, probably sitting symbolically in the Hague [the Tribunal has been set for February 27, 28, 29, 1992 in New York—*editor*]. That Tribunal will be chosen collegially from those who participated in all of these hearings and helped provide all the evidence that is being gathered for the Tribunal. The Tribunal itself will be composed of international leaders who will render a judgment on the basis of the nineteen charges and any others that have been developed in the interim.

Then we begin the real effort, to take those reports, to take those charges, back to the people from which they came in the countries and the cities of six continents to demand action. The action will include the creation of an international court of criminal justice for the future, so that any nation hereafter that dares to violate these laws against war crimes and crimes against peace will be immediately accountable. The court will require reform of the United Nations so that it is no longer a corrupt institution in which wealth and power and not principle dominate.

It will require worldwide disarmament so we can stop starving ourselves and then killing ourselves with the product of our energy. It will require the redistribution of wealth to the poor because we know there will be a billion more people on the planet before the end of this millennium, nine years away. Eighty percent will have beautiful darker skin and will be condemned to short lives of hunger, want, sickness, poverty and misery unless we act boldly now. It will include a new world information order, because the press has been an accomplice worldwide with this assault on humanity. We'll pull out the old Sean McBride report and we will demand that we obtain information from every part of the planet and every suffering person always so that we will never be kept in the dark again, never lied to again and never led into war again.

Each country will have the obligation for dealing with the matter of its own leaders because that is a domestic affair, and here in the United States, we will go to every congressional district and demand of our representatives that they begin the processing of resolutions of impeachment against George Bush and all other officials who led us into this war.

It's simply a matter of will. Our capacity to do it is abundant and manifest. It is the highest duty of every individual on this planet to see that his or her governmental officials are accountable for their acts, including acts of war in the immediate term and restrained in their pursuits of war for the future.

The highest form of patriotism, of love of country, is to stand up in a time of moral crisis such as this and say, "My country will not commit war crimes or crimes against humanity ever again."

Ramsey Clark served as U.S. Attorney General in the administration of Lyndon Johnson. He is the convener of the Commission of Inquiry and a human rights lawyer of world-wide respect. This report was given in New York, May 11, 1991.

This is what remains of a market in Basra, southern Iraq, after U.S. bombing. Unlike Baghdad which received mostly laser-guided bombs, Basra was subject to B-52 carpet bombing. (Photo: Commission of Inquiry for the International War Crimes Tribunal)

International Law
and War Crimes

Michael Ratner

In the work of this Commission, we are undertaking an historic task. We are here to inquire into and ultimately judge whether the United States has violated laws that are fundamental to a civilized world; laws that are designed to protect people, human beings, from the barbarity of war. These laws prohibit war except in the narrowest of circumstances; they severely restrict who can be killed, the types of weapons that can be used and the appropriate targets. An indicia of a civilized country is adherence to these laws, not only by pious words but through actions. To act outside these laws, to disobey these laws, to flaunt these laws is to become "hostis humani generis," an enemy of all mankind. In days past "enemies of all mankind" were slave traders and pirates. They could be brought to justice wherever found. Today such enemies include those countries and individuals who violate the fundamental laws that protect the peace and limit war. The testimony presented at the various Commissions of Inquiry here in New York and in other hearings throughout the world will determine whether the United States and its leaders are enemies of all mankind.

As people living in the United States we have an obligation not to close our eyes, cover our ears and remain silent. We must not and cannot be "good Germans." We must be, as Bertrand Russell said about the crimes committed by the U.S. in Vietnam, "Against the Crime of Silence." We must bear witness to the tens of thousands of deaths for whom our government and its leaders bear responsibility and ask the question—Has the United States committed war crimes with regard to its initiation and conduct of the war against Iraq? As investigators we believe that the United States and its leaders have committed international crimes. Although we cannot bring them to justice, we can reveal their criminal conduct to ourselves, to the people of the United States, and to the world with the hope that U.S. conduct will be repudiated, conduct, which by the way, still continues. The U.S. still occupies parts of Iraq, it continues an embargo against food, and it engages in battle after a cease-fire.

Today I want to outline for you the legal framework in which we are operating and explain some of the broad principles of law applicable to judging the United States' conduct.

War crimes are violations by a country, its civilians, or its military personnel of the international laws of war. The laws of war are laws that must be obeyed by the United States, its officials and its military, and by the UN. The laws are contained in treaties that the U.S. has signed, for example the Geneva Convention of 1949 on Prisoners of War. They are reflected in what is called customary international law. This law has arisen over hundreds if not thousands of years. All countries must obey it.

War crimes are divided into two broad categories. The first are called crimes against peace. Crimes against peace include the planning, preparation, or initiation of a war of aggression. In other words one country cannot make aggressive war against another country. Nor can a country settle a dispute by war; it must always, and in good faith, negotiate a settlement. The second category are what we can call crimes against humanity; I am including here crimes against civilians and soldiers. These are violations of the rules as to the means and manner by which war is to be conducted once begun. These include the following prohibitions: killing of civilians, indiscriminate bombing, the use of certain types of weapons, killing of defenseless soldiers, ill treatment of POWs and attacks on non-military targets.

Any violation of these two sets of laws is a war crime; if the violations are done on purpose, recklessly or knowingly, they are considered very serious and called grave breaches; Nazis and Japanese following World War II were hanged for such grave breaches.

First, I want to discuss crimes against peace and give you some sense of its application here. This prohibition is embodied in the Charter of the United Nations, the Nuremberg Charter, which is the law under which the Nazis were tried, and a treaty called the Kellogg-Briand pact. As the Nuremberg Charter defines,

(a) Crimes against peace:
  (i) Planning, preparation, initiation or waging of a war of aggression or a war in violation of international treaties, agreements or assurances;
  (ii) Participation in a common plan or conspiracy for the accomplishment of any of the acts mentioned under (i).

The United Nations Charter is the highest expression of this prohibition on aggressive war and sets down very rigorous rules for avoiding the use of force—rules which were flagrantly violated by the United States and a Security Council it controlled. Article 2(3) of the UN Charter requires that international disputes be settled by peaceful means so that international peace, security and justice are not endangered; Article 2(4) requires that force shall not by used in any manner that is inconsistent with the purposes of the UN and Article 33 requires that parties to a dispute shall first of all seek a solution by negotiation, inquiry, mediation, conciliation, arbitration, judicial settlement, resort to regional agencies, or other peaceful means. Not until all such means are exhausted can force be used.

So, taken together we have two basic rules: a nation cannot plan and make war, and second, if there is a dispute, the nations must exhaust every means of settlement—every means. Even then, only the UN can authorize war. There is strong evidence, some of which is presented in the papers here, that the U.S. violated both of these basic laws. These facts are not hidden. Much of the evidence indicating that the U.S. set up the war with Iraq is contained in U.S. Rep. Gonzalez's impeachment resolution and brief in support presented to Congress and printed in full in the *Congressional Record* (H. Res. 86, February 21, 1991, *see Appendix B, below, for the full text*). It is only the major commercial press which has ignored the facts. In part it includes the following revelations:

> As early as October 1989 the CIA representatives in Kuwait had agreed to take advantage of Iraq's deteriorating economic position to put pressure on Iraq to accede to Kuwait's demands with regard to the border dispute.
>
> ... Encouraging Kuwait to refuse to negotiate its differences with Iraq as required by the United Nations Charter, including Kuwait's failure to abide by OPEC quotas, its pumping of Iraqi oil from the Rumaila oil field and its refusal to negotiate these and other matters with Iraq.
>
> Months prior to the Iraqi invasion of Kuwait, the United States administration prepared a plan and practiced elaborate computer war games pitting United States forces against Iraqi armored divisions.
>
> In testimony before Congress prior to the invasion, Assistant Secretary Kelly misleadingly assured Congress that the United States had no commitment to come to Kuwait's assistance in the event of war.
>
> April Glaspie's reassurance to Iraq that the dispute was an 'Arab' matter and the U.S. would not interfere.

Even if we suspend judgment and believe that the U.S. neither planned nor prepared this war, it had no right to initiate war until all means of negotiation were at an end. The U.S., however, never wanted to negotiate. It wanted war. According to the *New York Times*, the U.S. wanted to "block the diplomatic track because it might defuse the crisis at the cost of a few token gains for Iraq."[1] Iraq at about this time made an offer to negotiate to settle the crisis. It offered to withdraw from Kuwait for some form of control over two uninhabited islands that would give it access to the Gulf and control over the Rumaila oilfield. The offer was, according to the some U.S. officials, "serious and negotiable." Offers continued until the eve of war and by that time Iraq was willing to withdraw totally from Kuwait. The U.S. instantly dismissed all offers to negotiate a settlement and refused to pursue them. "No negotiations" was the constant theme of U.S. President George Bush.[2] The U.S. and its allies wanted to see the crisis settled by force. It is the U.S. that chose war and not peace; it is the U.S. that committed a crime against peace.

I want to say a word about the UN Resolutions embargoing Iraq and supposedly authorizing the use of force. All of the UN Resolutions were suspect because of what Rep. Gonzalez called in his impeachment resolution the "bribing, intimidating and threatening of others, including members of the UN Security Council." Gonzalez cites the following outright bribes:

- Immediately after the November 29 vote in the UN authorizing force, the administration unblocked a $140 million loan for the World Bank to China and agreed to meet with Chinese government officials.
- The Soviet Union was promised $7 billion in aid from various countries and shipments of food from the United States.
- Zaire was promised forgiveness of part of its debt as well as military assistance.
- A $7 billion loan to Egypt was forgiven, a loan the President had no authority to forgive under U.S. law.
- Syria was promised that there would be no interference in its Lebanon actions.
- Saudi Arabia was promised $12 billion in arms sales.
- The U.S., which owes the most money to the U.N., paid off $187 million of its debt immediately after the vote authorizing the use of force.
- The administration attempted to coerce Yemen by threatening the cutoff of U.S. funds.[3]

But even were this not the case, can the UN apply measures of force such as the embargo, effectively a blockade and an act of war, and authorize all necessary means—which the U.S. saw as war—without negotiating first? It cannot do so according to the stipulations of its own Charter.

Nor was the UN permitted to embargo food and limit the importation of medicine. Neither the UN nor any country can take measures that intentionally or knowingly have the effect of starving and harming the civilian population. This is prohibited by every tenet of international law. It is well known that Iraq imports 60 to 70 percent of its food. As testimony presented elsewhere in book and in many reports from fact finding missions to Iraq since the end of the war, many children died because of the lack of infant formula and adequate food and medicine.

And what of this infamous resolution that authorized all necessary means to remove Iraqi forces from Kuwait? Did this authorize war? Not by its own terms. The resolution was left specifically vague, stipulating only "all necessary means." Nowhere did it mention war and certainly many other means were readily available for achieving the goals of the UN resolutions. All other means were never exhausted. From the U.S. standpoint, massively violent war was the first and only option. All other means had to be precluded at any cost.

Finally, on the point of the U.S. commission of crimes against peace even if we get over all of the other illegalities and assume that the UN had the authority to authorize war and did so in this case, what did it authorize? It authorized the use of force only to obtain the withdrawal from Kuwait. It certainly never authorized the incursion into, much less the occupation of, Iraq and the total subjection of that nation to the dictates of the UN acting out policies originating in the U.S. government. No one has authorized the U.S. to have even one soldier in Iraq. This is aggression in the classic sense. U.S. forces moved in from the north down to the 36th parallel and have set up camps for displaced Kurds. Nor did the resolution authorize any bombing of Iraq, certainly not the bombing of Baghdad or Basra or the near complete destruction of the economic infrastructure.

The second broad category we are concerned with are what are referred to as crimes against humanity. By this I mean both crimes against civilians and combatants. There is a long history of outlawing certain kinds of conduct once war has begun. The principle is that the means and manner of waging war are not unlimited. In other words, while it is of primary importance to prevent war, once war has begun there are limits on the types of targets that can be attacked and the weapons that can be employed. Central to these laws of war is the desire to protect civilians, noncombatants, soldiers who are no longer fighting, and the resources and infrastructure necessary to their survival. Again, at Nuremberg, the Nazis were tried for crimes against humanity which included killings of the civilian population and the wanton destruction of cities, towns or villages and devastation not justified by military necessity.

These laws are embodied in various treaties, including most importantly the Hague Convention of 1907, the Geneva Conventions of 1949, and Protocol I Additional to the Geneva Conventions. They all reflect a similar set of rules, violations of which are war crimes. They are built around two principles. First, military operations are to be directed at military objectives—the civilian population and civilian objects are not to be targets. So, massive bombing, as was engaged in by the U.S., which kills civilians and destroyed the water supply, is illegal. In fact, when the dispute was barely a month old, in September, Air Force chief of staff General Michael J. Duggan was fired for leaking to the press suggestions that the U.S. was already planning bombing targets which would include Iraqi power systems, roads, railroads, and petroleum plants.[4]

At the height of the war, this sort of bombing campaign was defended by Pentagon spokespersons in terms reminiscent of the Vietnam War. Many parts of Iraq became "free fire zones" in which everyone who remains in such a zone is declared unilaterally by the U.S. as a legitimate target for destruction. The entire city of Basra, Iraq's second largest, became such a free fire zone, as described by Brigadier General Richard I. Neal. The *Washington Post* story recounts: "In Riyadh, Marine Brig. Gen. Richard I. Neal gave a detailed explanation of why repeated allied pounding of the southern Iraqi city of Basra is causing 'collateral damage.' Basra, Neal said, 'is a military town in the true sense, it is astride a major naval base and a port facility. The infrastructure, military infrastructure, is closely interwoven within the city of Basra itself.' The destruction of targets in and around Basra is part of what Neal described as an 'intensifying' air campaign against all 'echelons of forces, from the front lines and all the way back . . . There is no rest for the weary, for any of them. . . . There is no division, no brigade, there is no battalion that really is spared the attacks from our pilots.' "[5]

The second limit international law places on the conduct of war is the principle of proportionality—you can only use the amount of force against military targets necessary to achieve your objective. So, for example, destroying the retreating Iraqi army was disproportional for it was not necessary to achieve the Iraqi withdrawal from Kuwait. The whole conduct of the war, in fact, violates every conceivable notion of proportionality.

International law lays down rules for how the civilian population is to be protected. Obviously civilians cannot be intentionally attacked, but, indiscriminate attacks are prohibited as well. Such attacks are defined as those that "employ a method of combat which cannot be directed at specific military objectives." While the mass media, especially TV news, gave the impression during the war that the U.S. was using only "smart" bombs that directly hit their military targets, in fact 93 percent of the bombs used were "dumb" bombs of which at least 60 to 70 percent missed their targets, killing lots of people. Such bombs cannot be directed exclusively at a military objective and in my view are illegal. Nor can bombs dropped from a B-52 flying at thirty to forty thousand feet hit their targets.

There is a special law protecting objects indispensable to the civilian population—the infrastructure of a country. This includes prohibitions on destroying food supplies, water and sewer systems, agriculture, power, medical services, transportation and similar essentials. These cannot be attacked even if there is some military goal, if the effect would be to leave civilians without the essentials for life. In fact, the U.S. government openly stated its goal of destroying the infrastructure of Iraq including water, food supplies, the sewer system, electricity and transportation. The story was not reported in U.S. newspapers until late June of 1991, but the facts were obvious to even a casual observer. According to the *Washington Post* story, U.S. officials admitted that "Some targets, especially late in the war, were bombed primarily to create postwar leverage over Iraq, not to influence the course of the conflict itself. . . . the intent was to destroy or damage valuable facilities that Baghdad could not repair without foreign assistance."[6] A report of the United Nations Mission to Iraq led by Under Secretary General Martti Ahtisaari said that Iraq had been bombed into the pre-industrial age (see Appendix B, below).[7] Thousands of additional people—all civilians and most children—are dying as a result.

Attacks are also to be limited to strictly military objectives. These are defined as those that make an effective contribution to military action and whose destruction offer a definite military advantage. Civilian objects are not to be attacked. In case of doubt, such as a school, it should be presumed that it is not used as a military object. What does this rule say about bombing of the al-Ameriyah shelter? At least 300 children and parents were incinerated in a structure that the U.S. knew was built as a shelter for civilians. Its possible use as a military communications center was only a matter of speculation and weak supposition. Or, what are we to make of the destruction of the baby milk factory at the beginning of the bombing campaign? Again, an American general has admitted that this was a mistake—a mistake that has cost many, many babies their lives.

There are also a series of very specific laws:

1. The use of asphyxiating gases is prohibited. The U.S. violated this by its use of fuel-air explosive bombs on Iraqi frontline troops; these bombs are terror bombs which can burn the oxygen over a surface of one or two square kilometers, destroying human life by asphyxiation.

2. These fuel-air bombs and the U.S. use of napalm are also outlawed by the Hague and Geneva Conventions, which prohibit the use of weapons causing unnecessary harm to combatants. The level of U.S. evil is demonstrated by the sending to the Gulf of a stingray blinding laser system which is supposed to knock out optics on enemy weapons, but has the side effect of blinding soldiers as well who operate the weapons.

3. The bombing of peaceful nuclear power facilities is forbidden and particularly so because of the dangers of the spread of radioactivity. The UN International Atomic Energy Agency classified the reactors as peaceful, yet the U.S. bombed them, not caring about the spread of radioactivity. The bombing was intentional and planned in advance, clearly in violation of international law.

4. Both the Hague Convention of 1954 and Protocol I to the Geneva Conventions prohibit attacks against historic monuments, works of art, places of worship and sites which constitute the cultural and spiritual heritage of a people. Catholic churches, a 4th century monastery and a Sunni Moslem mosque represent just some of the massive violations that occurred. [See Fadwa El Guindi's essay on archaeological destruction, below—editor.]

5. Protocol I of the Geneva Convention also requires protection of the natural environment against widespread and severe damage—the U.S. massive bombing, the blowing up of reactors, the hitting of oil storage facilities all violate this prohibition.

What I have tried to outline today is the broad framework in which we can evaluate the criminal conduct of the United States. I believe that these hearings will establish beyond doubt the criminal nature of American actions in this war. I want to close with the words of Bertrand Russell when he addressed the war crimes that had been revealed at the War Crimes Tribunal held in 1967 in Stockholm and in 1968 in Copenhagen to judge U.S. actions in Vietnam:

It is not enough, however, to identify the criminal. The United States must be isolated and rendered incapable of further crimes. I hope that America's remaining allies will be forced to desert the alliances which bind them together. I hope that the American people will repudiate resolutely the abject course on which their rulers have embarked. Finally, I hope that the peoples of the Third World will take heart from the example of the Vietnamese and join further in dismantling the American empire. It is the attempt to create empires that produces war crimes because, as the Nazis also reminded us, empires are founded on a self-righteous and deep-rooted belief in racial superiority and God-given mission. Once one believes colonial peoples to be *untermenschen*—'gooks' is the American term—one has destroyed the basis of all civilized codes of conduct.

Notes

See Appendix A of this book for relevant selections from international law.

1. *New York Times*, August 22, 1990.
2. Michael Emry, "How the U.S. Avoided the Peace," *The Village Voice*, March 5, 1991.
3. *Congressional Record*, January 16, 1991: H520.
4. Rick Atkinson, "U.S. to Rely on Air Strikes if War Erupts," *New York Times*, September 16, 1990: A1.
5. "Ground War Not Imminent, Bush Says: Allies to Rely on Air Power 'for a While,'" *Washington Post*, February 12, 1991: A14.
6. *Washington Post*, June 23, 1991: A1.
7. Martti Ahtisaari, "Report to the Secretary General on Humanitarian Needs in Kuwait and Iraq in the Immediate Post-Crisis Environment," United Nations Report No. S122366, March 20, 1991.

Michael Ratner is an attorney, former director of the Center for Constitutional Rights, and past president of the National Lawyer's Guild. He has filed a lawsuit challenging the constitutionality of the Gulf War. This report was given at the New York Commission Hearing, May 11, 1991.

War Crimes Committed
Against the People of Iraq

Francis Kelly

On November 15, 1990, President George Bush declared, "Let me repeat, we have no argument with the people of Iraq. Indeed, we have only friendship for the people there."[1] President Bush's "friendship" found a peculiar variety of expressions. In the course of his brief war against Iraq, president Bush killed thousands of civilians, hundreds of thousands of Iraqi soldiers, and left the country in ruins. In a nation whose level of development was the envy of the region, the electrical system is now crippled, the sanitation system is gone, the communication system destroyed, and famine and disease claim hundreds of lives a day. Besides being offensive to any standard of civilized conduct, this campaign of systematic destruction also violated international law repeatedly by disregarding the rights of non-combatants, destroying Iraqi infrastructure, and using excessive force against Iraqi troops.

President Bush popularized the myth of a clean war against Iraq and actively misinformed the public about what his policies really involved. While he asserted that he was at war with Saddam Hussein alone and indeed, that the U.S. military was utilizing technologies that would spare the civilian population, the bleak reality in the cities and towns throughout Iraq offers a painful refutation of the President's claims.

President Bush said of the allied bombing raids:

> This has been fantastically accurate and that's because a lot of money went into this high technology weaponry—these laser guided bombs and a lot of other things—stealth technology—many of these technologies ridiculed in the past now coming into their own and saving lives, not only American lives, Coalition lives but the lives of Iraqis.[2]

The air war against Iraq was accurate only in so far as the bombs always hit the ground; any more stringent criteria makes the President's statement invalid. The Pentagon later conceded that only seven percent of all bombs used against Iraq were the so-called "smart bombs." These weapons hit their targets about 80 to 90 percent of the time, while their "dumb" counterparts missed their targets 75 percent of the time. In the end, 70 percent of the bombs dropped on Iraq missed their intended targets.[3] Witnesses to the destruction said that the Coalition bombing leveled entire blocks of civilian homes.[4] A group of refugees fleeing Baghdad early in the war claimed that the neighborhoods of Jadriyyah and Qadissiyya were hit, the bus station in Doura was hit as well as a bus full of people.[5] In the city of Basra, Louise Cainkar, the director of the Palestine Human Rights Information Center, reported visiting five different sections of Basra where bombs had struck civilian homes. She said that the residents of the Ma'kel neighborhood reported that 400 civilians in that section alone had died from the U.S.-led Coalition bombardment.[6]

Although 80-90 percent of the smart bombs may have enjoyed a deadly precision, the remaining 10-20 percent did not. One such wayward missile exploded in a civilian area of Fallujah, a city about forty miles west of Baghdad. Civil defense officials claimed that one hundred and thirty people, mostly tenants of an apartment complex, were killed by the attack.[7] Twelve year-old Abdullah Mehsan now has two stumps where his legs used to be. He is arguably one of the lucky ones in his family; his father, an uncle, and a cousin all perished in that raid.[8] Likewise, a failed assault on a bridge in the southern city of al-Nasiriya reportedly killed forty-seven people.[9]

Some of the Coalition attacks betrayed a particularly pronounced disregard for civilian lives. Refugees fleeing Iraq reported that Coalition warplanes strafed the highway leading west to Jordan. Bernd Debusmann of Reuters said that "Of at least half a dozen burned or damaged vehicles on the desert highway, only one vehicle was clearly a military vehicle" and that "local residents told me that the bombing of the road was frequent and the targets almost always seemed to be civilian trucks or private cars."[10] In one of their more arrant violations of the Geneva Convention, Coalition planes attacked a convoy of medical vehicles despite the fact that they bore the symbols of the United Nations, the Red Cross and the Red Crescent.[11] Louise Cainkar reported seeing "no less than forty bombed out civilian cars and freight trucks and two buses laying on their sides, most of them between the border and the 200km road marker" and claims that "the Jordanian authorities said twelve Jordanian truck drivers were killed on this road."[12] Pentagon officials, while offering excuses, do not deny that civilian vehicles on the road between Baghdad and Amman have been hit.[13] So too in southern Iraq, the Coalition attacked civilian vehicles; they bombed a bus traveling on the highway to Basra and between thirty and forty people burned to death.[14]

The most egregious attack on civilian, however, remains the bombing of al-Amariyah bomb shelter in Baghdad. At 4:30 am on February 13, 1991, U.S. pilots sent a laser-guided ordnance down a ventilation shaft, destroying the shelter and killing at least three hundred people and possibly as many as 1600.[15,16] The U.S. military claimed that the structure was a command and control center and thus a legitimate target. However, the military steadfastly refused to provide any hard evidence of their assertion.[17] Moreover, reporters who visited the scene after the bombing saw no evidence to support the Coalition's claim. Indeed, retired Air Force Chief of Staff, General Michael Dugan told the *London Times* that the intelligence information about the shelter was out of date at the time of the attack.[18] When questioned about the civilian deaths, the Coalition claimed ignorance. Lt. General Thomas Kelly responded that "We didn't know that the Iraqis had civilians in there."[19] The response is puzzling given that the U.S. military authorities knew that the structure was originally built as a bomb shelter.[20] Survivors of the attack claim that the facility had been used as a shelter since the second week of the war.[21,22] hence the suggestion by intelligence officers that Iraqi authorities had moved civilians into the shelter at night, when U.S. photographic satellites cannot see, is patently absurd. Furthermore, officials conceded that the last aerial photos of the structure may have been taken a full week before its attack.[23] While the real motive for the attack may never be known, one point is clear: when it came to respecting Iraqi lives, the Coalition just couldn't be bothered. Louise Cainkar estimates that in the end between 11,000 and 24,500 civilians died as an immediate result of the Coalition bombing[24] and the United Nations estimates that Coalition bombing caused the destruction of 2,500 homes in Baghdad leaving 20,000 people homeless.[25]

President Bush's prattle about friendship only adds insult to mortal injury. The relentless bombing of Iraq is repugnant to our basic sense of decency and it reveals an utter disregard for human life by the Coalition forces. However, it also betrays a contempt for international law in the a campaign whose putative motivation was the enforcement of that very body of law. The most salient example of this is the tragedy at al-Amariyah. Article 57 of the Geneva Convention delineates the responsibility that the parties to a conflict owe the non-combatants: it states that anyone conducting military operations must "do everything feasible to verify that the objectives to be attacked are neither civilian or civilian objects and are not subject to special protections but are military objectives." As outlined above, the U.S. military either knew that civilians were present and lied or just did not bother to check. If the latter is true, they are in violation of the Convention. If they did know that civilians were in the shelter, then while they might advance some specious argument that the military end justified the slaughter of innocents, nevertheless Article 57 mandates that they give advance warning of "attacks which may affect the civilian population," which they failed to do. Given that survivors of the attacks spoke of listening to Voice of America, the Coalition clearly had the option of saving those civilian lives; they simply chose not to exercise it.[26] So too with the attacks on the highways, the Coalition ignored their moral and legal duty. As a party to the conflict they were under an obligation to make every effort to avoid civilian casualties and furthermore to abide by the Geneva Convention's restriction on indiscriminate attacks. The Convention unambiguously proscribes attacks of the variety witnessed on the Iraqi highways. Indeed, Article 51 states that

> 4. Indiscriminate attacks are prohibited. Indiscriminate attacks are: a) those which are not directed at a specific military objective. . . .
> 5. Among others, the following types of attacks are to be considered as indiscriminate: a) an attack by bombardment by any method or means which treats as a single military objective a number of clearly separated and distinct military objectives located in a city, town, village, or other area containing a similar concentration of civilians or civilian objects.

The attacks on the highways and bridges provide an ideal illustration of the motive behind these restrictions: while the highways carry military vehicles, they also carry civilian vehicles and probably in greater numbers, based on the eyewitness testimony to the destruction. The Pentagon's pathetic justification that civilians shouldn't have been using those roads and bridges since their pilots can't distinguish civilian vehicles from military ones in no way exculpates the Coalition for its crime. In fact it only further proves the guilt since the Geneva Convention also stipulates that when doubt exists whether a potential target is civilian or military the favor must go to the civilian use and the attack be cancelled.

If the treatment of civilians was harsh, the assault on the Iraqi army plumbed the depths of depravity. In the first two days of the ground phase, the U.S. Army employed tanks and earthmovers to bury thousands of Iraqi soldiers alive. The tactic of ploughing sand into the trenches was designed to destroy the trenches and terrify the soldiers into surrendering, only surrender was almost impossible because the earthmovers were flanked by armored vehicles pouring machine-gun fire into the ditches as the sand was piled over. Colonel Anthony Moreno, who participated in the assault said that "What you saw was a bunch of buried trenches with people's arms and things sticking out of them."[27]

In the early morning of February 26, 1991, the Iraqi forces began a panicked flight from Kuwait. U.S. forces left open only two roads out of Kuwait City. All retreating soldiers were forced onto these roads and it was made known that soldiers moving north would not be attacked. Later, the U.S. military feigned ignorance of the troops' intentions and floated the possibility that they sought to reinforce the Republican Guards just over the border in Iraq. Thus, the Pentagon argued, the possibility of a serious threat from this retreating force left the Coalition no choice but to attack its adversary.[28] However, the Coalition did not merely attack its foe; it massacred them. The fleeing Iraqi troops took two roads that meet near the Kuwaiti town of al-Mutlaa and their exodus quickly became a trafic jam of immense proportions. U.S. Marines allowed the convoy of cars, trucks, and every sort of vehicle to get out of Kuwait City before bombing the front and the end of the convoy. Kill zones were assigned along the seventy miles of highway so that planes would not crash into each other.[29,30] The Coalition forces were under orders to "find anything that was moving and take it out"[31] and thus began the orgy of slaughter. When the devastation finally ceased, the roadways were literally awash in blood. One reporter wrote that "As we drove slowly though the wreckage, our armored personnel carrier's tracks splashed through great pools of bloody water."[32] Both soldiers and civilians alike perished on the Basra road as North Carolina Guardsman Mike Ange described:

> I actually went up close and examined two vehicles that basically looked like refugees maybe trying to get out the area. You know you had like a little Toyota pick-up truck that was loaded down with you know the furniture and the suitcases and you know rugs and you know the pet cat and you know that type of thing all over the back of this truck and those trucks were taken out just like the military vehicles.[33]

The BBC's Stephen Sackur said that among the dead on the highway were contract workers from the Indian subcontinent as well as Palestinians fleeing an intolerant, "liberated Kuwait."[34] The army estimates that 25,000 people were slaughtered on those highways.[35]

The Coalition immediately sought to provide a justification for the carnage. The Army pleaded that they couldn't be sure these fleeing troops weren't going to join the Republican Guard and strike back at Coalition forces. A U.S. military spokesman claimed that the Coalition had "no real evidence of any withdrawal at this time." Specifically, he said, "There's no significant Iraqi movements to the north." His comments were utterly false; half a day before that report had been issued, Iraqi troops had begun their exodus from Kuwait.[36] Furthermore, U.S. troops observed that the Iraqi forces were "trying to escape up the highway."[37] One Navy pilot even claimed that the Iraqis had affixed white flags to their tanks, though it failed to save them.[38] The retreat was not an orderly attempt to withdraw from Kuwait and re-group but rather a terrified run from a marauding foe. The fleeing soldiers were conscripts who had been forced to fight and never posed any threat to the U.S. forces.[39] Furthermore, the Iraqis in their frenzied departure were in fact complying with UN resolution 660 which called for them to "withdraw immediately and unconditionally all its forces to the positions in which they were located before August 1, 1990."

The U.S. generals could not, in the end, conceal their true agenda. General McPeak said that the Coalition sought to disarm the Iraqis, a goal that exceeded the bounds of the UN mandate. Clearly, the Coalition was not protecting itself from a soon-to-be reinforced Republican Guard; it was exploiting the Iraqi panic in order to further its own objectives, and Coalition soliders took tens of thousands of lives in the process. As McPeak put it when he spoke of the retreat: "It's during this phase that the true fruits of victory are achieved from combat, when the enemy is disorganized."[40]

Of course, the Coalition later sought to soften the perception of the attack on the convoy as a massacre. McPeak had the gall to claim that the U.S. forces made every effort to avoid killing the Iraqi troops, seeking to destroy their equipment instead. He stated, "I think we tried to disarm the Iraqi Army as humanely as possible."[41] However, the *London Independent* correspondent Richard Dowden said in a televised interview,

> The lorries further down the line would have tried to crash off the motorway and just get away, just get off the road and [the American pilots] would have chased them, and you saw them in the desert, and then you would see bodies going from those lorries so they'd actually hunted down people who were just running away.[42]

The attitude of those participating in the killing seems to bear out Dowden's comment. Lt. General George Patrick told a reporter, "I think we're past the point of just letting him [i.e., Iraqi soldiers—Americans developed the habit of referring to them in the singular] get in his tanks and drive them back to Iraq and say, 'I'm sorry.' I feel fairly punitive about it." Cmdr. Sweigart said,

> One side of me says, 'That's right, it's like shooting ducks in a pond.' Does that make me uncomfortable? Not necessarily. Except that there is a side of me that says, 'What are they dying for? For a madman's cause? And is that fair?' Well, we're at war—it's the tragedy of war. But we do our jobs.[43]

We wonder if someday, Cmdr. Sweigart will claim that he was only following orders as Nazi war criminals did at the Nuremburg Tribunals.

Even after the cease-fire between Iraq and the Coalition was signed, the U.S. continued to disarm the Iraqi army. On March 1, 1991, an Iraqi convoy allegedly fired on a platoon of the 24th Infantry Division. Many Iraqi soldiers, due to their loss of communication lines, were unaware of the cease-fire agreement. Hence it is possible that the Iraqis really did fire upon U.S. forces. Even so the U.S. had loudspeakers, which they chose not to use, which would have allowed them to broadcast news of the cease-fire and possibly avert any bloodshed. Instead, they annihilated the convoy and killed 2,000 Iraqi soldiers without suffering a single death on the American side.[44] Had the Iraqis fired first and gotten some sort of advantage on the U.S. forces, surely someone would have been killed. One U.S. soldier quipped, "Say hello to Allah" as he obliterated his target with a Hellfire missile. The post-cease-fire massacre as this "battle" came to be called, like the slaughter near al-Mutlaa, Kuwait, is remarkable for its needlessness;

so many lives sacrificed for nothing.[45]

It has become perfunctory for proponents of the war, especially when talking about these kinds of massacres, to punctuate their remarks with comments about the brutality, the inhumanity, the nastiness of war. Interviewed about the war, former ambassador Robert Neumann argued for the destruction of Iraq's infrastructure as a military necessity, adding that "War is rough business."[46] These self-evident and self-serving observations seek to obfuscate the fact that the conduct of war is regulated by international law and that the obligations of the combatants cannot simply be swept aside with some essentially trivial remark. The obligations include respect for the rule of proportionality which the U.S. ignored in its treatment of the Iraqi forces both on the Basra highway and after the cease fire. The rule of proportionality granted the Coalition the right only to use as much force as is necessary to achieve its legitimate military aim. However, the violent destruction of the Iraqi army clearly exceeded the UN mandate under which the Coalition operated. The goal of the Coalition forces was to drive Iraq from Kuwait; they did not need to massacre them to accomplish this, much less destroy the economic infrastructure.

Only after the cease-fire was signed and the rebellions had ended, did the full dimensions of Iraq's situation became apparent. The horror caused by the bullets and bombs was replaced by other, equally deadly forms of extermination. What the Pentagon spokespeople politely termed "collateral damage" is no less than annihilation of the infrastructure of Iraq and this destruction has caused what the International Committee of the Red Cross has termed a "public health catastrophe of immense proportions."[47]

On March 20, 1991, Under-Secretary General of the UN, Martti Ahtisaari submitted a report on the post-war situation in Iraq. In the report, he writes that

> It should, however, be said at once that nothing that we had read had quite prepared us for the particular form of devastation which has now befallen the country. The recent conflict has wrought near-apocalyptic results upon the economic infrastructure of what had been, until January 1991, a rather highly urbanized and mechanized society.

The *UN Report* chronicles the nature of the damage inflicted by unrelenting allied assault. The bombing virtually eliminated Iraq's capacity to generate electrical power. At the time the report was published, all electrically operated installations had ceased to function and only diesel-powered plants produced power. Public sanitation is jeopardized by the elimination of garbage collection. The bombing destroyed all modern forms of communication, and transmission of information occurs only by person-to-person contact. When hostilities within Iraq finally ceased, the city of Erbil had only five of its forty-two community health centers functioning; Basra had five out of nineteen; and Sulamaneiya had six out of twenty.

Likewise, in Baghdad four hospitals were destroyed. Iraq lost its only laboratory for producing veterinary vaccines as well as all its available stores of animal vaccines in the bombardment.[48,49]

This infrastructural damage has profound implications: Iraq is experiencing a public health disaster on a scale heretofore unimaginable. The crux of the disaster lies in the destruction of the electrical system. At the end of the war, Iraq's electrical output was four percent of its prewar level; in May the level was twenty-two percent. The reduction in generating capacity is already producing a lethal effect. A team of medical professionals from Harvard visited Iraq and in their report they write: "There is a link in Iraq between electrical power and public health. Without electricity, water cannot be purified, sewage cannot be treated, water borne diseases flourish, and hospitals cannot cure treatable illnesses." This absence of electricity, coupled with direct damage to the sewage treatment facilities, has rendered the sewage treatment system as a whole inoperable, Richard Reid, the regional director of UNICEF, described the result, "You can go into places like Amara and Basra and walk for blocks and blocks almost knee deep in liquid sewage and it's in people's homes obviously. It's everywhere."[50] Among other things, it's in the Tigres River, a main source of drinking water for Baghdad. The water system, too, has been paralyzed. Iraqis, once accustomed to using 450 liters of water a day, now find themselves limited to between thirty and forty liters a day. The water they manage to obtain is probably contaminated. They lack of electricity has greatly affected hospitals which depend on electricity for refrigeration, sterilization, lighting, and sanitation. Doctors complain of having to perform operations by candlelight.[51] There is a particularly savage irony here. President Bush accused the Iraqis of removing babies from incubators in Kuwait (a charge which later proved false) while it was the Coalition which by rendering incubators useless actually perpetrated the crime in Iraq.

While all of Iraq will pay dearly for the destruction, children will suffer most acutely. President Bush declared 1990 the "Year of the Child." In Iraq, 1991 is clearly not the year of the child. The *Harvard Report*, in what it describes as a conservative estimate, claims that by May of 1992 170,000 Iraqi children under the age of five will perish form health problems directly related to the destruction of Iraqi society. The pollution of the water supply has led to epidemics of typhoid, cholera, and gastroenteritis which threaten the entire population, and children in particular. The *UN Report* notes that immunization of children has stopped, that there is a high incidence of upper respiratory illnesses, diarrhea, and psychological problems for children under five.

As the Iraqi people confront this crisis, their medical system is especially ill-equipped to cope. The report claims that the "Iraqi health system is currently operating at a fraction of its capacity before the gulf crisis." Before the war, Iraq had 131 hospitals and 851 community health centers

(Above) Former residential area in Babylon Province which was bombed at 3:00 a.m. on February 26, 1991. Seventeen people were killed, including four children. (Below) A common scene throughout Iraq after the bombing: women washing and taking drinking water from an irrigation ditch. This photo comes from Kufa, an agricultural town south of Baghdad. This area was completely electrified and every home had running water before the U.S. bombing. Some 26,000 necessary civilian and industrial facilities were destroyed by U.S. bombing. Electrical grids were targeted thus making the preservation of food and medicine impossible as well as the purification of water and the treatment of sewage. (Photos: Commission of Inquiry)

nationwide. According to Ezio Murzi, the director of the United Nations Children's Fund, ninety-five percent of Iraq's population had easy access to medical care.[52] Iraqi hospitals were well equipped with sophisticated medical technology but such progress has been tragically reversed.[53] Iraqi physicians who once used multi-million dollar CAT scanning devices now suffer severe shortages of everything: drugs, IV fluids, needles, syringes, bandages, and blood for transfusions.[54,55] Syringes are now often reused, even when not properly sterilized, a practice which raises the specter of hepatitis epidemic as well.[56] Iraq used to import sixty percent of its medicines. The trade embargo, coupled with inoperability of Iraq's only two pharmaceutical factories means a severe shortage of drugs of any sort. Of course, this includes painkillers; one victim of an air raid reportedly had his leg amputated without anesthetic.[57]

A whole range of medical practices have become impossible. Louise Cainkar reported that the necessity of using kerosene lamps has dramatically increased the number of burned children, but the normal treatment for burns has become unavailable. The standard procedure of bathing the children and applying a salve is impossible; neither clean water, nor any kind of lotion is available. If the children can survive the risk of infections, which there are no antibiotics to treat, they will still be covered in scar tissue as skin grafts have become infeasible.[58] In fact, the treatment of such victims usually extends no further than flapping a towel to keep away the flies.[59] A host of other problems has arisen. Women are suffering physical stress from carrying water, a chore imposed upon them with the destruction of the water system.[60] Dr. David Levinson cites anecdotal evidence that increased levels of stress are causing psychological problems.[61]

As though the collapse of the healthcare system were not enough, it is in fact only part of the problem: famine has begun to aggravate an already dire situation. The *UN Report* warned back in March that Iraq's food supply was critically low. While Iraq used to import seventy percent of its food, it can no longer do so because of the United Nation's sanction. The report cautioned that even if Iraqi agriculture enjoyed a bumper crop, the country would probably only enjoy a portion of the yield because the destruction of the infrastructure has made harvesting crops very difficult. The scarcity of food has dramatically inflated food prices. The same package of powdered infant formula that cost one dollar before the war now costs fifty dollars.[62] The cost of rice has increased twenty-five times. The caloric intake for the average Iraqi has been cut in half and the entire population is beginning to suffer from acute malnutrition.[63] Richard Reid, the regional director of UNICEF said of the situation,

> We're seeing also in Iraq now a couple of manifestations of hunger that you had seen only before in Africa, never in our region, never in the Middle East or North Africa and that is marasmus, the condition

that makes kids under two suddenly look like wizened old men, the bony face, the skull; and kwashiokor, the malnutrition that turns a child's hair a rusty red and gives him a pot belly. That's unimaginable in Iraq and yet you see it all over the place now, even in Baghdad.[64]

Even as he was presiding over the dismemberment of Iraqi society, President Bush continued to peddle his notion of a humane and surgical war: "And we are not trying to systematically destroy the functions of daily living in Iraq. That's not what we're trying to do or are we doing it."[65] In fact, such systematic destruction was one component of the complex architecture of the war; Bush's remark was his own desperate attempt to continue to mask what was becoming obvious to anyone who listened to the grisly stories coming from Iraq. Pentagon planners now admit that they chose certain targets within Iraq in order to gain leverage over Iraq following the war. The military acknowledged that they sought to intensify the effect of the sanctions by bombing Iraq.[66] Senior Pentagon officials now also concede that it was neither "dumb" bombs nor failed "smart" bombs that caused the crucial damage to Iraq. Rather, it was the laser-guided missiles which struck their intended targets—electrical plants, oil refineries, and transportation networks—that have brought Iraq so much misery.[67] Article 54 of the Geneva Convention states that,

> It is prohibited to attack, destroy, remove or render useless objects indispensable to the survival of the civilian population, such as foodstuffs, agricultural areas for the production of foodstuffs, crops, livestock, drinking water installations and supplies and irrigations works, for the specific purpose of denying them of their sustenance value to the civilian population or to the adverse Party, whatever the motive, whether in order to starve out civilians or cause them to move away, or for any other motive.

Hence, these admissions by the U.S. military are nothing short of a confession to war crimes.

The continuing use of sanctions against Iraq adds another sinister dimension to the crisis. Not only has the Coalition brought Iraq to the brink of famine, but it is still actively aggravating the situation by refusing to lift the UN sanctions. While Iraqis suffer and die, U.S. officials trivialize the situation. U.S. ambassador to the UN, Thomas Pickering, even after the publication of the *UN Report* describing the onset of starvation, said that Iraq's food supply was "minimal but adequate."[68] Pentagon spokeperson, Lt. Col. T. P. Mazer downplayed the urgency of the crisis, "When you first see a car wreck, it looks really bad. But then the body guy gets there and pretty soon the car runs like new."[69] Besides the contemptuousness of the analogy, it fails to address the situation at all: under the UN sanctions, the "body guy" wouldn't even be allowed to go into Iraq. Even band-aid measures of relief have met with resistance. A shipment of ibuprofen from the Fellowship of Reconciliation was delayed by customs officials[70] and a shipment of medical supplies sent by the Mennonite Central Committee met bureaucratic obstacles from the State Department.[71]

Even when the sanctions finally do end and food and medicine can flow freely into Iraq, the suffering will not be done. For most people in Iraq life will continue to be a struggle. George Bush may have vilified Saddam Hussein, but he punished the people. It has been the average Iraqi who has suffered: the children whose fathers died on the Basra highway, the people whose loved ones burned to death in al-Amariyah, and the parents who cannot feed their children. The level of misery and grief in Iraq are completely foreign to the people of the United States, but perhaps if they try to imagine what this war has meant on an individual level, they will be forces to ask themselves, "How did we let this happen?"

Notes

1. Bill Moyers, "PBS Special Report: After the War," Spring 1991.
2. Ibid.
3. Jack Colhoun, "U.N.: Iraq Bombed Back to Stone Age," *Guardian*, April 3, 1991.
4. Mark Fineman, "Eyewitnesses Describe Allied Raids' Devastation," *San Francisco Chronicle*, February 5, 1991.
5. Mark Fineman, "Refugees Carry Tales of Terror from Baghdad," *Los Angeles Times*, January 23, 1991.
6. Louise Cainkar, "Desert Sin," in *Beyond the Storm: A Gulf Crisis Reader*. Michel Moushabeck and Phyllis Bennis, eds. (An advance copy of the article was used for this report.)
7. "Death Comes to a Town Almost Forgotten by War," *Manchester Guardian Weekly*, February 24, 1991.
8. Ed Vulliamy, "Bombs Blast Away Lives and Limbs," *Manchester Guardian Weekly*, May 12, 1991.
9. Bernd Debusmann, "Many Civilians Die in Bridge Bombing Raids," *Financial Times*, February 8, 1991.
10. "News Reports That Allied Bombs Have Hit Civilians on Highway," *San Francisco Chronicle*, February 1, 1991.
11. Nora Boustany, "In Baghdad, Surgery by Candlelight," *Washington Post*, February 10, 1991.
12. Cainkar, "Desert Sin."
13. Gerald F. Seib, "Heavy Civilian Casualty Toll of Raid on Iraq has U.S. Scrambling to Keep Alliance United," *Wall Street Journal*, February 4, 1991.
14. Frank Smyth, "Rider: Kuwait Buses Bombed," *San Francisco Examiner*, February 10, 1991.
15. Edward Cody, "U.S. Briefers on Attack Concede No Quarter," *Washington Post*, February 14, 1991.

16. Cainkar, "Desert Sin."

17. Doyle McManus and James Gerstenzang, "Structure Built to Shelter Iraqi Elite, U.S. Says," *Los Angeles Times*, February 15, 1991.

18. William Arkin, Damian Durrant, and Marianne Cherni, *On Impact: Modern Warfare and the Environment—A Case Study of the Gulf War* (Washington, DC: Greenpeace, 1991). Hereafter cited as *On Impact*.

19. "Kelly: 'We Knew This To Be' a Military Facility," *Washington Post*, February 14, 1991.

20. see McManus and Gerstenzang, above.

21. Cainkar, "Desert Sin."

22. Caryle Murphy, "Amariya Where One Raid Killed 300 Iraqis," *Washington Post*, June 23, 1991.

23. see Seib, above.

24. Cainkar, "Desert Sin."

25. Martti Ahtisaari, *Report to the Secretary-General on Humanitarian Needs in Kuwait and Iraq* (New York: United Nations, 1991). Hereafter cited as *UN Report*.

26. Cainkar, "Desert Sin."

27. Patrick J. Sloyan, "U.S. Officers Say Iraqis Were Buried Alive," *San Francisco Chronicle*, September 12, 1991.

28. "Trapped in the Killing Ground at Mutlaa," *Manchester Guardian Weekly*, March 17, 1991.

29. Ibid.

30. See *On Impact*, p. 107

31. See *On Impact*, p. 109.

32. See *On Impact*, p. 108.

33. See Moyers, above.

34. Alexander Cockburn, "Unlimited Violence Wins Out," *Los Angeles Times*, March 11, 1991.

35. See *On Impact*, p. 108.

36. See "Trapped in the Killing Ground," above.

37. See *On Impact*, p. 108.

38. See *On Impact*, p. 110.

39. See Moyers.

40. See *On Impact*, p. 111.

41. See *On Impact*, p. 111.

42. See Moyers.

43. See "Trapped in the Killing Ground," above.

44. See *On Impact*, p. 112.

45. Patrick J. Sloyan, "War's Fiercest Ground Battle Was After Cease Fire," *Oakland Tribune*, May 8, 1991.

46. See Moyers.

47. Jessica Matthews, "A New Meaning for the Term Germ Warfare," *Manchester Guardian Weekly*, April 28, 1991.

48. *Harvard Study Team Report: Public Health in Iraq After the Gulf War*. Hereafter cited as *Harvard Report*.

49. See Colhoun, above.

50. See Moyers.

51. See Boustany, above.

52. See Caryle Murphy, "Doctors in Postwar Iraq Teetering Between Hope and

Terror," *Washington Post,* June 20, 1991.

53. Patrick Tyler, "Iraqi Hospitals Struggle With Wounds of War," *New York Times,* July 5, 1991.

54. See *Harvard Report.*

55. See Boustany.

56. Walter V. Robinson, "Iraq Since the War: A Hell of Hunger and Privation," *San Francisco Examiner,* March 24, 1991.

57. See Boustany.

58. Louise Cainkar, "Iraq Was a New Kind of War—Biological Warfare," *Guardian,* May 15, 1991.

59. See Matthews, above.

60. "Hunger, Disease Stalk a Ravaged Iraq," *Guardian,* March 13, 1991.

61. David Levinson, "Healthcare Effects of the War Against Iraq," see Part Three of this volume.

62. Patrick E. Tyler, "Disease Spirals in Iraq as Embargo Takes Its Toll," *New York Times,* June 24, 1991.

63. Joyce Price, "Embargo and Air War Diminish Iraq's Food Supply to a Record Low," *Washington Times,* February 28, 1991.

64. See Moyers.

65. See Moyers.

66. Barton Gellman, "Allied Air War Struck Broadly in Iraq," *Washington Post,* June 23, 1991.

67. Ibid.

68. "Hunger, Disease Stalk a Ravaged Iraq," *Guardian,* March 13, 1991.

69. Dennis Bernstein and Larry Everest, "Apocalypse Later," *East Bay Guardian,* June 1991.

70. See Colhoun.

71. Press release from the Mennonite Central Committee, March 12, 1991.

This essay was presented at the San Francisco Commission of Inquiry, September 14, 1991 and published in *High Crimes and Misdemeanors: U.S. War Crimes in the Persian Gulf* by the Research Committee of the San Francisco Commission of Inquiry (2849 Mission Street, #28, San Francisco, CA 94110).

Part Three:

Testimony and Evidence

Bomb damage in a residential neighborhood in Basra, Iraq's second largest city with a population of about 800,000 people. There are no military targets anywhere near. (Photo: Commission of Inquiry for the International War Crimes Tribunal)

Provoking Iraq

Gautam Biswas and Tony Murphy

The picture the U.S. paints of the war against Iraq is that its impetus was the invasion of Kuwait by Iraq. The U.S. was apparently only responding to a madman's actions, a madman who would take over Saudi Arabia if given the chance. However, there is strong evidence that the U.S. has had designs on Iraq for a long time; that rather than the Persian Gulf War being sparked by Hussein's actions, the conflict was actually part of a long-term strategy of the U.S. designed to weaken Iraq.

When the long record of U.S.-Iraq relations is studied, the war would actually seem to be premeditated on the part of the U.S. The premeditated aspect of the war is evident from the simultaneous support by the U.S. for Hussein and by the U.S. cooperation with Kuwaiti efforts to weaken Iraq. War would be the inevitable outcome of such double dealing. The goal of war would be the destruction of Iraq as a power center in the Middle East. A history of CIA operations reveals designs to destabilize Iraq dating back to the 1950s, and it includes statements made as early as 1985 that showed U.S. intent to depose Hussein.

Supporting Iraq and Weakening Iraq

Intentions to create a situation which would cause Iraq to invade Kuwait are evident from the dual policy the U.S. pursued with both countries; tilting toward Iraq near the start of the Iran-Iraq war, with increasing favoritism as the 80s progressed, but secretly cooperating with Kuwait to economically weaken Iraq.

Just before 1980, the U.S. retreated from its position that Iraq was a terrorist state and tool of the Soviets and began a process of support and cooperation.[1] According to authoritative Kuwaiti sources, in late 1979, U.S. Secretary of State Zbigniew Brzezinski urged Saddam Hussein to attack Iran and seize Khuzistan, the U.S. objective being to roll back the Iranian revolution under the Ayatollah Khomeini. Hussein, if successful, could have access to the Gulf through the Shatt-al-Arab, a strait between Iraq and Iran.[2]

In late 1980, Hussein, now with the tacit approval of the Bush-Reagan administration, invaded Iran in order to regain that territory, conceded to Iran in 1975.[3]

The Iran-Iraq war lasted eight years; Saudi Arabia and Kuwait provided financial support while the U.S. (among other nations) provided arms. The U.S. Senate Committee on Foreign Relations reported in June 1990 that "From the start of the Iran-Iraq war . . . the world's arms dealers gathered like carrion to pick on the corpse of conflict. . . . In 1982, the Reagan-Bush administration removed Iraq from the list of those countries which supported terrorism and in 1984 restored full diplomatic relations. This was a clear signal to the Western world that Iraq was back in the fold."[4]

But the U.S. embrace of Iraq was not all public. In fact, the U.S. sent $50 billion in shipments of U.S. weapons to Iraq through third countries— including Egypt, Jordan, and Kuwait—in violation of the arms embargo previously slapped on Iraq in response to reports of Iraqi human rights abuses.[5] Another illegal military aid program to Iraq was funneled through a credit program in the Agriculture Department—$5.5 billion in credit guarantees between 1983 and 1990.[6] Legally, Iraq was only supposed to receive credit for loans to buy U.S. food and agricultural products, like seeds and tobacco.[7]

Most of the hardware shipped to Iraq was "dual use" equipment: trucks, machinery, and parts easily used for either civilian or military purposes. Yet, Rep. Charlie Rose (Dem-NC) talking to the media about the program, said that there was evidence that some U.S. agriculture companies might have provided guns, ammunition, and other military aid.[8] Rose said of the program, "The Administration decided to funnel aid to Iraq through a quiet little sleepy loan program in the Agriculture Department because they thought it wouldn't attract too much attention. And now that the whole thing has blown up in their face, they are petrified about people finding out."[9]

The U.S. support for Iraq extended to encouragement of Iraq's economic policies. The *London Observer* reported on October 21, 1990 that at a secret meeting in early 1990 in New York between an Iraqi minister and a U.S. former ambassador, Hussein was advised to push for higher oil prices. Hussein, saddled with an $80 billion debt after the war with Iran, consulted the Center for Strategic and International Studies (CSIS) to determine an appropriate price.[10] In January 1990, the oil price was $21 per barrel and expected to plummet to $15 per barrel—as it did. The recommendation to Hussein by CSIS was to adopt an aggressive campaign to push the price of oil up to $25 per barrel.[11]

The Bush administration continued to express sympathy for Hussein's economic woes, and worked to stave off Congressional efforts at sanctions and suppress State Department reports mildly critical of Iraq's government.[12] But Hussein's economic problems were steadily being worsened as a result of coordinated efforts by the CIA and Kuwait to glut the oil market.[13] This had been happening since the mid-1980s. As Iraq became increasingly embroiled in the war with Iran, Kuwait took advantage of Iraq's preoccupation to encroach on Iraqi territory until the southern tier of the Rumaila oil reserves was in Kuwaiti hands. In all, Kuwait annexed 900 square miles of Iraqi land.[14] Kuwait then purchased the Santa Fe Drilling Corporation, a company that specializes in "slant drilling" (drilling horizontally or at an angle rather than vertically) and proceeded to pump out billions of dollars of Iraqi oil. This action glutted the oil market and prices came tumbling down.[15]

In the second quarter of 1990, Kuwait's excess overproduction was eighteen percent of OPEC's total excess.[16] It was around this time that Hussein accused OPEC of waging economic war against him. Documentation for this claim does exist. A top-secret Kuwaiti intelligence memorandum described a meeting in November 1989 between Brig. Fahd Ahmad Fahd, the director general of state security in Kuwait and CIA Director William H. Webster. It states the following,

> We agreed with the American side that it was important to take advantage of the deteriorating economic situation in Iraq in order to put pressure on that country's government to delineate our common border. The Central Intelligence Agency gave us its view of appropriate means of pressure, saying that broad cooperation should be initiated between us on condition that such activities are coordinated at a high level.[17]

The above facts suggest that the U.S. was working with Kuwait to intentionally provoke Iraq. How else to explain the lack of concern by Kuwaiti government officials when Iraqi soldiers began massing on their country's northern border? Congress held hearings about the dangerous situation of the troop deployment; only the Bush administration and the Kuwaitis seemed unconcerned. In a July 30, 1990, meeting between the Jordanians and Kuwaitis, Kuwaiti Foreign Minister Sheikh Sabeh Ahmed al-Jaber al Sabah, the Emir's brother, wasn't the least worried about an Iraqi invasion. Instead he was reported to be making sarcastic remarks: "We are not going to respond [to Iraq]. . . . If they don't like it, let them occupy our territory. . . . We are going to bring in the Americans."[18]

Later that week, the crown prince of Kuwait confirmed that Kuwaitis had known all along about American intentions.[19] He said he had told his senior military officers that if an invasion were to occur, their responsibility was to hold off the Iraqis for twenty-four hours and then "American and foreign forces would land in Kuwait and expel them."[20]

In the months preceding the invasion, Hussein had grown increasingly hostile. On April 12, 1990, Hussein met with four Senators, including Robert Dole and Alan Simpson. Hussein complained about increasing American hostility and especially a Voice of America broadcast that criticized the Iraqi government, as well as the efforts in Congress for economic sanctions against Iraq for human rights violations. Dole and Simpson reassured Hussein that the U.S. press was "spoiled and conceited," and that neither the VOA broadcast nor the congressional sanctions issues accurately reflected Bush administration sentiment.[21] Dole said that the VOA commentator had been fired—which turned out to be a lie. Shortly thereafter, Hussein instructed his military officers to prepare a plan for the invasion of Kuwait.[22]

On May 28, 1990 at an Arab League Summit meeting, Hussein accused fellow Arabs of economic warfare through depression of the price of oil. He also hinted that if other Arab countries were not willing to help him with his war debt, he would be willing to resort to force against them.[23] Hussein's intentions during the months leading up to the invasion actually were quite clear, yet the U.S. maintained its policy of privately encouraging Hussein while publicly denouncing Iraq and supporting similar hostile actions toward Iraq by other nations. On April 25, 1990 April Glaspie, U.S. Ambassador to Iraq flatly told Hussein: "We have no opinion on the Arab-Arab conflicts, like your border disagreement with Kuwait. . . . James Baker has directed our official spokesmen to emphasize this instruction."[24] This comment was made in the context of near catastrophic hostility between Iraq and Kuwait. Iraqi troops were already staging on the border. Nearly a year after her meeting with Hussein, Glaspie claimed to the Senate Foreign Relations Committee that something had been lost in the translation, that Iraq had "maliciously" edited the transcript of the meeting "to the point of inaccuracy."[25] Her warnings that the U.S. would not tolerate the use of force against Kuwait had been deleted, she said. Later, however, when actual transcripts of cables Glaspie sent to the State Department immediately after the meeting were released, it became apparent that Glaspie lied to the Senate and that the original transcripts released by Iraq were quite accurate [see Appendix B for transcripts of the cables—editor]. She had, in effect, given Hussein a green light just at the moment before the invasion by saying that the U.S. would not interfere in border disputes between Iraq and Kuwait.[26]

If the Iraqi government had edited out Glaspie's warning, her positions would have been grossly out of synch with other official U.S. statements made to Iraq at the time. On the day before Glaspie's meeting with Hussein, State Department Spokesperson Margaret Tutweiler told reporters at a press briefing, "We do not have any defense treaties with Kuwait and there are no special defense or security commitments to Kuwait."[27] And on July 31, 1990, two days before the Iraqi invasion, Assistant Secretary of State for Near Eastern Affairs John Kelly reiterated that the U.S. was uninterested. Questioned by Rep. Lee Hamilton in Congress, "If Iraq . . . charged across the border into Kuwait—what would be our position with regard to the use of U.S. forces? . . . Is it correct to say, however, that we do not have a treaty commitment which would obligate us to engage U.S. forces there?" Kelly's answer was, "That is correct."[28] Iraq was monitoring these discussions carefully and was well aware of these official pronouncements.

U.S. officials went as far as to punish senior CIA official Charles Eugene Allen for repeatedly warning that Iraq would invade Kuwait. Warning was Allen's job; his actual title "National Intelligence Officer for Warning" meant that he had to take seriously his prediction of an invasion. Yet two of Allen's government colleagues assert he was stripped of his authority because of his warning. His bi-weekly report on developing trouble spots was suspended and his staff at the Pentagon and National Intelligence Council shrunk.[29] Kuwait's government behaved much the same way. On March 7, 1991, Kuwaiti officials broke up a press conference at which a Kuwaiti military attaché based in Iraq before the invasion accused his government of ignoring his repeated warnings in July 1990 that an Iraqi invasion was imminent.[30]

Kuwait and the U.S. seemed to have something to hide regarding why the warnings of Iraq's imminent invasion were ignored. It is clear that some serious warning to Iraq by the U.S. that an invasion of Kuwait would meet with U.S. military opposition would have deterred Hussein. The Iraqi president seems to gone out of his way to find out whether or not the U.S. would respond before giving the signal to begin the invasion. While Hussein did have a complaint against Kuwait, he did not have any reason for wanting to provoke the U.S. Clearly, the U.S. war with Iraq was not sparked by the Iraqi invasion of Kuwait. Rather, through cooperation with Kuwait that included economic pressure, provocation and deceit, the U.S. worked to create the invasion as a pretext for a war against Iraq—a major war which General Norman Schwarzkopf had been planning and simulating for at least a year before it actually occurred.

Thirty Years of Anti-Iraq Covert Action

Since Iraq gained independence through the revolution in 1958, the U.S. has consistently engaged in covert operations designed to destabilize it. And these operations continue even now after the war has officially ended. In the Middle East the pattern is familiar. The democratic government of Iran in 1953 was overthrown by the CIA because it had nationalized its oil fields. Iranian leader Mohammed Mossadegh was over thrown and the former Shah of Iran, Muhammad Reza Pahlevi, returned to his throne as a U.S. puppet, embarking on a 25-year reign of U.S. financed repression and torture.[31]

In 1958 Brig. Gen. Abdul Karim Kassem replaced the royal family's Premier Nuri Said as the Iraqi leader. Soon the CIA had formed the Health

Alteration Committee, euphemistically named for the planned assassination of Kassem. Dr. Sidney Gottlieb of the CIA's technical services division mailed a monogramed, poisoned handkerchief to "an Iraqi colonel." The CIA told the Church Committee that the ploy did not work—but that the target had "suffered a terminal illness before a firing squad in Baghdad."[32] That is an accurate description of Kassem's death; he was killed by the Ba'athist coup in 1963.[33]

As the U.S. became embroiled in Vietnam, its destabilization program against Hussein lagged. In 1972, Nixon found reason to renew the campaign. On June 1, 1972, Iraq had announced the nationalization of this oil industry.[34] The Ba'ath Party's slogan—"Arab Oil for Arabs"—just did not sit well with the U.S. On May 31, 1972, Nixon and National Security Advisor Henry Kissinger planned with the Shah of Iran to arm Kurds in northern Iraq.[35] Uncovered by the House Select Committee on Intelligence which published its findings in the suppressed Pike Report, the plan called for $16 million in arms to the Kurds in a program so secret that the State Department was not even told about it.[36] The stated goal of the program was to weaken Iraq, but neither the U.S. nor the Shah wanted the Kurds to win autonomy. The Pike Report states: "Neither the foreign heads of state (the Shah) nor the President and Dr. Kissinger desired victory for our clients (the Kurds). They merely hoped to insure that the insurgents would be capable of sustaining a level of hostility just high enough to sap the resources of the neighboring state."[37] The Report goes on to say that "the strategy was not imparted to our clients, who were encouraged to continue fighting. Even in the context of covert action, ours was a cynical enterprise."[38]

In 1975 the Shah of Iran and Hussein reached an agreement whereby Iran would stop arming the Kurds in exchange for territorial concessions by Hussein; namely, the Shatt-al-Arab waterway. All aid to the Kurds was cut off, and Iraq's military launched a search-and-destroy mission in Kurdish Iraq.[39] U.S. strategies to weaken Iraq came to a temporary halt with the rise of Islamic fundamentalism and the overthrow of the Shah in February 1979. But the U.S. soon found a way to continue its covert war with Iraq, even as it supported Iraq in the war against Iran. U.S. arms sales to both sides of the war were undertaken, using Oliver North's secret weapons supply team.[40] Setting the stage for the U.S. war with Iraq, the U.S. helped Iran by sharing intelligence on Iraq and assistance in trying to depose Saddam Hussein. The Congressional report on the Iran-Contra scandal states:

> The United States simultaneously pursued two contradictory foreign policies—a public one and a secret one. . . . The public one was to improve relations with Iraq. At the same time, the United States secretly shared military intelligence on Iraq with Iran, and North told the Iranians in contradiction to United States policy that the United

States would help promote the overthrow of the Iraqi head of government. . . . As the negotiations continued, North returned to the fate of President Hussein. He declared that '[We] also recognize that Saddam Hussein must go,' and North described how this could be accomplished.[41]

North elaborates during a conversation with Iran-Contra players Richard Secord, Albert Hakim, and an Iranian government official in Frankfurt in 1985:

One of the things that we would like to do is that we would like to become actively engaged in ending this war [Iran-Iraq] in such a way that it becomes very evident to everybody that the guy who is causing the problem is Saddam Husain [sic]. . . . If I were to talk to any other Moslem leaders, they wouldn't say Saddam Husain [sic] is the problem. They'd say Iran is the problem. . . .

What we're talking about is a process by which all the rest of the Arab world comes very quickly to realize that Iran is not a threat to them. Iran is not going to overrun Kuwait. Iran is not going to overthrow the government of Saudi Arabia. That the real problem in preventing peace in the region is Saddam Husain [sic], and we'll have to take care of that.[42]

North's statements underscore the role of the demonization campaign launched against Hussein after the invasion of Kuwait. One of the effects of this campaign was to obscure to the U.S. public the true nature of Hussein's relationship with other Arab states. Jordan's King Hussein corrects that image in an interview about his stand on the Gulf War with author Michael Emery:

. . . various leaders of the Arab states—even the Saudis—were worried about Iraq's strength. . . . But I went and brought this question up with every single one of them: 'Look, had this country not defended you [from Iran] these last many years, the whole situation would be different. Their strength is for you.'[43]

Saddam Hussein was seen as beneficial to the region, not a threat. The U.S. portrayal of Iraq as ready to invade Saudi Arabia—the justification for the first deployment of troops there—must be seen in the light of North's and King Hussein's statements. Defense Secretary Richard Cheney in a December 1990 speech explained that had Bush not "moved aggressively as he did last August . . . Saddam Hussein would control not only Kuwait, but, my own firm conviction is, he'd also control the eastern province of Saudia Arabia."[44]

Yet, a U.S. official who was closely monitoring intelligence reports from the CIA during the early part of the crisis concluded that, while the Iraqis possessed the capability of moving into Saudi Arabia, they never had the intention of doing so.[45] Another intelligence official receiving daily intelligence briefings on the Persian Gulf crisis told *New York Newsday* on August 9, 1990 that the CIA was "questioning whether they've got the intention. I tend to agree with them [the CIA]. I don't think it was their intention from Day One to invade Saudia Arabia."[46]

But U.S. administration officials claimed Iraqi troops were actually massing on the Saudi Border. However, when independent sources examined satellite pictures of the border they could find no evidence of troop buildup. When Defense Department officials were questioned about the discrepancy and asked to produce photographs showing the buildup, they refused.[47]

It appears that the portrayal of Hussein as a threat had to be consciously manufactured by the U.S. in its latest phase of anti-Iraq activity. With the end of the Iran-Iraq war and the concomitant decline of the Soviet Union as a military presence, the U.S. was able to pursue its deceptive policy of encouragement/provocation in earnest. The U.S. was absolutely adamant about using force against Iraq. Any hint of compromise was summarily rejected. The Soviets proposed a plan whereby Iraq was to withdraw unconditionally, and in return the Soviets would guarantee that Iraq would maintain its present borders. In addition, there would be a comprehensive Middle East conference on the Palestinian question. According to the Soviet plan, after the pullout, there would be no sanctions levied against Iraq, and Saddam Hussein would not be punished. The Bush administration was not moved. It steadfastly maintained that unconditional withdrawal or war were the only two possible resolutions.[48]

The evidence suggests, then, that the war against Iraq was pre-planned and pre-meditated. Far from being waged solely in reaction to Iraq's invasion of Kuwait, the U.S. war against Iraq was a continuation of a 30-year policy. The policy to weaken Iraq has been waged through covert activity, provocation, and dishonesty. The timing of the war has to do with the reduced role in the world of the Soviet Union as a military power.

Many critics of the war with Iraq focus on western dependence on oil as the reason for U.S. dishonesty about its motives in the Gulf. Indeed, the U.S. under Bush has weakened programs for the investigation of alternatives sources even more than when Reagan was president.[49] But some argue that a more general U.S. policy of control of Third World resources—whether in Iraq or Latin America—is the motive; that the decline of the Soviet Union as a military power has given the U.S. freer reign in the Third World as an imperialist power and caused the U.S. military industry to reformulate its reason for existence—a re-focusing from east-west conflict to north-south conflicts.

In fact, Professor Michael Klare has documented the debate in 1989 that occurred as Gorbachev dismantled the Warsaw Pact. The military high command in the Pentagon saw the "peace dividend" as coming out of their pockets. The changes in the USSR prompted an intense discussion among members of the Pentagon, White House, and conservative think tanks as to how to maintain control over government funding.[50] It is important to note that one of the biggest products of the U.S. is military hardware. The Pentagon's spending on hardware and supplies represents more that twenty percent of U.S. manufactured goods.[51] In his article, "Learning the Wrong Lessons from the Gulf Crisis," journalist William Greider notes that

> Since the beginning of the cold war, the defense budget has always served as a kind of back door socialism for patriots. Though no one would admit this, the federal government used national defense as the unassailable cover for massive intervention in the private economy—both by stimulating the economy through heavy spending and by choosing certain industries for subsidy and growth.[52]

Two camps emerged from the debate over what to do with the money that had previously subsidized cold war weapons. One side said that $300 – 500 billion a year should be given to private enterprise in order to strengthen productivity and competition with Germany and Japan. The other side, whose argument won out with Pentagon planners, said that military subsidies should be maintained but that military policy should be redefined.[53]

The U.S. military will now be geared toward low-intensity conflict fighting capability. This will mean that the Pentagon's new mission is to protect continued access to strategic raw materials which are needed by northern industrial states, including the Soviet Union. Speaking in Santa Barbara about Michael Klare's research, Daniel Sheehan of the Christic Institute describes the stance of the northern industrial states: "It is the northern industrial states that believe that they have the right to privileged access to these resources, to pull through their industry, to manufacture, and then to sell to the world."[54] He then cites strategic papers—the U.S. Army's "A Strategic Force for the 1990s and Beyond" (January 1990) and the Air Force's "Global Reach, Global Power" (June 1990): "These are the documents," Sheehan states, "that in the early period before Saddam Hussein had made any moves whatsoever, specifically designated the Persian Gulf and explicitly named Iraq and Saddam Hussein as 'likely candidates' for the . . . new mission of the military."[55]

Notes

1. *Covert Operations, the Persian Gulf, and the New World Order* (Washington, DC: Christic Institute, 1991), p. 8.
2. Ralph Schoenman, "How the U.S. Set Up Iraq's Invasion of Kuwait," *Socialist Action Magazine*, December 1990: p. 4.
3. "Covert Operations," Christic Institute, p. 8.
4. Ibid.

5. Ibid.

6. Jonathan Broder, "U.S. Stuck for Bad Iraq Loans," *San Francisco Examiner*, November 21, 1990: A1.

7. Ibid.

8. Ibid.

9. Ibid

10. Helga Graham, "Exposed: Washington's Role in Saddam's Oil Plot," *London Observer*, October 21, 1990.

11. Ibid.

12. Ibid.

13. See Schoenman, above.

14. Ibid.

15. Ibid.

16. See Graham, above.

17. See "Covert Operations," Christic Institute.

18. Michael Emery, "How the U.S. Avoided Peace," *Village Voice*, March 3, 1991: 22.

19. Ibid.

20. Ibid.

21. Murray Waas, "Who Lost Kuwait?" *Village Voice*, January 22, 1990.

22. Ibid.

23. Ibid.

24. "Covert Operations," Christic Institute.

25. Christopher Ogden, "In From the Cold," *Time*, April 1, 1991: 6.

26. Elaine Sciolino, "Envoy's Testimony on Iraq is Assailed," New York Times, July 13, 1991.

27. "Covert Operations," Christic Institute.

28. See Waas, above.

29. Michael Wines, "CIA Sidelines Gulf Cassandra," *New York Times*, January 24, 1991: D22.

30. William Claiborne, "Envoy Recounts Warning in July of Invasion: Kuwaitis Cut Him Off," *Washington Post*, March 8, 1991: A26.

31. "Covert Operations," Christic Institute.

32. David Wise, "A People Betrayed," *Los Angeles Times*, April 14, 1991: M1.

33. Ibid.

34. "Violence and Sorrow: The History of the Kurds," *Covert Action Information Bulletin*, Summer 1991: 56.

35. Gerard Chaliand and Ismet Seriff Vanly, *People Without A Country: The Kurds and Kurdistan* (London: Zed Press, 1980), p. 184.

36. Daniel Schorr, "1975: Background to Betrayal," *Washington Post*, April 7, 1991: D3.

37. Christopher Hitchens, "Minority Report," *The Nation*, May 6, 1991: 582.

38. Ibid.

39. See Schorr, above.

40. "Covert Operations," Christic Institute.

41. *Report of the Congressional Committees Investigating the Iran-Contra Affair* (Washington, DC: Government Printing Office, 1987), p. 12.

42. Ibid, Volume 1, Appendix A: Source Documents, Frankfurt Meeting

Tape 12, page 1500.

43. Michael Emery, "Jordan's King Hussein on the Gulf War," *San Francisco Chronicle*, March 13, 1991: Z-3.

44. Knut Royce, "A Trail of Distortion Against Iraq," *New York Newsday*, January 21, 1991.

45. Ibid.

46. Ibid.

47. Jean Heller, "Public Doesn't Get the Picture with Gulf War Satellite," *In These Times*, February 27 – March 19, 1991: 7.

48. Serge Ridgeway, "Gorbachev Gives Iraqi a Peace Proposal," *New York Times*, February 19, 1991: A1.

49. James Ridgeway, "Repo Job for Iraq," *Village Voice*, April 16, 1991: 19.

50. Daniel Sheehan, "The Persian Gulf War: Covert Operations and the New World Order," (speech), Santa Barbara, CA, March 21, 1991.

51. Ibid.

52. William Greider, "Learning Wrong Lessons from the Mideast Crisis," *Rolling Stone Magazine*, October 4, 1990: 53.

53. See Sheehan, above.

54. Ibid.

55. Ibid.

"Provoking Iraq" was presented at the San Francisco Commission of Inquiry of the International War Crimes Tribunal and originally published in the Commission's report: *High Crimes and Misdemeanors: U.S. War Crimes in the Persian Gulf* by the Research Committee, 2489 Mission Street, #28, San Francisco, CA 94110. A report on Palestinians in Kuwait will be published soon. Contact the Research Committee for information.

U.S. Conspiracy to Initiate the War Against Iraq

Brian Becker

Even before the first day of the Persian Gulf crisis George Bush and the Pentagon wanted to wage war against Iraq.

What was the character of this war? Iraq neither attacked nor threatened the United States. We believe that this was a war to redivide and redistribute the fabulous markets and resources of the Middle East, in other words this was an imperialist war. The Bush administration, on behalf of the giant oil corporations and banks, sought to strengthen its domination of this strategic region. It did this in league with the former colonial powers of the region, namely Britain and France, and in opposition to the Iraqi people's claim on their own land and especially their natural resources.

As is customary in such wars, the government is compelled to mask the truth about the war—both its origin and goals and the nature of the "enemy"—in order to win over the people of this country. That's why it is important to get the facts. There is ample evidence that the U.S. was eagerly planning to fight the war even before the Iraqi invasion of Kuwait on August 2, 1990. With its plans in tact, we must determine if it is possible that the U.S. government actually sought a pretext for a military intervention in the Middle East.

Information that has come to light suggests that the United States interfered in and aggravated the Iraq-Kuwait dispute, knew that an Iraqi military response against Kuwait was likely, and then took advantage of the Iraqi move to carry out a long-planned U.S. military intervention in the Middle East. This evidence includes:

1) The tiny, but oil-rich sheikdom of Kuwait became the tool of a U.S.-inspired campaign of economic warfare designed to weaken Iraq as a regional power once the Iran-Iraq war ended. During 1989-1990, the Kuwaiti monarchy was overproducing and driving down the price of oil, a policy that cost Iraq $14 billion in lost revenue.[1] Iraq also complained that the Kuwaitis were stealing Iraqi oil by using slant drilling technology into the gigantic Rumaila oil field, most of which is inside Iraq. Kuwait also refused

to work out arrangements that would allow Iraq access to the Persian Gulf.

In May of 1990 at an Arab League meeting, Saddam Hussein bitterly complained about Kuwait's policy of "economic warfare" against Iraq and hinted that if Kuwait's over-production didn't change Iraq would take military action. Yet the Emir of Kuwait refused to budge. Why would an OPEC country want to drive down the price of oil? In retrospect, it is inconceivable that this tiny, undemocratic little sheikdom, whose ruling family is subject to so much hostility from the Arab masses, would have dared to remain so defiant against Iraq (a country ten times larger than Kuwait) unless Kuwait was assured in advance of protection from an even greater power—namely the United States. This is even more likely when one considers that the Kuwaiti ruling family had in the past tread lightly when it came to its relations with Iraq. Kuwait was traditionally part of Iraq's Basra Province until 1899 when Britain divided it from Iraq and declared Kuwait its colony.

Coinciding with Kuwait's overproduction of oil, Iraq was also subjected to the beginning of *de facto* sanctions, instituted incrementally by a number of western capitalist governments. Hundreds of major scientific, engineering, and food supply contracts between Iraq and western governments were canceled by 1990.[2]

2) The U.S. policy to increase economic pressure on Iraq was coupled with a dramatic change in U.S. military doctrine and strategy toward Iraq. Starting in the summer of 1989, the Joint Chiefs of Staff revamped U.S. military doctrine in the Middle East away from a U.S.-Soviet conflict to target regional powers instead. By June 1990—two months before the Iraqi invasion of Kuwait—General Norman Schwarzkopf was conducting sophisticated war games pitting hundreds of thousands of U.S. troops against Iraqi armored divisions.[3]

3) The Bush administration lied when it stated on August 8, 1990, that the purpose of the U.S. troop deployment was "strictly defensive" and necessary to protect Saudi Arabia from an imminent Iraqi invasion. King Hussein of Jordan reports that U.S. troops were actually being deployed to Saudi Arabia in the days before Saudi Arabia "invited" U.S. intervention.[4] Hussein says that in the first days of the crisis Saudi King Fahd expressed support for an Arab diplomatic solution. King Fahd also told King Hussein that there was no evidence of a hostile Iraqi build-up on the Saudi border, and that despite American assertions, there was no truth to reports that Iraq planned to invade Saudi Arabia.[5] The Saudis only bowed to U.S. demands that the Saudis "invite" U.S. troops to defend them following a long meeting between the king and Secretary of Defense Richard Cheney. The real substance of this discussion will probably remain classified for many, many years.

On September 11, 1990, Bush also told a joint session of Congress that "following negotiations and promises by Iraqi dictator Saddam Hussein not to use force, a powerful army invaded its trusting and much weaker neighbor, Kuwait. Within three days, 120,000 troops with 850 tanks had poured into Kuwait and moved south to threaten Saudi Arabia. It was then I decided to act to check that aggression." However, according to Jean Heller of the *St. Petersburg Times* (of Florida), the facts just weren't as Bush claimed. Satellite photographs taken by the Soviet Union on the precise day Bush addressed Congress failed to show any evidence of Iraqi troops in Kuwait or massing along the Kuwait-Saudi Arabian border. While the Pentagon was claiming as many as 250,000 Iraqi troops in Kuwait, it refused to provide evidence that would contradict the Soviet satellite photos. U.S. forces, encampments, aircraft, camouflaged equipment dumps, staging areas and tracks across the desert can easily be seen. But as Peter Zimmerman, formerly of the U.S. Arms Control and Disarmament Agency in the Reagan Administration, and a former image specialist for the Defense Intelligence Agency, who analyzed the photographs for the *St. Petersburg Times* said:

> We didn't find anything of that sort [i.e. comparable to the U.S. buildup] anywhere in Kuwait. We don't see any tent cities, we don't see congregations of tanks, we can't see troop concentrations, and the main Kuwaiti air base appears deserted. It's five weeks after the invasion, and from what we can see, the Iraqi air force hasn't flown a single fighter to the most strategic air base in Kuwait. There is no infrastructure to support large numbers of people. They have to use toilets, or the functional equivalent. They have to have food. . . . But where is it?

On September 18, 1991, only a week after the Soviet photos were taken, the Pentagon was telling the American public that Iraqi forces in Kuwait had grown to 360,000 men and 2,800 tanks. But the photos of Kuwait do not show any tank tracks in southern Kuwait. They clearly do show tracks left by vehicles which serviced a large oil field, but no tank tracks. Heller concludes that as of January 6, 1991, the Pentagon had not provided the press or Congress with any proof at all for an early buildup of Iraqi troops in southern Kuwait that would suggest an imminent invasion of Saudi Arabia. The usual Pentagon evidence was little more than "trust me." But photos from Soviet commercial satellites tell quite a convincing story. Photos taken on August 8, 1990, of southern Kuwait—six days after the initial invasion and right at the moment Bush was telling the world of an impending invasion of Saudi Arabia—show light sand drifts over patches of roads leading from Kuwait City to the Saudi border. The photos taken on September 11, 1990, show exactly the same sand drifts but now larger and deeper, suggesting that they had built up naturally without the disturbance of traffic for a month. Roads in northern Saudi Arabia during this same period, in contrast, show no sand drifts at all, having been swept clean by heavy traffic of supply convoys. The former DIA analyst puts it this way: "In many places the sand goes on for 30 meters and more." Zimmerman's analysis is that "They [roads] could be passable by tank but not by personnel or supply vehicles. Yet there is no sign that tanks have used those roads. And there's no evidence of new roads being cut. By contrast, none of the roads in Saudi Arabia has any sand cover at all. They've all been swept clear."[6]

It would have taken no more than a few thousand soldiers to hold Kuwait City, and that is all satellite evidence can support. The implication is obvious: Iraqi troops who were eventually deployed along the Kuwait-Saudi Arabian border were sent there as a response to U.S. build up and were not a provocation for Bush's military action. Moreover, the manner in which they were finally deployed was purely defensive—a sort of Maginot Line against the massive and offensive mobilization of U.S. and Coalition forces just over the border with Saudi Arabia.

A War to Destroy Iraq as a Regional Power

That the Bush administration wanted the war is obvious by its steadfast refusal to enter into any genuine negotiations with Iraq that could have achieved a diplomatic solution. Iraq's August 12, 1990, negotiation proposal, which indicated that Iraq was willing to make significant concessions in return for a comprehensive discussion of other unresolved Middle East conflicts, was rejected out of hand by the Bush administration.[7] So was another Iraqi offer made in December that was reported by Knut Royce in *Newsday*.

President Bush avoided diplomacy and negotiations, even refusing to send Secretary of State Baker to meet Saddam Hussein before the January 15, 1991 deadline as he had promised on November 30, 1990. Bush also rejected Iraq's withdrawal offer of February 15, 1991, two days after U.S. planes incinerated hundreds of women and children sleeping in the al-Ameriyah bomb shelter. The Iraqis immediately agreed to the Soviet proposal of February 18, 1991—that is four days before the so-called ground war was launched—which required Iraq to abide by all UN resolutions.

The U.S. ground war against Iraqi positions resulted in the greatest number of casualties in the conflict. As many as 50,000 to 100,000 Iraqi soldiers may have died after the Iraqi government had fully capitulated to all U.S. and UN demands. It is thus obvious that the U.S. government did not fight the war to secure Iraq's eviction from Kuwait but rather proceeded with this unparalleled massacre for other foreign policy objectives. These objectives have never been defined for the broader public but only referred to euphemistically under the rubric of the New World Order.

What is the New World Order, what does the U.S. expect to get out of it and what is the "new thing" in the world that makes a new order possible? It is Bush's assumption that the Soviet Union is willing, under the Gorbachev leadership, to support U.S. foreign policy in the Third World. The U.S. figures that if the Soviets are willing to abandon Iraq and their other traditional allies in the Third World then the U.S. and other western capitalist countries can return to their former dominant position in various areas of the world. How the U.S. conducted the war shows that the permanent weakening of Iraq is a key part in the New World Order.[8]

Although the Soviet role has changed dramatically, the goals of U.S. imperialism in the Middle East have remained basically the same, with some shifts in tactics based on varied conditions. The basic premise of U.S. policy has been to eliminate or severely weaken any nationalist regime that challenges U.S. dominance and control over the oil-rich region. The military strategy employed against Iraq not only aimed at military targets, but the "bombing raids have destroyed residential areas, refineries, and power and water facilities, which will affect the population for years."[9] As early as September 1990, the administration, according to a speech by Secretary of State James Baker, changed the strategic goals of the U.S. military intervention to include not only the "liberation of Kuwait" but the destruction of Iraq's military infrastructure.[10]

Iran-Iraq War and U.S. Strategy

That the U.S. sought to permanently weaken or crush Iraq, as a regional power capable of asserting even a nominal challenge to U.S. dominance over this strategic oil-rich region, fits in with a longer historical pattern. Since the discovery of vast oil deposits in the Middle East, and even earlier, the strategy of the U.S. and other European colonial powers was to prevent the emergence of any strong nationalist regime in the region. The U.S. has relied on corrupted and despised hereditary monarchies and dictatorships in the Middle East. Such regimes have served as puppets for U.S. interests in exchange for U.S. protection. When the Shah of Iran was overthrown in 1979 by a massive popular revolution, it came as a complete shock to U.S. oil companies, the CIA, and the Pentagon, which used the hated Shah as a pro-U.S. policeman of the Gulf region.

The Iran-Iraq war was seen as a new opportunity to recoup U.S. losses from the Iranian revolution. Starting in 1982 the U.S. encouraged and provided arms and satellite information to the Iraqi government in its fight against Iran—the Reagan/Bush administration's principal goal was to weaken and contain Iran in order to limit its regional influence. The Iran-Iraq war did indeed weaken Iran, squandering much of the human and material resources of the revolution.

Having weakened Iran, the goal was then to weaken Iraq and make sure that it could not develop as a regional power capable of challenging

U.S. domination. After the war ended, U.S. policy toward Iraq shifted, becoming increasingly hostile. The way U.S. policy shifted is quite revealing; it bears all the signs of a well-planned conspiracy. The cease-fire between Iran and Iraq officially began on August 20, 1988. On September 8, 1988, Iraqi Foreign Minister Sa'dun Hammadi was to meet with U.S. Secretary of State George Schulz. The Iraqis had every reason to expect a warm welcome in Washington and to begin an era of closer cooperation on trade and industrial development. Instead, at 12:30 p.m., just two hours before the meeting and with no warning to Hammadi whatsoever, State Department spokesman Charles Redman called a press conference and charged that "The U.S. Government is convinced that Iraq has used chemical weapons in its military campaign against Kurdish guerillas. We don't know the extent to which chemical weapons have been used but any use in this context is abhorrent and unjustifiable. . . . We expressed our strong concern to the Iraqi Government which is well aware of our position that the use of chemical weapons is totally unjustifiable and unacceptable."[11]

Redman did not allude to any evidence at all nor was the Iraqi government warned of the charges by the State Department. Rather, when Hammadi arrived at the State Department two hours later for his meeting with Schulz, he was besieged by members of the press asking him questions about the massacre. Hammadi was completely unable to give coherent answers. He kept asking the reporters why they were asking him about this. Needless to say the meeting with Schulz was a dismal failure for Iraq's expectations of U.S. assistance in rebuilding after the Iran-Iraq war. Within twenty-four hours of Redman's press release, the Senate voted unanimously to impose economic sanctions on Iraq which would cancel sales of food and technology. Following September 8, 1988 is a two year record that amounts to economic harassment of Iraq by the American State Department, press, and Congress. Saddam Hussein alluded to this period many times during the lead-up to the war and the war itself. On February 15, 1991, in the preamble to his cease-fire proposal, he said "The years 1988 and 1989 saw sustained campaigns in the press and other media and by other officials in the United States and other imperialist nations to pave the way for the fulfillment of vicious aims [i.e., the present war].[12] The *Washington Post's* story on the cease-fire proposal of February 15, 1991 was titled simply: "Baghdad's Conspiracy Theory of Recent History."[13] Some conspiracies theories just happen to be true!

The Bush administration has never presented any evidence whatsoever for its charges that Iraq used poison gas on its own citizens. Rather it has simply repeated the charges over and over in the press. This event is analyzed in considerable detail in a study published by the Army War College called, *Iraqi Power and U.S. Security in the Middle East*. The authors of that study conclude that the charges were false but used by the U.S. government to change public opinion toward Iraq. They even go so far as to suggest a conspiracy against Iraq: "The whole episode of seeking to impose sanctions on Iraq for something that it may not have done would be regrettable but not of great concern were this an isolated event. Unfortunately, there are other areas of friction developing between our two countries."[14]

If the first part of the strategy was to create hostility and economic hardships, then the war was the second phase. The massive bombardment of Iraq coupled with the continued economic sanctions after the war completes a two-part strategy designed to leave Iraq both in a weakened state and dependent on western aid and bank loans for any reconstruction effort. The U.S. will want to have a puppet government in Baghdad, and even if it is impossible to impose a Shah-type government on the Iraqi people, the Bush administration assumes that a war-ravaged country that is economically dependent on the U.S. and European capitalist powers or on UN humanitarian aid will be forced into a subservient position.

The New World Order and Big Oil

We believe that the real goal of the United States war against Iraq is to return to the "good old days" when the U.S. and some European countries totally plundered the resources of the Middle East. Five of the twelve largest corporations in the United States are oil monopolies. Before the rise of Arab nationalism and the anti-feudal revolutions that swept out colonialist regimes in Iraq and other Middle Eastern countries in the 1950s and 1960s, U.S., British, and Dutch oil companies owned Arab and Iranian oil fields outright. Between 1948 and 1960 U.S. oil companies received $13 billion in profit from their Persian Gulf holdings. That was half the return on all overseas investment by all U.S. companies in those years.

In recent decades U.S. companies no longer directly own the oil fields of the Middle East, but they still get rich from them. That is because the royal families of the oil-rich Arabian peninsula, who were put on their thrones by the British empire and are kept there by the U.S. military and the CIA, have loyally turned their kingdoms into cash cows for Wall Street banks and corporations.

This is one way it works. Money spent on Saudi Arabian oil, for example, once went into the accounts of Rockefeller-controlled oil corporations at the Rockefeller-controlled Chase Manhattan Bank. Now it is deposited in the Saudi king's huge account at Chase Manhattan which reinvests it at a hefty profit to the Rockefellers. Chase Manhattan also manages the Saudi Industrial Development Fund and the Saudi Investment Bank. Morgan Guaranty Trust Company, which is linked to Mobil and Texaco, has a representative on the Board of the Saudi Monetary Authority and controls another big chunk of the kingdom's income. Citicorp handles much of the Emir of Kuwait's $120 billion investment portfolio.[15] The total amount that the Gulf's feudal lords have put at the disposal of the western bankers is conservatively estimated at $1 trillion. It is probably much more.

While the big oil companies have a going partnership with the feudal rulers of Saudi Arabia, the United Arab Emirates, etc., they are relatively locked out of Iraq, Iran, Libya, Yemen, and Algeria. The goal of the U.S. war is to roll back the Arab revolution and all the other revolutionary movements that have swept the region since World War II.

The New World Order that Bush has in mind is, in fact, not so new. It is an attempt to turn the clock back to the pre-World War II era of unchallenged colonial domination and plunder of the land, labor, and resources of Africa, Asia, Latin America, and the Middle East by a handful of industrialized capitalist countries. Unlike the old world order of outright colonialism, the new world order will be imposed by Stealth aircraft, guided missiles, smart bombs, and tactical nuclear weapons—not 19th-century gunboats. This is based on grand geopolitical strategy that flows like water from Pentagon-sponsored think tanks in Washington. It leaves out the most important factor in the equation of the Middle East—the broad mass of the people whose hatred for foreign domination and capacity to struggle remains as powerful as ever.

The U.S. and its imperialist allies have won a temporary victory in the Middle East. But their policy of military domination to stop the natural progression of history—for people to liberate themselves from the yoke of colonialism—cannot succeed.

Notes

1. *New York Times*, September 3, 1990.

2. Stated to Brian Becker and other members of the Muhammad Ali Peace Delegation on November 30, 1990 by Iraqi Deputy Prime Minister Ramadan.

3. *Newsweek*, January 28, 1990; for more information on the revamping of Pentagon strategy in early 1990 see Michael T. Klare, "Policing the Gulf— And the World," *The Nation*, October 15, 1990.

4. *New York Times*, October 16, 1990.

5. *New York Times*, October 16, 1990.

6. Jean Heller, "Public Doesn't Get Picture with Gulf Satellite Photos," *St. Petersburg Times*, January 6, 1991. Rpt. *In These Times*, February 27-March 19, 1991: 7.

7. *Newsday*, August 20, 1991.

8. See James Ridgeway, "Third World Wars: Iraq is a Model for Post-Cold War Colonies," *Village Voice*, January 29, 1991.

9. *Newsday*, February 4, 1991—our emphasis.

10. Speech by Secretary of State James Baker, *New York Times*, September 4, 1990.

11. *American Foreign Policy: Current Documents* (Washington, DC: Department of State, 1991), p. 260.

12. *New York Times*, February 16, 1991: A5.

13. Don Oberdorfer, *Washington Post*, February 16, 1991.

14. Stephen C. Pelletiere, et al. *Iraqi Power and U.S. Security in the Middle East* (Carlisle, PA: Strategic Studies Institute, U.S. Army War College, 1990), p. 53.

15. *Liberation and Marxism*, #7 (1990).

_____

Brian Becker was a member of the Muhammad Ali Peace Delegation which travelled to Iraq in late November 1990 in an effort to prevent the war. This report was presented at the New York Commission hearing on May 11, 1991.

U.S. Bombing—
The Myth of Surgical Bombing in the Gulf War

Paul Walker

I first want to thank Ramsey Clark and the National Coalition for having the courage to undertake an event of this nature. I hope as we continue to dig for the truth in this war, the inquiry will be repeated and repeated and repeated hundreds of times over, not only in the United States but around the globe.

Let me try to give you a brief account of the weapons and the war as a military analyst like myself is trying to discover. I must say first that our research at the Institute for Peace and International Security in Cambridge has been going on for several months at this point, ever since the war began and to a certain extent before it began. And there still is a large amount of stonewalling in Washington. Much of the information is unavailable. Much of the information takes an inordinate amount of time to come out. Much of it given out by the various services is in fact contradictory.

The first images of the 42-day Mideast war mesmerized most viewers— nighttime television pictures of targeted Iraqi bunkers and buildings, many in downtown Baghdad, being surgically destroyed by precision-guided bombs dropped by stealthy aircraft. The crosshairs of an aircraft high-tech laser targeting system lined up on the rooftop of the Iraqi Ministry of Defense, moments later a laser-seeking 2,000-pound bomb blew the building apart. Then the cameras would turn to U.S. General H. Norman Schwarzkopf, commander of the anti-Iraq coalition, who described the attack "on his counterpart's headquarters" with a wry, amused smile—you'll all remember this from the first night as I do. Hundreds of military news reporters in the Saudi briefing room laughed with nervous interest as if viewing Nintendo games, although thousands of individuals were killed, possibly, by that weapon. High-tech warfare had, indeed, come of age.

Back in Washington, General Colin Powell, Chairman of the U.S. Joint Chiefs of Staff, announced that he was "rather pleased that we appear to have achieved tactical surprise" against Iraqi forces in a sudden early morning first strike on January 17, 1991. Coalition forces undertook, in short, thousands of aircraft sorties and missile strikes in the first days of war. A select number of the successful ones with laser-guided bombs were portrayed daily back home on Cable News Network, Nightline, and other regular news programs.

Some 50 of the new F-117A batwing stealth fighter bombers were flown in early attacks, apparently achieving better success in Baghdad than they had one year earlier when they missed their targets in Panama City. Over 200 Tomahawk cruise missiles were fired from ships and submarines for the first time in combat, also reportedly achieving successful "surgical strikes" on high-value Baghdad targets, including the Ministry of Defense and Saddam Hussein's presidential palace. American technological prowess was again displayed graphically several days later when Patriot air-defense missiles successfully intercepted attacking Iraqi missiles launched against Saudi Arabia and Israel.

These and other images of war, perhaps more than anything else, I believe, created an illusion of remote, bloodless, pushbutton battle in which only military targets were assumed destroyed. Pentagon officials stressed throughout their daily briefings that Coalition war planners were taking great pains to marry the right weapon with the right target in order to minimize "collateral damage," that is, injury to innocent civilians in Iraq and Kuwait, particularly in populated areas such as Baghdad and Kuwait City.

Halfway through the war, one journalist described the conflict as a "robo war" in which "the raids are intense, unremitting, and conducted with the world's most advanced non-nuclear weaponry but are unlikely to cause the sort of general destruction being anticipated by commentators." A *Wall Street Journal* article proclaimed, "Despite public perceptions, the recent history of high-tech conventional warfare has been to steadily reduce general destruction."

Despite all these public proclamations about limited casualties from so-called surgical and precision strikes there would appear to be much greater destruction and much higher numbers of dead and injured in Iraq and Kuwait. Early first-hand accounts provided glimpses of the possibilities of more than surgical damage to Iraqi targets. From my discussions with Ramsey Clark, this is certainly the case. For example, Captain Steven Tait, pilot of an F-16 jet fighter which escorted the first wave of bomber aircraft and who was the first American to shoot down an Iraqi plane, described his bird's eye view of Baghdad after the first hour of allied bombardment: "Flames rising up from the city, some neighborhoods lit up like a huge Christmas tree. The entire city was just sparkling at us."

The sheer amount of explosive tonnage dropped over Iraq and Kuwait also, I think, tends to undermine any assumption of surgical strikes. Air Force General McPeak, Air Force commanding general, proudly proclaiming,

"Probably the first time in history that a field army has been defeated by air power," estimated that some 88,500 tons of bombs have been dropped in over 109,000 sorties flown by a total of 2,800 fixed-wing aircraft. Of these flights somewhat over half were actual bombing raids while the remainder involved refueling, bomber escort, surveillance, and so forth. Of the actual bombing missions, about 20,000 sorties were flown against a select list of 300 strategic targets in Iraq and Kuwait; about 5,000 were flown against SCUD missile launchers, and some 30,000 to 50,000 against Iraqi forces in southern Iraq and Kuwait. In all, more than 3,000 bombs (including sea-launched cruise missiles) were dropped on metropolitan Baghdad. The total number of bombs dropped by allied forces in the war comes to about 250,000. Of these only 22,000 were the so-called "smart bombs" or guided bombs. About 10,000 of these guided bombs were laser-guided and about 10,000 were guided anti-tank bombs. The remaining 2,000 were radiation guided bombs directed at communication and radar installations.

The most complete survey of all the different bombs, missiles, shells, and weapons so far appears in Appendix A of *On Impact: Modern Warfare and the Environment*, a report prepared by William Arkin, Damian Durrant, and Marianne Cherni for Greenpeace. This report was prepared for the "Fifth Geneva Convention on the Protection of the Environment in the Time of Armed Conflict (London, June 3, 1991). The authors infer the total weapons used from the 1991 fiscal year supplemental budget request to Congress which lists weapons required to replenish U.S. stockpiles. The numbers are revealing and staggering. In part, they include:

- 2,095 HARM missiles
- 217 Walleye missiles
- 5,276 guided anti-tank missiles
- 44,922 cluster bombs and rockets
- 136,755 conventional bombs
- 4,077 guided bombs[1]

The conventional unguided bomb (so-called "dumb bomd") was the most commonly used weapon in the massacre. These come in four types: the Mk 82 (500 lbs), Mk 83 (1,000 lbs), Mk 84 (2,000 lbs), and the M117 (750 lbs). In all some 150,000 to 170,000 of these bombs were dropped during the war.

The U.S. arsenal contains eight kinds of guided bombs:

- AGM-130, an electro-optically or infrared-guided 2,000 pound powered bomb,
- GBU-10 Paveway II, a 2,000 pound laser-guided bomb based on a Mk 84,
- GBU-101 Paveway II, a 2,000 pound laser-guided bomb with I-2000 hard target munition, employed exclusively on the F-117A and used in small numbers,

- GBU-12 Paveway II, a 500 pound laser-guided bomb, used against tanks,
- GBU-24 Paveway III, a 2,000 pound laser-guided, low-level weapon (with BLU-109 bomb and mid-course auto pilot) used against chemical and industrial facilities, bridges, nuclear storage areas, and aircraft shelters,
- GBU-27 Paveway III, a 2,000 pound laser-guided bomb with I-2000 hard target munition on the BLU-109/B, a "black program" adapted version of the GBU-24, used exclusively by F-117A fighters to attack aircraft shelters, bunkers, and other targets in Baghdad, and
- GBU-28, a 5,000 pound "bunker busting" laser-guided bomb, fabricated especially for the war against Iraq "in an effort to destroy extremely hardened, deeply buried Iraqi command and control bunkers, kill senior military officials and possible kill Saddam Hussein."[2]

As if explosive bombs were not enough, the U.S. used massive amounts of fire bombs and napalm, although U.S. officials denied using napalm against Iraqi troops, only on oil filled trenches (this raises the question of who set all the oil wells on fire in Kuwait and southern Iraq). These trenches, of course, in many cases surrounded bunkers where Iraqi soldiers were hiding. Perhaps the most horrifying of all bombs was the Fuel Air Explosives (FAE) which were used to destroy minefields and bunkers in Iraq and Kuwait. These fire bombs were directly used against Iraqi soldiers, although military spokesmen and press reports have consistently tried to downplay their role.[3] Perhaps this is only because press reports were too descriptive before the war when the Pentagon was leaking stories about possible Iraqi use of FAEs, along with nuclear, chemical, and biological weapons—none of which ever appeared on the Iraqi side. The FAE is composed of an ethelene oxide fuel which forms an aerosol cloud or mist on impact. The cloud is then detonated, forming very high overpressures and a blast or shock wave that destroys anything within an area of about 50,000 square feet (for a 2,000 pound bomb). The U.S. also used "daisy cutters" or the BLU-82, a 15,000 pound bomb containing GSX (gelled slurry explosive). This, too, is a concussion type bomb which military spokesmen and the U.S. press said was used to detonate pressure sensitive mines. The mines, of course, surrounded Iraqi troop deployments and the concussive force of the bomb would surely also rupture internal organs or ear-drums of Iraqi soldiers pinned down in their bunkers. This is not even to mention incineration and asphyxiation, as the fire storm of the bomb sucks all of the oxygen out of the area. President Bush continually warned about Iraqi weapons of mass destruction, but it is clear that U.S. forces alone used weapons of mass destruction against Iraqi troops in both Iraq and Kuwait.

Among other controversial weapons are cluster bombs and anti-personnel bombs which contain a large number of small bomblets inside a large casing. Upon impact the little bombs are dispersed over a wide area and then explode. Using cluster bombs, a single B-52 can deliver more than 8,000 bomblets in a single mission. A total of about 60,000 to 80,000 cluster bombs were dropped.[4]

What all of this means to anyone who thinks about the numbers is simply that the bombing was not a series of surgical strikes but rather an old fashioned mass destruction. On March 15, 1991, the Air Force released information stating that 93.6% of the tonnage dropped were traditional unguided bombs. So we have something like 82,000 tons of bombs that were non-precision guided and only 7,000 tons of guided bombs. This is not surgical warfare in any accurate sense of the term and more importantly in the sense that was commonly understood by the American public. Bombs were, moreover, not the only source of explosives rained down upon Iraq. Artillery shells from battleships and rocket launchers amounted to an additional 20,000 to 30,000 tons of explosives.

While the F-117 Stealth fighter captured the fascination of the news media, massive B-52s carried out the bulk of the work. Flying out of bases in Diego Garcia, Spain, United Kingdom, the United States, Saudi Arabia, and other places, B-52s dropped about thirty percent of the total tonnage of bombs. B-52s were used from the first night of the war to the last. Flying at 40,000 feet and releasing 40 – 60 bombs of 500 or 750 pounds each, their only function is to carpet bomb entire areas. General McPeak told *Defense Week*, "The targets we are going after are widespread. They are brigades, and divisions and battalions on the battlefield. It's a rather low density target. So to spread the bombs—carpet bombing is not my favorite expression—is proportionate to the target. Now is it a terrible thing? Yes. Does it kill people? Yes."[5] B-52s were used against chemical and industrial storage areas, air fields, troop encampments, storage sites, and they were apparently used against large populated areas in Basra.

Language used by military spokesman General Richard Neal during the war made it sound as if Basra had been declared a "free fire zone"—to use a term from the Vietnam war for areas which were declared to be entirely military in nature and thus susceptible to complete bombing. On February 11, 1991, Neal told members of the press that "Basra is a military town in the true sense. . . . The infrastructure, military infrastructure, is closely interwoven within the city of Basra itself"[6] He went on to say that there were no civilians left in Basra, only military targets. Before the war, Basra was a city of 800,000 people, Iraq's second largest. Eyewitness accounts suggest that there was no pretense at a surgical war in this city. On February 5, 1991, the *Los Angeles Times* reported that the air war had brought "a hellish nightime of fires and smoke so dense that witnesses say the sun hasn't been clearly visible for several days at a time . . . [that the bombing is] leveling some entire city blocks . . . [and that there are] bomb craters the size of football fields and an untold number of casualties."[7] Press reports immediately following the cease-fire tried to suggest that the massive destruction of Basra was caused by Iraqi forces suppressing the Shiite rebellion or was simply left over from the Iran-Iraq war. This would not be the first time the press and the U.S. government covered up the extent of its war destruction—the case of Panama comes immediately to mind.

The use of B-52s and carpet bombing violates Article 51 of Geneva Protocol I which prohibits area bombing. Any bombardment that treats a number of clearly separated and distinct military objectives located within a city as a single military objective is prohibited. Basra and most of southern Iraq and Kuwait where Iraqi forces were deployed were treated by U.S. military planners as a single area or to use McPeak's phrase "a low density target." The same is true for General Norman Schwarzkopf's order at the start of the ground war "not to let anybody or anything out of Kuwait City."[8] The result of this order was the massive destruction that came to be known as the "Highway of Death." In addition to retreating soldiers, many of whom had affixed white flags to their tanks which were clearly visible to U.S. pilots,[9] thousands of civilians, especially Palestinians, were killed as they tried to escape from Kuwait City. An Army officer on the scene told reporters that the "U.S. Air Force had been given the word to work over that entire area [roads leading north from Kuwait City] to find anything that was moving and take it out."[10]

By now it should be clear to anyone that claims of a surgical or a precise war are no more than the kind of excuses which the guilty always give to deflect blame elsewhere. The destruction of Iraq was near total and it was criminal. The fact that Baghdad was not carpet bombed by B-52s does not mean that the civilian population was not attacked and killed. On top of the massive bombing, we have now a new kind of war: bomb now, die later. The precision bombs which did manage to hit their targets destroyed precisely the life-sustaining economic infrastructure without which Iraqis would soon die from disease and malnutrition. George Bush's remark on February 6, 1991, that the air strikes have "been fantastically accurate" can only mean that the destruction of the civilian economic infrastructure was, indeed, the desired target and that the U.S. either made no distinction between military and civilian targets or defined the military area in such a broad manner as to include much civilian property. In both cases, it is a war crime.

Finally, comments about the surgical nature of the war tend to neglect the outright massacre which occurred in southern Iraq and Kuwait. The only way to describe what happened there would be a killing frenzy. No accurate numbers of people killed in these areas exist but with the massive bombing of bunkers, especially by FAEs, it is likely that most of the Iraqi soldiers were killed by the saturation bombing. This number could go as high as several hundred thousand. These soldiers were defenseless from air attacks and cut off from communication with leaders in Baghdad. They were simply isolated by the U.S.-led coalition, brutally killed, and then bulldozed into some forty-nine mass graves. That is what General Colin Powell said in November with regard to the Iraqi army: "First you cut it off, then you kill it." There is nothing surgical about that.

Notes

1. William M. Arkin, Damian Durrant, and Marianne Cherni, *On Impact: Modern Warfare and the Environment—A Case Study of the Gulf War* (Washington, DC: Greenpeace, May 1991), p. 160, fn 377.

2. John D. Morrocco and David Fulghum, "USAF Developed a 4,700-lb. Bomb in Crash Program to Attack Iraqi Military Leaders in Hardened Bunkers," *Aviation Week & Space Technology*, May 6, 1991: 85.

3. John Morrocco, "Looming Budget Cuts Threaten Future of Key High-Tech Weapons," *Aviation Week & Space Technology*, April 22, 1991: 66-67. Eric Schmitt, "Why Iraqi Battle Threat Fizzled: Allied Strengths and Enemy Weaknesses," *New York Times*, March 4, 1991: A9. Barbara Starr, "FAEs Used to Clear Mines," *Jane's Defense Weekly*, February 23, 1991: 247.

4. Arkin, Durrant, and Cherni, *On Impact*, Appendix A.

5. Tony Capaccio, "McPeak: Unclear If Air War has Sapped Iraqi Will," *Defense Week*, February 4, 1991.

6. *Washington Post*, February 2, 1991: A14.

7. Mark Fineman, "Smoke Blots Out Sun in Bomb-Blasted Basra," *Los Angeles Times*, February 5, 1991.

8. Bill Gannon "Pool Report with the Tiger Brigade Outside Kuwait City," *Newark Star-Ledger*, February 27, 1991.

9. Rowan Scarborough, "Pool Report Aboard the USS Blue Ridge," *Washington Times*, February 27, 1991.

10. Michael Kelly, "Highway to Hell," *New Republic*, April 1991: 12.

Paul Walker is the director of the Institute for Peace and International Security at the Massachusetts Institute of Technology. His report was given at the New York Commission hearing, May 11, 1991 and at the Boston Commission hearing on June 8, 1991.

The Massacre of Withdrawing Soldiers on "The Highway of Death"

Joyce Chediac

I want to give testimony on what are called the "highways of death."
These are the two Kuwaiti roadways, littered with remains of 2,000 mangled
Iraqi military vehicles, and the charred and dismembered bodies of tens
of thousands of Iraqi soldiers, who were withdrawing from Kuwait on
February 26th and 27th 1991 in compliance with UN resolutions.

U.S. planes trapped the long convoys by disabling vehicles in the front,
and at the rear, and then pounded the resulting traffic jams for hours. "It
was like shooting fish in a barrel," said one U.S. pilot. The horror is still
there to see.

On the inland highway to Basra is mile after mile of burned, smashed,
shattered vehicles of every description—tanks, armored cars, trucks, autos,
fire trucks, according to the March 18, 1991, *Time* magazine. On the sixty
miles of coastal highway, Iraqi military units sit in gruesome repose,
scorched skeletons of vehicles and men alike, black and awful under the
sun, says the *Los Angeles Times* of March 11, 1991. While 450 people
survived the inland road bombing to surrender, this was not the case with
the 60 miles of the coastal road. There for 60 miles every vehicle was strafed
or bombed, every windshield is shattered, every tank is burned, every truck
is riddled with shell fragments. No survivors are known or likely. The cabs
of trucks were bombed so much that they were pushed into the ground,
and it's impossible to see if they contain drivers or not. Windshields were
melted away, and huge tanks were reduced to shrapnel.

"Even in Vietnam I didn't see anything like this. It's pathetic," said
Major Bob Nugent, an Army intelligence officer. This one-sided carnage,
this racist mass murder of Arab people, occurred while White House
spokesman Marlin Fitzwater promised that the U.S. and its coalition
partners would not attack Iraqi forces leaving Kuwait. This is surely one
of the most heinous war crimes in contemporary history.

The Iraqi troops were not being driven out of Kuwait by U.S. troops,
as the Bush administration maintains. They were not retreating in order

to regroup and fight again. In fact, they were withdrawing, they were going home, responding to orders issued by Baghdad, announcing that it was complying with Resolution 660 and leaving Kuwait. At 5:35 p.m. (Eastern Standard Time) Baghdad radio announced that Iraq's Foreign Minister had accepted the Soviet cease-fire proposal and had issued the order for all Iraqi troops to withdraw to postions held before August 2, 1990 in compliance with UN Resolution 660. President Bush responded immediately from the White House saying (through spokesman Marlin Fitzwater) that "there was no evidence to suggest the Iraqi army is withdrawing. In fact, Iraqi units are continuing to fight. . . We continue to prosecute the war." On the next day, February 26, 1991, Saddam Hussein announced on Baghdad radio that Iraqi troops had, indeed, begun to withdraw from Kuwait and that the withdrawal would be complete that day. Again, Bush reacted, calling Hussein's announcement "an outrage" and "a cruel hoax."

Eyewitness Kuwaitis attest that the withdrawal began the afternoon of February 26, 1991 and Baghdad radio announced at 2:00 AM (local time) that morning that the government had ordered all troops to withdraw.

The massacre of withdrawing Iraqi soldiers violates the Geneva Conventions of 1949, Common Article III, which outlaws the killing of soldiers who are out of combat. The point of contention involves the Bush administration's claim that the Iraqi troops were retreating to regroup and fight again. Such a claim is the only way that the massacre which occurred could be considered legal under international law. But in fact the claim is false and obviously so. The troops were withdrawing and removing themselves from combat under direct orders from Baghdad that the war was over and that Iraq had quit and would fully comply with UN resolutions. To attack the soldiers returning home under these circumstances is a war crime.

Iraq accepted UN Resolution 660 and offered to withdraw from Kuwait through Soviet mediation on February 21, 1991. A statement made by George Bush on February 27, 1991, that no quarter would be given to remaining Iraqi soldiers violates even the U.S. Field Manual of 1956. The 1907 Hague Convention governing land warfare also makes it illegal to declare that no quarter will be given to withdrawing soldiers. On February 26, 1991, the following dispatch was filed from the deck of the U.S.S. Ranger, under the byline of Randall Richard of the *Providence Journal*:

> Air strikes against Iraqi troops retreating from Kuwait were being launched so feverishly from this carrier today that pilots said they took whatever bombs happened to be closest to the flight deck. The crews, working to the strains of the Lone Ranger theme, often passed up the projectile of choice . . . because it took too long to load.

New York Times reporter Maureen Dowd wrote, "With the Iraqi leader facing military defeat, Mr. Bush decided that he would rather gamble on a violent and potentially unpopular ground war than risk the alternative: an imperfect settlement hammered out by the Soviets and Iraqis that world opinion might accept as tolerable." In short, rather than accept the offer of Iraq to surrender and leave the field of battle, Bush and the U.S. military strategists decided simply to kill as many Iraqis as they possibly could while the chance lasted. A *Newsweek* article on Norman Schwarzkopt, titled "A Soldier of Conscience" (March 11, 1991), remarked that before the ground war the general was only worried about "How long the world would stand by and watch the United States pound the living hell out of Iraq without saying, 'Wait a minute—enough is enough.' He [Schwarzkopf] itched to send ground troops to finish the job." The pretext for massive extermination of Iraqi soldiers was the desire of the U.S. to destroy Iraqi equipment. But in reality the plan was to prevent Iraqi soldiers from retreating at all. Powell remarked even before the start of the war that Iraqi soldiers knew that they had been sent to Kuwait to die. Rick Atkinson of the *Washington Post* reasoned that "the noose has been tightened" around Iraqi forces so effectively that "escape is impossible" (February 27, 1991). What all of this amounts to is not a war but a massacre.

There are also indications that some of those bombed during the withdrawl were Palestinians and Iraqi civilians. According to *Time* magazine of March 18, 1991, not just military vehicles, but cars, buses and trucks were also hit. In many cases, cars were loaded with Palestinian families and all their possessions. U.S. press accounts tried to make the discovery of burned and bombed household goods appear as if Iraqi troops were even at this late moment looting Kuwait. Attacks on civilians are specifically prohibited by the Geneva Accords and the 1977 Conventions.

How did it really happen? On February 26, 1991 Iraq had announced it was complying with the Soviet proposal, and its troops would withdraw from Kuwait. According to Kuwaiti eyewitnesses, quoted in the March 11, 1991 *Washington Post*, the withdrawal began on the two highways, and was in full swing by evening. Near midnight, the first U.S. bombing started. Hundreds of Iraqis jumped from their cars and their trucks, looking for shelter. U.S. pilots took whatever bombs happened to be close to the flight deck, from cluster bombs to 500 pound bombs. Can you imagine that on a car or truck? U.S. forces continued to drop bombs on the convoys until all humans were killed. So many jets swarmed over the inland road that it created an aerial traffic jam, and combat air controllers feared midair collisions.

The victims were not offering resistance. They weren't being driven back in fierce battle, or trying to regroup to join another battle. They were just sitting ducks, according to Commander Frank Swiggert, the Ranger Bomb Squadron leader. According to an article in the March 11, 1991 *Washington Post*, headlined "U.S. Scrambles to Shape View of Highway of Death," the U.S. government then conspired and in fact did all it could to hide this war crime from the people of this country and the world. What the U.S. government did became the focus of the public relations campaign managed by the U.S. Central Command in Riyad, according to that same issue of the *Washington Post*. The typical line has been that the convoys were engaged in "classic tank battles," as if to suggest that Iraqi troops tried to fight back or even had a chance of fighting back. The truth is that it was simply a one-sided massacre of tens of thousands of people who had no ability to fight back or defend themselves.

The *Washington Post* says that senior officers with the U.S. Central Command in Riyad became worried that what they saw was a growing public perception that Iraqi forces were leaving Kuwait voluntarily, and that the U.S. pilots were bombing them mercilessly, which was the truth. So the U.S. government, says the *Post*, played down the evidence that Iraqi troops were actually leaving Kuwait.

U.S. field commanders gave the media a carefully drawn and inaccurate picture of the fast-changing events. The idea was to portray Iraq's claimed withdrawal as a fighting retreat made necessary by heavy allied military pressure. Remember when Bush came to the Rose Garden and said that he would not accept Saddam Hussein's withdrawal? That was part of it, too, and Bush was involved in this cover up. Bush's statement was followed quickly by a televised military briefing from Saudi Arabia to explain that Iraqi forces were not withdrawing but were being pushed from the battlefield. In fact, tens of thousands of Iraqi soldiers around Kuwait had begun to pull away more than thirty-six hours before allied forces reached the capital, Kuwait City. They did not move under any immediate pressure from allied tanks and infantry, which were still miles from Kuwait City.

This deliberate campaign of disinformation regarding this military action and the war crime that it really was, this manipulation of press briefings to deceive the public and keep the massacre from the world is also a violation of the First Amendment of the U.S. Constitution, the right of the people to know.

Joyce Chediac is a Lebanese-American journalist who has traveled in the Middle East and writes on Middle East issues. Her report was presented at the New York Commission hearing, May 11, 1991.

The Effects of the War on Health Care in Iraq

David Levinson, M.D.

The following general observations are based on a trip I made to Iraq shortly after the cessation of the war. It was clear that the bombing war against Iraq has been a war directed against the civilian population through massive destruction of the country's infrastructure. "Iraq has, for some time to come, been relegated to a pre-industrial age, but with all the disabilities of post-industrial dependency on an intensive use of energy and technology." This is the conclusion reached by Martti Ahtisaari, Undersecretary General of the United Nations in his report on the health conditions in Iraq and Kuwait [*see Appendix B, below*].

The extent of infrastructure damage threatens to cause a health catastrophe of immense proportions. This disaster may be inevitable since the entire health care system is severely crippled as a result of the war and serious health care consequences are already visible throughout the country. Conditions in Baghdad, although very serious, are better than in the rest of the country, and have improved recently.

Specific points

1. Iraq's electrical production and telecommunications systems have been destroyed. The transportation system has been critically damaged by massive bombing of bridges and lack of fuel due to sanctions and bombing of Iraq's oil refining centers. In addition, the lack of fuel seriously impairs Iraq's ability to use generators as alternative sources of electrical power. Iraq is a country of rivers and the destruction of bridges, traditionally used by civilians, hampers transport of medical supplies as well as civilian commerce.

These factors have severely affected health care. Health care facilities throughout Iraq have little or no access to electrical power. Although some facilities use generators, they are able to use them for only several hours each day due to lack of fuel. Communication between facilities and between facilities and mobile health units does not exist. Many health centers lack intra-facility telephone service. Without electricity, most of the technology of modern health care cannot be used: laboratory services, blood banking, culturing of media, sterilization of equipment, storing of medicines, radiography equipment, and so forth.

2. There is a critical shortage of medical supplies and medicine throughout the country. Diagnostic and therapeutic equipment is frequently unavailable or cannot be used because of lack of power, shortage of supplies and spare parts. These problems are due to several factors: transportation difficulties as already mentioned, destruction of equipment and supply depots which occurred primarily in the civil war, and sanctions. The effect of the sanctions is difficult to assess. There is a large number of orders for supplies and medicines from before August 2, 1991, which have been paid for by the ministry of Health and have not been delivered. It is claimed that these items have been prevented from reaching Iraq in part by inappropriate application of sanctions to many shipments regardless of content.

In addition, it is claimed that the U.N. sanctions committee has delayed the flow of medical shipments to Iraq through over-strict inspection of all shipments in order to exclude sanctioned items. Perhaps the most crucial impact of sanctions is in preventing Iraq from exporting oil and thereby generating the revenue necessary to purchase needed medical supplies. Medical supplies which are presently being received come entirely from donations from United Nations' relief organizations and other non-governmental organizations such as the Red Cross and Red Crescent Societies. According to the Ministry of Health, these donations supply only 2.5 percent of the country's medical needs.

3. The primary health care threat is that of gastro-intestinal disease caused by water-born infectious illnesses resulting from consumption of contaminated or inadequately treated water. In Baghdad the water supply is drastically reduced, primarily as a result of lack of power needed to move water through pipe systems and purification systems. Water is rationed and the risk of contaminated water is increased with the opening and closing of pipe systems. In Baghdad only three out of seven water treatment plants are functioning due to lack of power. These are running on generators at ten percent capacity. Plants producing aluminum phosphate and chlorine gas have been destroyed by bombing, and sewage treatment plants have been damaged. Water quality is poor to contaminated in many, if not most, areas outside of Baghdad. The ability to test water is limited or non-existent because of lack of reagents. Some neighborhoods in Baghdad and many rural areas are still without water after several months. In many areas, the people as well as health care facilities have to use unsafe water for daily needs. Despite urgent relief efforts in Baghdad which are producing running water to many neighborhoods for a few hours a day, the amount available to each

person is only about 20 liters per person per day—normal use being 200 liters per person per day.

Health care workers report markedly increased numbers of cases of diarrheal illnesses, particularly among children, with unusually high mortality rates of up to 40 percent. Such illnesses were rarely seen in winter months before, but now have been occurring in increased numbers, presumably from the consumption of contaminated water. Warmer summer temperatures optimize conditions for the spread of these illnesses. The threat of serious diseases such as cholera and typhoid is high. In the early Spring when I was in Iraq, cases of cholera were being reported, but I was unable to confirm them personally.

All of the parameters for severe epidemics exist in Iraq: poor sanitation, no communication, lack of food, lack of medicines, lack of transportation, and a poor water supply.

4. The percentage of functioning health care facilities is drastically reduced. Those functioning do so at a minimal level, essentially treating only emergency cases. Many centers have had to significantly reduce hours, and some have closed because of the previously mentioned problems of power, supplies, and transportation. Care of patients is compromised because patients often arrive late in the course of their illnesses and are therefore more severely ill, and they must often be discharged early. These problems are also due to lack of transportation, supplies, reduced hours and staffing difficulties.

5. Hospitals report a significant increase in malnutrition illnesses such as marasmus or progressive emaciation and kwashiorkor, a severe malnutrition in infants and children caused from a diet high in carbohydrates and low in protein. I saw several cases in just one pediatric hospital in Baghdad where I was told that such cases had rarely been seen in the past. Factors which might contribute to this problem are a decreased food supply, particularly in rural areas and decreased transport of food. There appears to be an increased case fatality rate from these illnesses.

6. Morbidity and mortality from chronic illness is increased due to a lack of critical medicines such as insulin, cardiac medicines and chemo-therapeutic agents. Surgeons report increased post-operative complications such as infection, including septicemia, as a result of poor sterile technique caused by unclean water, reusing of surgical gowns and gloves, and inability to adequately sterilize equipment. There has been a marked increase in serious burn injuries from inexperienced handling of kerosene appliances which people must now substitute for electrical appliances. Burn complications—infection and dehydration—have also increased due to lack of antibiotics, sterile dressing materials, and clean water.

7. There have been direct civilian casualties from bombing. Civilian homes and businesses in the vicinity of infrastructure targets were frequently damaged or destroyed with resultant civilian casualties. In

addition, there are many documented cases of civilian neighborhoods and structures which have been bombed and which are not located near any military or infrastructure targets. I saw many examples of both kinds of destruction. It is not possible to ascertain the total number of civilians killed in such bombing, but they appear to be in the thousands to tens of thousands for the entire country.

8. There has been an undetermined number of damaged or destroyed health care facilities—hospitals, clinics, ambulances—from both the bombing and/or civil war. There are reports of casualties, including deaths, among health care workers, but these are not confirmed.

9. There is a serious threat of an increase in routine childhood illnesses as a result of decreased vaccination programs due to a limited supply of vaccines, inability to refrigerate vaccines and decreased ability to transport vaccines.

10. There has not been any assessment of the potential health hazards resulting from damage to chemical plants and nuclear reactors.

11. Anecdotal reports raise the possibility of an ensuing breakdown in the social fabric as a result of a significant increase in stresses caused by living within such a damaged infrastructure, and from the deteriorating economic conditions of increasing unemployment and rising prices. Individuals and families report increased family dysfunction, child behavior problems, increased crime and manifestations of psychological illness.

Comments

The primary focus to improve the health care crisis in Iraq must be directed towards rebuilding the electrical, communications and transport systems. To accomplish this, sanctions must be lifted completely and immediately to permit the free flow of medical supplies and non-medical equipment and to allow Iraq to generate revenues necessary to purchase supplies and equipment. Provisions in the recent United Nations' cease-fire agreement which continue sanctions pending destruction of armaments, impound part of Iraq's oil revenue and require Iraq to pay reparations critically limit Iraq's ability to significantly address its health care needs.

In order to reduce damage to the health care system and allay the threat of infectious disease epidemics, there must be an immediate and massive delivery of potable water, fuel, and generators to all parts of Iraq. Such an effort would require the active participation of governments in addition to the non-governmental organizations presently involved in medical aid. The continued refusal of the United States and the United Nations to address these catastrophic needs can only be interpreted as an intention on their part to allow the destruction of Iraq to continue toward the fulfillment of the real but unstated goal of the total destruction of Iraq as a nation.

In a real sense, the bombing war against Iraq has been a war against the health of the Iraqi people. This highly technological war against the infrastructure of a country raises the specter of future warfare which, like this one, may be readily condoned in its disguise of being "surgical." In truth, such warfare is horrifying in its capacity to cause long-term suffering, with high and unpredictable numbers of casualties from illness and disease.

David Levinson is a doctor of internal medicine living in California. He travelled to Iraq immediately after the war to assess the health care needs of Iraqi people.

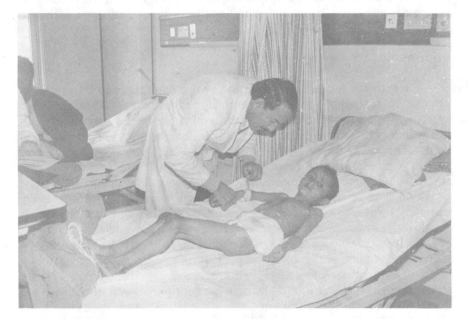

A hospital in Baghdad. One of thousands of children hospitalized for malnutrition and for dehydration caused by drinking polluted water.

Impact of Sanctions on Baghdad Children's Hospital

Ann Montgomery

As a member of the Gulf Peace Team, I was in Iraq for twenty-six days. But most of that, nineteen days, were spent on the border between Iraq and Saudi Arabia at Wadi Aurora. Because we were trying to remain neutral—a neutral presence between the two opposing armies—we remained within the compound there and could not see too much because we were very isolated. However, on Monday, January 7, 1991, before the war began, we were in Baghdad for a couple of days waiting for transport down to the camp. One of the places that the Iraqis took us, because they wanted all visitors to see it, was the Children's Teaching Hospital. It's a hospital just for children and babies.

I think what is relevant here is the effect the embargo was having even before the war started. Later you will hear plenty of testimony about what happened to the hospitals afterwards. What I saw was a very specific fact for me. I think for a fact, to come home to me, it has to involve individual human beings. These were individual babies and small children that I saw in that hospital.

I think I knew when I left that hospital why I was going to the camp. There were very small wards, about six beds in each, and I could see the doctor who escorted us around didn't want to be taken away from his work because he had so little help. But he could speak English, so he took us into several of these wards. In each one of them, there were babies lying on beds, very listless. Some of them you could see were right on the edge between life and death. Beside every bed was either a mother or a sister sitting there with the child because there wasn't enough nursing help. I was surprised at how friendly they were toward us, how they wanted to smile and have their pictures taken and welcome us, even us Americans, to Baghdad because they knew we were there for peace.

The doctor told us that forty babies were dying a day, not from wounds, not from any extraordinary illness, but because there was no milk and no very simple medications. Nothing extraordinary, just simple medications, especially for diarrhea. You know how little it takes to get rid of diarrhea if you just have what it takes. I have no medical knowledge, so I can't give the chemical terms. But the doctor was very angry, and his words to us were, "Please tell them not to make war on children." It was as plain as that. Whenever I hear that we should have let the embargo work, that's what I think of. The embargo was war, the embargo still is war when you hear about these ships being stopped.

For the sake of this investigation, I'd just like to read a couple of quotations to back up what I saw. This was from Ramsey Clark's letter to the Secretary General of the United Nations. Ramsey Clark arrived in Baghdad the day we left, so it was sort of a direct follow-up.

Dr. Abrahim Al-Nouri has been head of the Red Crescent and Red Cross for Iraq for 10 years. He is a pediatrician by training who interned at the Children's Hospital in London, later headed Children's Hospital in Baghdad, and served in the Ministry of Health for some years, rising to deputy minister. Doctor Al-Nouri estimates that there have been 3,000 infant deaths since November 1, 1990, in excess of the normal rate, attributable solely to the shortage of infant milk formula and medicines. Only 14 tons of baby formula have been received during that period. Prior monthly national consumption was approximately 2,500 tons.

When we got back to Baghdad, ten or eleven days after the war had started, we were taken to the infant milk factory. The milk was ground into the mud. The only milk we saw, even though we were staying in the El Rashid Hotel, was the milk we brought back from that milk factory. So we knew that if we weren't getting milk in the El Rashid, certainly nobody else in Baghdad was.

The Gulf Peace Team report made after the war points out what is not generally reported in the press: "Despite being excluded from the sanctions embargo, medical supplies are being prevented from entering Iraq for civilian use. Over fifty shipments of paid medical supplies, ordered long before the sanctions were in place, remained locked in ports and borders because the governments involved refused to release the shipments for transport to Iraq. Many pharmaceutical companies continue to refuse to sell medicines to Iraq. All medicines originating in the United States require a license from the Treasury Department before they can be shipped via humanitarian convoys to Iraqi civilians. The volume of medicines reaching Iraq via humanitarian channels is perhaps one-thirtieth of that required by the Iraqi civilian population." I know when we got back to Amman, we were told by a pharmacist that medicines were piling up, waiting to go.

So I think the image that stayed with me, because I think what touches us is the concrete, is that of one old grandmother. Apparently the mother couldn't be with the baby. She looked to me like the mother of sorrows, one of those faces you would see in a portrait, a very wrinkled, lined face, very impassive, very stoic. She was sitting cross-legged on the bed with an infant, a very tiny infant between her hands. At first I could get no reaction from her. Finally she turned around and smiled. She couldn't speak any English. But I knew that she had been sitting there all day, and would probably sit there for the rest of the day, absolutely quiet.

As we left somebody said to the doctor, "You're always at war, how do you feel about it?" He said, "Well, it is our fate." I think that's what we felt from the Iraqi people—there's a sense of a very sad and tragic fate. And just sadness more than anger. So I think that is the picture that stays with me.

Ann Montgomery was a member of the International Gulf Peace Team based in Iraq during U.S.-led bombing. She delivered this testimony at the New York Commission hearing.

Impact of the War on Iraqi Society

Adeeb Abed and Gavrielle Gemma

Our delegation to Iraq included Adeeb Abed, National Coalition to Stop U.S. Intervention in the Middle East and the Palestine Aid Society; Gavrielle Gemma, Coordinator, National Coalition; and Elisa Chavez, a videographer with Haiti Films. We were joined for four days by Dr. David Levinson. We were in Iraq from April 3, 1991 to April 14, 1991, and in Amman, Jordan, from March 30 to April 2 and from April 15 to 22. We went to every part of Baghdad, and went to Babylon, Najaf, Hilla, and Karbala in the South. Our trip was undertaken as part of a continuing investigation into the effects of the U.S.-led coalition bombing and sanctions for the Commission of Inquiry for the International War Crimes Tribunal. Our task was to assess the effects of the bombing and the condition of the population one month after the bombing had ceased; to acquire written and visual documentation and direct testimony; and to assess the effects on other countries, especially Jordan.

Throughout the trip we had the cooperation of officials and spoke to whomever we chose. Our movement was hindered only by the time-consuming problems of procuring sufficient gasoline each day, inability to make appointments because there was no telephone or postal service, various offices had moved due to the bombing, and of course the intense, urgent work of surveying and repair that was being undertaken in the country by officials, experts, and the general population. Also, everyone had to spend long hours every day ensuring that their families had food and other necessities. All of our interviews were done directly, some in English but most in Arabic by Adeeb Abed.

This report's aim is to summarize our experience. The information it contains, including any historical background or opinions, was acquired directly in Iraq and Jordan. Only where such information was repeatedly told to us did we include it. We spoke to many government officials but concentrated on talking to the people themselves in neighborhood after neighborhood. Transcripts of interviews, video testimony, and photos wherein Iraqi, Palestinian, and Jordanian victims of the war speak directly are available from the Commission. Most importantly, we want to thank the Iraqi people for their kindness and assistance to us and their determination and courage in the face of the suffering inflicted upon them by the United States government.

We arrived on April 3, 1991, in a car loaded with enough gasoline, water, and bread to last what we thought would be four or five days in Iraq. Given the difficult conditions, we extended that stay. At the time we arrived some newspapers in the West had reported that life was back to normal in Baghdad. Nothing could be further from the reality we witnessed.

The country was without electricity except for intermittent short periods of time in small sections of the city. There was no domestic or international telephone service, no postal service, trains, or Iraqi planes, passenger or cargo. Gasoline was scarce. Rationing was still in effect for almost everything. The majority of workers were unemployed due to lack of electricity, transportation, spare parts, and raw materials and the destruction of facilities by bombing. There were no military targets in sight.

The medical situation was devastating. The children who had survived eight months of sanctions, bombing, and terror were getting sick in increasing numbers. In every city we visited we documented the destruction or severe damage to homes, electrical plants, fuel storage facilities, civilian factories, hospitals, churches, civilian airports, vehicles, transportation facilities, food storage and food testing laboratories, grain silos, animal vaccination centers, schools, communication towers, civilian government office buildings, and stores. Almost all facilities we saw had been bombed two or three times, ensuring that they could not be repaired. Most of the bridges we saw destroyed were bombed from both ends.

It is important to know what social conditions were like before the embargo and bombing. Although it varied in different parts of the country, again and again people described to us the following: the entire country was electrified (we saw that even in the more rural towns and farms there were electrical lines direct to people's homes). After the Iran-Iraq war billions were spent on developing the technology and infrastructure and services of the country.

Since 1982, eighteen major hospitals had been built. Some were renowned in the Middle East. Medical care was basically free with a token payment of half a dinar upon admission and one dinar each day regardless of care. Illiteracy had been substantially reduced, education was universal and free through college. Water was supplied to all parts of the country. Pre-natal and post-natal care and vaccinations for children were available throughout the country including in rural areas. The social position of women was advancing. Food was abundant and inexpensive. People came from other countries to shop in Iraq and baby formula and cooking oil were often transported to Amman. Low-interest loans for homes were provided by the government, which had also started a program to give land to people who promised to produce within five years. Doctors had not seen cases of malnutrition in Baghdad for over a decade.

Although Iraq had a staggering debt, its oil production—giving it direct income or allowing it to directly exchange oil to pay off debts—enabled it to purchase advanced communications technology from foreign companies. In Baghdad, the public transportation system was cheap and widespread. Iraq was just beginning to develop its own manufacturing capabilities in technology and other production. Although it was 70% dependent on imported food, Iraq was making a priority of internal food production. While it was still emerging from colonial exploitation, and relatively poor, Iraq was developing rapidly and its standard of living and extent of public services was among the highest in the Middle East. The functioning and well-being of society was dependent on technology.

The embargo, freezing of Iraq's bank accounts, and bombing have not only destroyed between 125,000 and 225,000 lives—including those of thousands of children—they have destroyed all that the people were so enormously proud of wherever we went. The effects will last for decades.

The Bush administration's claims that its bombing was solely directed at military targets was contradicted by everything we saw. In every city we saw civilian homes and stores bombed. Despite the high percentage of bombs the Pentagon admits missed their targets, the U.S. deliberately and with chilling and deadly precision bombed the entire infrastructure necessary to sustain life and society.

As almost all facilities in Iraq were constructed by foreign companies based in countries that were part of the U.S.-led coalition, the plans and locations of these facilities were available to the Pentagon. We were told that altogether 26,000 facilities had been destroyed, including 61 bridges and 80% of oil refineries.

Baghdad

It was an odd feeling to be in a major city, to look up into the sky and see no civilian aircraft and to know that anytime you saw a plane it was a U.S. military jet. Everyone would stop and look up with anger. On our second night there, and several other times, at about 2:30 a.m. U.S. jets flew low over the city, deliberately creating an enormous sonic boom that sounded as if the bombing had started again. The next morning people would describe how their children had awakened in terror. Families we spoke to everywhere described what it felt like for forty days and nights to hear and see bombing.

Before the bombing, Baghdad used 9,000 megawatts of electricity per day. After the bombing it was reduced to 700 megawatts per day for more than three months. According to the Water Department, the complete cutoff of water and/or potable water was due to the lack of electrical power and the scarcity of chemicals to treat the water. Bombing had destroyed some of the machinery necessary for water purification and supply. There were no spare parts. Three of the six bridges in Baghdad had been bombed. One was partially repaired; the other two, including the suspension bridge, were completely destroyed. Both Saddam International Airport and Al Muthana, the domestic airport, were bombed, and passenger and cargo planes were destroyed.

Twenty minutes outside of the city in Al Taji, we saw the country's largest frozen-meat storage and distribution center—one of two main centers for the entire country, which also included a laboratory for testing meat quality. It had been completely obliterated by the bombing. The center held 14,000 tons of frozen meat. The workers had all left the apartment complex next to the plant to stay with their families. The only one left was the plant engineer, who just sat for hours at the front gate. Twenty-five meters from the plant, women were collecting water from a ditch. The plant had been bombed three times—at 8 a.m., 3 p.m and 8 p.m., and workers inside the plant had been killed.

Throughout Baghdad, communication towers, the main communication centers, were destroyed. Civilian government office buildings destroyed included the City Hall, the Supreme Court and the Justice Department. The Blessed Virgin Church was bombed, as was the new convention and conference center and the transportation hub and bus parking area. We went to many homes and stores in various parts of the city that had been destroyed in the bombing. Baghdad is a sprawling city. While it was certainly not leveled by the bombing, the cumulative effect of seeing so many major facilities and institutions just twisted metal and demolished everywhere was chilling.

Baghdad, a city of three million, was dark except for gasoline-powered portable generators. The traffic was light and there were no traffic lights. The water-pumping and purification systems were not working. Non-potable water was beginning to return. A neighborhood would get water for one hour—not past the first floor in apartment buildings—and all the neighbors would come with receptacles. Sewage was backed up in drains and flowing into the rivers.

We visited al-Ameriyah shelter that was destroyed by two bombs in February 1991. You could still smell death inside and envision the terror and panic of people unable to get out. On one side of this shelter was a school, on the other a supermarket. Estimates of those killed on the night it was bombed—the majority of them women and children—range as high as 1,500 people. Only eleven survived, many of them severely burned. All through the surrounding completely residential neighborhood banners were hung outside of homes listing family members who died. One banner named seventeen dead. We met in their homes with surviving family members who seemed to be still in shock. Once school had resumed, some classes had lost half their students. Outside the shelter, women still mourned at the gates for loved ones whose bodies had never been recovered or identified. The Bush administration and media had said they thought this was a military bunker. Anyone spending five honest minutes in this neighborhood would know that was untrue. Many expressed to us that this was a deliberate bombing to terrorize the population.

Dr. Abrahim Al-Nouri, President of the Iraqi Red Crescent, gave us an overview of the medical situation. He said there were serious shortages of all medicines, including antibiotics and anesthetic drugs, surgical equipment, disposable gloves, antiseptics, face masks, intravenous fluids, whole blood and plasma. Incubators were useless because there was no electricity or no spare parts. Laboratory testing was basically unavailable, hemodialysis was impossible. Dr. Al-Nouri stressed the necessity of repairing the electrical system and its link to providing health care. Clean water remained a major problem and he emphasized his fear that major epidemics of cholera and typhoid would appear as the temperatures climbed. As of April 13, 1991, the International Red Cross had brought in a million liters of purified water, 70 water trucks and seven mobile water-purification systems, which were mostly sent to the South. However, even combined with other efforts, water in Baghdad was limited to one liter per person per day.

Hospitals had been closed in Baghdad due to lack of supplies. Polio, measles, hepatitis, diphtheria, meningitis, malnutrition, gastroenteritis, and nervous disorders were reappearing. Miscarriages and infant mortality were way up. On April 4, 1991, we visited Kindi Hospital, a neighborhood hospital in a working class area of Baghdad. By flashlight we interviewed the head nurse, who reported that of the thousand people brought in during the bombing, half had already died. Dr. Saad Sallal told us the hospital had been without electricity since the bombing, using generator power for surgery and emergency cases twelve hours a day.

Because of the lack of insulin, amputations had been necessary for diabetic patients, and heart patients had died for lack of medicine. All specialty clinics were closed. There was a lack of certain drugs imported from American and other Western countries, especially those drugs used for treating diabetes, hypertension and heart problems. Three to four thousand bags of blood had spoiled with no refrigeration. Dr. Sallal said, "The American propaganda says that nobody was killed by their attack, but we have a file and their location. One hospital was bombed. I don't know why certain localities, nowhere near the military buildings, were attacked."

"Right now," said Dr. Sallal, "the big problems are malnutrition in children, hygiene, and impure water. Right now I and my family are living without electricity. I couldn't eat."

Basic sterilization procedures have been dropped since the bombing. "I am a plastic surgeon. We cannot dress skin grafts; there is a high level of infection. You come later to my locker and you will see the same cap and mask used continuously. One disposable mask, used since last month."

Saddam Hussein Pediatric Hospital in Baghdad, with 300 beds, is a very modern facility with all the latest technology, famous in the region. It had gasoline-powered generators, sufficient only to run lights and smaller equipment. The hospital was accepting only serious or emergency cases. We interviewed Dr. Talaat Talal, who took us through the hospital. A very warm, sensitive man, he broke down and cried while describing the situation, and beamed when showing us a child they had saved. He described children who had died from lack of medicines and fluids including insulin. He said they were receiving patients from many cities, most of whom had been unable to get to the hospital sooner. These children were very sick by the time they came in especially from marasmus, dehydration, malnutrition, kidney disease. Many had died.

One mother came from Najaf in the South with a baby extremely ill with renal disease. No laboratory testing could be done due to the lack of electricity and necessary supplies, not even the simple blood urea test this baby needed. Dr. Talal said, "I can use clinical judgment, but we should have a document [test results]. What century are we in, what hospital are we in? Previously we had everything." We saw child after child with gastroenteritis caused by drinking impure water, and many suffering from malnutrition. Dr. Talal said, "You can't believe it, I had a case of kwashiorkor. I have been a doctor for eight years in Iraq and I have not seen one case of kwashiorkor. For six months the baby had only sugar and water." This child lived in Baghdad.

In the premature baby ward the incubators were not working nor the micro-drip for infants due to lack of electricity and spare parts. They were using an adult drip. We saw a mother standing next to a broken incubator using a candle on the incubator to raise the temperature.

There was no oxygen. The centralized oxygen supply was not working and oxygen tanks in the wards were empty. The factory that replenishes the tanks was closed due to lack of electricity. There were no X-ray machines operating nor was the CAT scan. The doctor described one case in which a neurosurgeon had to operate on a car accident victim without even an X-ray to determine whether there was bleeding in the brain. There was no bleeding, the operation was unnecessary.

Dr. Talal was greatly concerned about hospital conditions without air conditioning in summer heat that goes over 100 degrees fahrenheit. Dr. Talal described the lack of even basic items such as disposable gloves. He said, "Gloves, we don't have gloves, imagine just with our hands we do the puncture [spinal tap]. It is a tragedy. We may save the life of a patient with meningitis and then induce infection. You know we have progressed a lot, really, in our country. Every woman, even in the rural areas, had pre- and post-natal care. We had reached a very high level. And now everything has changed."

Everyday Life

It had become a daily struggle to obtain the necessary items to sustain life. This was especially true for the women. Many people had to sell belongings to buy items on the underground market. Finding water, flour or bread, cooking oil, gasoline or kerosene became an ordeal. On top of this people were unable to learn whether family members were alive or dead in other parts of the country due to the lack of communications. Schools were closed for months, and when they reopened they were overcrowded and without electricity or potable water. Everyone spoke about how terrible it was that instead of the public buses they had used for decades now people were forced to use open and crowded trucks.

Although rationing was carried out on a widespread and fairly equal basis, the amounts available to distribute were insufficient to meet people's needs. Some items would run out completely. During our stay, the government cracked down on price gouging and prices of items were dropping fast. After we left, the gasoline refinery in Dura began operating to provide gasoline internally. This gasoline is now being given free, and also sent to the south. This is a great achievement and important for the Iraqi people's lives. There was much bitterness when we were there that Iraq, an oil-producing country, had no gasoline due to the bombing.

Prior to the U.S. embargo which started in August and the freezing of Iraq's bank accounts, three Iraqi dinars equaled one U.S. dollar. At the time we were there it was 7D to $1. 1,000 fils equals 1D. Average income was 100-150D a month. 1 litre = about 1 quart, 1 kilogram = 2.2 lbs.

- 1 litre gas was 40 fils, went to 7D, now free
- 30 eggs were 2-3D, went to 15D
- 50K flour was 3D, went to 1,000D back down to 150D
- 5K lamb was 6D, went to 13D
- 1K rice was 200 fils, went to 7D
- 1K sugar was 200 fils, went to 10D
- 1K tea was 15D, went to 40D
- 5K cooking oil was 2.5D, went to 40D
- candle 50 fils, went to 500 fils, later they were not available
- butane was 750 fils, went to 25D but was unavailable
- an average taxi ride was 2.5D, went up to 20D
- kerosene 20 litres was 1D, went up to 5D, sometimes unavailable

Rationing was organized through local merchants or the local people's congress which assigned them to merchants who received the rationed items. Water was distributed at thirty sites in Baghdad. The nationwide rationing system, which had taken thirty to forty-five days to set up, had been disrupted by the rebellions in the north and south. The amounts, especially for baby formula and milk, were insufficient to prevent malnutrition. The items came partially from stores within the country, relief organizations, efforts by peace groups throughout the world and general collections among the people especially in Jordan. Once the bombing started amounts were decreased as major food stocks, including baby formula, were destroyed in the bombing. Despite well known shortages, Turkey refused to deliver 12,000 tons of nutrients and 32,000 tons of milk that had been purchased and paid for before the embargo or to pay for 100 million barrels of oil already delivered.

Ships and vehicles carrying medicine and food that was supposedly exempted from the embargo were bombed, confiscated and prevented from entering Iraq. Many of the drivers carrying relief supplies were killed and wounded by U.S. bombing. In Jordan we met with the widow and seven children of a truck driver who had brought UN approved frozen meat into Iraq. His truck was bombed and his relief driver burned in the cab. When he fled the truck he was strafed and killed.

Gas was rationed at twenty litres for three weeks at ten dinars per litre on the market. Babies under one year received three cans of formula a month. Babies over one year received two sacks of dry milk per month. The ration of one-fourth of a kilogram of oil was decreased in March; one kilo of rice per person was decreased to one-half in March; one and a half kilos of sugar was decreased to three-quarters; one bar soap to 200 grams per month.

People were out of work everywhere. The primary causes were lack of electricity, embargo on raw materials and spare parts, destruction from bombing, lack of transportation, and displacement. Many had turned to street sales, but this too became difficult because of lack of essential goods. An engineer turned to selling falafel, but had to stop because he could not get cooking oil. Many independent construction workers were unemployed due to the high prices of materials they needed. For example, lumber went from 7D to 1,700D (lumber was 100% imported from U.S.), cement went from 2D to 250D.

We were told many times by working class Iraqis that before the war everything was plentiful and cheap. People from other countries used to shop in Iraq. They used to take oil and baby formula to Amman, Jordan.

Again medical care was a vast problem and heartbreak. One man described how his mother had a heart ailment; she was paralyzed and he carried her to a taxi which was expensive. At the hospital, they could only give her one dosage and said she should come back three days later for another. She died.

One man described the social breakdown: "Theft became a new phenomenon. Iraq never had theft. My neighbor left because of the bombing and everything in his house was completely stolen. Food was stolen from houses. People sold furniture to purchase food, now there is nothing to sell. Now we see prostitution and gambling, new to Iraq."

People described going to the river for water. One said: "I went with a wheelbarrow rented for 5D. I took my son who almost drowned. Some young neighbors came by chance and saved his life. After all that the water I brought back was barely enough to take a bath and get rid of all the mud on us." One family from Beldiyat in Baghdad went to the salt springs to drink and wash. The ponds are like swamps and their son slipped and drowned. Others got water from a swamp that stinks and boiled it for washing. We saw many people collecting branches and sticks they used to boil water. Even doing this entire families had diarrhea.

The bombing and hardships caused and still cause terrible psychological problems. One man said, "During that time I became easily angered and irritated and my relationship with my children was filled with a lot of anger, the children too. When the bombing raids came my daughter yells mommy, mommy, they're coming. My 3-year-old son told his mother, we will die together."

One man of Palestinian background said, "What happened in 1948, I will not let it happen again. I will not leave. We used to sit and watch the clock between 7-8 p.m. waiting for the bombing to start. My daughter LuLu would say, 'Bush is coming.' She came to the point where now she sits in my lap and my wife's lap constantly. Tens of planes would go by, cruise missiles the first night. Everyone went outside to see what was happening. "That one night was the equivalent of a lifetime. I live by Muthana airport. My house was shaking continuously. I have eleven people in my house during the bombing. Everyone was crying and screaming huddled around mother. Now my daughter she is wetting the bed. All the children say Bush is coming. Not America, Bush."

Kerbala and Najaf

We visited Hussaini hospital in Kerbala, which was destroyed in the rebellion in the south. Medical personnel there said the rebels massacred wounded soldiers in their beds. Blood was all over the walls by patients' beds. Thirteen ambulances had been destroyed. Doctors there blamed the embargo and bombing for the deaths of many children due to deficiency in treatment.

The holy shrines were used as headquarters for the opposition, and there was much damage to them. We were shown a room with ropes still hanging said to be used to execute government officials, Sunni or Shiite, that had been rounded up. There were bloodstains everywhere. These shrines were over 1,100 years old. At the time of the rebellion the government was renovating the shrine, making additions, remolding gold trim on the minarets and dome. At the time we were there, the shrine was guarded by soldiers. An intense clean-up and repair was taking place. We were told plans had already been drawn up to expand the plaza in front and make all repairs. The Hussein Shrine, the most renowned in the world, had been burglarized. Gold plating in the domes and minarets was peeled off, the library was vandalized and gifts from Muslims around the world were stolen. We saw a room used as a hospital for the rebels, with material taken from civilian hospitals.

Kerbala had enormous destruction. We saw stores, civilian homes, and communication towers destroyed by the bombing. Most of the destruction was caused by door to door fighting during the rebellion, destroying every block. The situation in Najaf was similar although the destruction from the rebellion was not as great. Again we saw civilian homes, and commercial stores and structures bombed.

Hilla

In Hilla the student health clinic was bombed on the third day of the bombing as well as the school. The school was hit in the day, the clinic at 1:00 a.m. The local government administration buildings were bombed.

Student Health Center in Hilla, Babylon Province, was destroyed by U.S. bombs. (Photo: Commission of Inquiry, April 5, 1991)

Babylon

We were the first foreign delegation to visit Babylon, according to the Military Governor Duri. There were two types of destruction—from the bombing and from the internal fighting. In all of the Southern towns we visited it was quite obvious which was the cause. In addition, local guides made no attempt to characterize destruction from internal fighting as being caused by bombing. If anything they were anxious to show the depth of hardship and destruction caused by the rebellion.

In Babylon, as elsewhere in Iraq, bombing targeted the infrastructure and civilian facilities necessary to survival and the general life of society. We visited a textile weaving plant which had been built up in the last seven years and was completely demolished. It employed over 2,400 workers, mostly women. The employment of women in industry is very important to their overall advancement economically and socially in any country, and especially in the Middle East. The plant was bombed at 3 p.m. in the afternoon, and two women were killed while working at their station. This plant, according to Mr. Hassan, the plant manager, was built by an Italian company. The new structure next door, containing no equipment, was untouched.

All the machinery and raw materials were demolished. Mr. Hassan told sorrowfully how proud the local people were of this plant, its importance to the city and country. He said it was like seeing a child destroyed. He explained how in much of Iraq industry was organized in a reverse process than it was in the industrialized West. The first stage for the Iraqis to have any industrial capacity was just to assemble a finished product from imported processed materials. Their next step was to be able to process raw materials and later to produce the raw materials themselves.

Mr. Hassan felt that the U.S. air command knew exactly what they were hitting, and were provided the plans for industrial facilities all across the country. Almost all facilities in Iraq were built by foreign companies; Iraq purchased them with oil revenues. Basic industrial production was their next step and just beginning. He told us that the auto assembly plant was also bombed. This plant imported parts from foreign manufacturers and assembled them. The next step was domestic car production. But now they faced a total crisis because of the embargo; there were no spare parts for the foreign autos in the country.

We also visited Marjan hospital, which was bombed, repaired and bombed again. There were huge bomb craters on the grounds as well. The Health Clinic in Katheia was bombed. Two hundred meters from the hospital, a telephone and communication tower was completely destroyed. Across the street the kerosene storage tanks were bombed. Eyewitnesses we interviewed said they burned for three days. Thirty-nine civilians lost their lives in that bombing. There were no military installations in the area. We drove by a bombed grain silo and the town bakery. Governor Duri said of the allied bombing, "They wanted to put us backwards and destroy our civilization."

We were told that nineteen civilian homes were bombed and we visited most of the areas where this took place. We counted more than nineteen. We spoke to neighborhood residents and family survivors who gave us the times, dates, and numbers of people killed. Most devastating was the destruction of eight homes which shared a common courtyard. People's possessions were still in the rubble. We dug out a child's textbook, giving his name, age and grade. Sixty-four people were killed in this bombing, including fourteen children. The homes were bordered by a school on one side and an artists union on the other. Both were shut down. Residents came out to describe it to us and the children told us about lost friends. The bombing took place 4:00 a.m. on February 11, 1991. We visited three other residential neighborhoods and spoke at random to residents and survivors. There were no military installations. Some neighborhoods had open sewers.

Everywhere we went we saw military detachments cleaning the streets, clearing rubble and even planting trees. Their priority was a survey of needs in the town. They had partially restored the electricity and water pumping, but not the purification systems and water and food was being rationed. According to the governor, the rebellion lasted only one and onehalf days in Babylon. The city was active. In the downtown area, a telephone relay station was bombed twice and cut in half. It was right in the middle of the market area, as well as homes. Dozens of small older shops and homes next to the relay station were destroyed. This took place on February 18, 1991. Sixteen people were killed.

Kurdish Rebellion

We met with Kurdish tribal leaders in Baghdad. They were supporters of Kurdish autonomy within the framework of a unified Iraq. They opposed a military uprising at this time particularly because of hardships the people were already suffering caused by the U.S. bombing and sanctions. They opposed leaving the towns and said the rebels had told people they would be killed by the army and threatened if they did not leave. There were no provisions made about how to feed them or protect them from the freezing cold in the mountains.

According to reports we received in Iraq, the bombing had caused similar damage and conditions of deprivation in the north as in other parts of the country. Once the rebellion started, relief supplies that had been coming in from the government were unable to get to the people.

Turkish troops had entered northern Iraq and reports were coming in of beatings and shootings of Kurds and the theft of their possessions by hostile Turkish troops. There are twelve million Kurds in Turkey, seven million in Iran and two million in Iraq. The Kurdish language is banned in Turkey. In northern Iraq it is the official first language. By law in Iraq, a percentage of the Parliament must be made up of Kurdish representatives, and a form of autonomy, however insufficient, had been developing. Also reported was aid, coordination and incitement for the rebellion from the U.S., Iran, Turkey and Syria. Iran and Turkey are adamantly opposed to an independent Kurdistan.

We found that almost all non-Kurdish Iraqis we spoke to had been favorable to greater rights and were sympathetic to the Kurds. However, they were now becoming bitter that some Kurds were working with the U.S. Among the Iraqis there was intense hatred of the Bush administration because of the bombing and sanctions and U.S. interference in their affairs. The U.S. announcement of aid to the Kurds (real or not), when everyone was suffering increased that bitterness. Getting the U.S. out of Iraq and maintaining the country's sovereignty and independence was people's first priority.

While we were in Iraq the government was attempting to set up meetings with all Kurdish political opposition leaders even those with long known links to the C.I.A. to attempt a settlement. An extended amnesty was announced. Convoys of trucks sent to the north carrying water, food and medicine were turned back at the 36th parallel by the U.S.

The widely held feeling in Iraq and among all progressive Palestinian, Jordanian, and Arab organizations and individuals was opposition to the armed rebellion, although all supported Kurdish self-determination, which they stressed could never come about by working with the U.S. As Taysir Zebri, General Secretary of the Jordanian Peoples Democratic Party said, "The main reason for this situation in the north and south of Iraq is directly the result of the Coalition aggression against Iraq. The Kurdish and Shia communities were the victims of a conspiracy without knowing. The help that is being provided to the opposition forces is nothing short of a cover-up of the viciousness of the crimes against all the people of Iraq."

It was understood by some that this was an attempt by the U.S. to alienate and divide the people of Iraq on regional, religious, and tribal bases, enabling the U.S. to extend its occupation of Iraq and insuring its domination of the people of the region. It was pointed out to us that the main oil producing centers of Iraq lie in the north, with major refineries and the oil pipeline through Turkey and in the south, with major oil fields, refineries and the oil pipeline through Saudi Arabia. It was felt it was also a goal of the U.S. to control these areas.

Economic Aspects of the War

Minister of Trade Mohammed Mahdi Saleh said Iraq had $200 billion in damages inflicted by the U.S.-led coalition and had lost $20 billion in oil revenues in 1990 alone.

Minister Saleh described the recent history of trade relations with the U.S. and its relationship to the war. He explained that from 1982 to 1987 trade with the U.S. had grown from $300 million to $1.1 billion in 1988, almost all of it in food imports from the U.S. Iraq imported 100 percent of its needs in corn and 90 percent of its needs in rice from the U.S. Seventy percent of food in Iraq was imported. The U.S. sold no technology to Iraq. The minister explained that their relatively high technology was purchased from other countries and that they were beginning to develop their own internal production of high technology items.

The relationship did not change until 1990. On March 3, 1990, the U.S. cancelled $500 million in credit to Iraq for food imports. Minister Saleh said, "Okay, we told them, we are going to buy food from other countries. . . . They tried to interfere in the internal affairs of Iraq and passed a resolution on economic sanctions on Iraq before the Kuwaiti problem, in July. . . . After August 2, 1990, they went further. It [the war] was well prepared, it was not born on August 2."

Immediately after August 2, 1990, the U.S got a resolution to boycott all trade and to freeze all financial assets in the U.S. The largest portion of Iraq's bank assets are in the U.S. Saleh said, "We have concluded that it was well prepared by the U.S. and it was a good chance for them to use the Kuwaiti problem to fulfill their objectives. Totally it is not the question of Kuwait. If any other country, Iran or Saudi Arabia, had taken Kuwait, the U.S. would never move at all. . . . They thought that because we are largely dependent on them in food . . . they had a good weapon to press on us."

When Iraq told the U.S. they would buy elsewhere, Minister Saleh explained, then the U.S. went for a worldwide boycott to disable Iraq. Saleh went on, "Imagine capturing American people in a desert for nine months and not allowing any new supplies of food or baby milk to their children in Arizona, the desert. So they kept Iraq, as it is in a desert, nobody can pass, nobody can talk, nobody, nobody. . . . They analyzed what we have in our stock . . . then the destruction of Iraq would come four or five months from the beginning of sanctions. . . . If it had been possible the Bush administration would have prevented the air from coming in."

The minister described as "inhuman" the U.S. decision to stop shipments of food and medicine that were purchased and paid for before the embargo. The U.S. allowed oil purchased before August 2nd to enter the U.S. But they "ordered" Turkey to not deliver baby milk that had been bought from Nestlé in Switzerland. As of April 1991 these items have not been delivered.

Dr. Riad Al Qaysi, undersecretary, Ministry of Foreign Affairs, said: "The attempt [by the U.S.] is to decrease the living standard of the people of the entire region, depress wages, create competitiveness for jobs, and chop off development, particularly of attempts for industrial capacity at home."

Jordan

During our stay in Jordan, we met with a great many political, union, and professional leaders in the country who explained the following points. The effect on the economy of Jordan is considerable and has caused great hardships to the population. They were affected three ways. One, the effect of sanctions against Iraq, which included cut-off of oil and nondelivery of raw materials; this closed factories or reduced their operating hours and led to layoffs of workers in Jordan. Seventy percent of the shipping in Aqaba, Jordan's major port city, was to Iraq. Other commerce through Aqaba was hindered and discouraged by Coalition searches of ships, which are still continuing, and by exorbitant insurance required on ships. The port is one of Jordan's main sources of income, adding $44 million to its annual income.

Jordan's economy lost $1.5 billion in 1990 alone. Some 55,000 Jordanian workers lost jobs. Tourism practically ceased. The lack of oil from Iraq, which Jordan paid for by reducing Iraq's debt to Jordan, meant it had to purchase oil at higher prices with cash. According to a UNICEF report released in Jordan, what the "Gulf crisis has done to Jordan is make it instantly a less developed country from a middle income country."

The second effect was the influx of refugees from Iraq and especially from Kuwait. It is estimated 250,000 refugees came, including Palestinians from Kuwait and an unknown number of returning Jordanians. They have neither jobs nor homes, and many are without passports from any country.

The third effect was the cut-off of aid from international financial institutions and from the U.S. At a recent meeting, the Gulf States Cooperation Council decided to exclude Jordan from a $5 billion fund established for assistance to countries impacted by the Gulf war. Yemen and the Sudan were also excluded from the fund, despite the expulsion of 950,000 Yemenis from Saudi Arabia during the crisis and Sudan's own desperate needs.

As a result, there is a growing medical crisis developing in Jordan as well as a rise in hunger, malnutrition, infant mortality, and miscarriages. Because of growing unemployment, Jordan enacted a policy of replacing immigrant workers with Jordanians, and Egyptian, Syrian and other workers were forced to leave the country.

Kuwait—Persecution of Palestinians

250,000 Palestinians have fled Kuwait due to persecution, including many who lived and worked there all their lives. Remittances to families in Jordan, the West Bank and Gaza have stopped. Kuwaiti and Gulf states contributions to Palestinian relief projects has ended.

[In the Occupied Territories, according to the UN Emergency Relief and Works Agency, West Bank and Gaza Strip schools lost half their class days due to military closures or curfew during the war. These areas were put under a 24 hour curfew for the duration of the war, 45 days. Even Mosques and churches were closed to worshippers.]

In Amman we met with Palestinians who were victims of Kuwaiti torture and spoke to Palestinians by phone in Kuwait. To date [April 1991] there are 628 confirmed deaths, several hundreds missing and feared dead, 7,000 imprisoned and twenty-four "officially" deported. Death squads were operating in Kuwait, especially targeting Palestinians. Witnesses reported that Jordanians, Sudanese, Filipinos and South Asians, and Kuwaitis opposed to the royal family were also victims of arrest and torture after the Kuwaiti and U.S. military took control.

All the victims we interviewed reported the presence of U.S. military officers in a position of responsibility in the detention and torture centers. They said they were visited by American officers who saw the injuries they had received.

Muenis Khatib, age 23 years, spoke with us at Al-Bashir Hospital in Amman where he is recovering. He said, "Then an American officer came. The American officer put us in a separate room for three days. And when the U.S. officer would come in they (the Kuwaitis) would remove the blindfold from our eyes. The Kuwaitis tortured us with cigarettes, electrical wires, electricity was running through my legs." During the time he was under torture no medical treatment was given.

Another Palestinian victim is Omar Abdullah, who after being tortured was thrown across the border into Iraq. He had a severe head injury, no money or shoes, and was unable to walk. Fellow victims carried him until they were found by Iraqi soldiers who gave them food and transported them to Basra.

One of the Palestinians who left Kuwait before the U.S. bombing was a dairy cattle specialist for over 40 years in Kuwait. He was personally responsible for cross breeding that produced cattle stock that supplied forty percent of Kuwait's need for fresh milk. He had lost everything, including his savings, and was prevented from returning to Kuwait.

Conclusion

The U.S.-led coalition's embargo and bombing was deliberately aimed at the population of Iraq and to destroy the country's infrastructure, independence, and standard of living. This was a high technology war against all the people of Iraq and most especially the children. The Iraqi military was defenseless in the face of the massive aerial bombardment. There was no regard for the health, nutrition, or economic condition of the people. This was a policy of starvation, poverty and terror. There is no end in sight yet for the Iraqi people—how many will die in the future as a direct or indirect result of the embargo and bombing?

What we witnessed constituted the most flagrant and deliberate war crimes by any standard of decency or international law.

The almost complete destruction of any and all life sustaining or economically necessary facilities, the continuation of the embargo, the freezing of Iraq's assets and the U.S. occupation of areas of Iraq show that the aim was not the withdrawal of Iraq from Kuwait but U.S. domination over Iraq. In the process the U.S. successfully lowered the standard of living for people of the entire region, and set back their struggle for development.

The U.S. now has its long sought after direct military presence in every Gulf state—Kuwait, Saudi Arabia, Kuwait, Bahrain, Oman, Qatar, and the United Arab Emirates—in addition to expanded forces in Turkey, troops in Iraq and nuclear aircraft carriers in the Persian Gulf. It has shored up Israel against the Palestinians and emboldened Israel in its repression, settlements, and continued illegal occupation of the West Bank, Gaza and the Golan Heights. The U.S. now has domination over sixty percent of the world's oil reserves.

Dr. Al Qaysi said, "No home remained untouched, no family unharmed, if not through death in the war, through malnutrition, disease, or new found poverty. This is a return to colonialism. The U.S. is asking for terms like another Treaty of Versailles [in which following World War I the victors imposed such severe conditions on the defeated Germany that economic recovery was not possible at all until the rise of Hitler]. Iraq is dependent on the outside world to repair its infrastructure and I fear Iraq will be in a state of permanent human bondage."

For the sake of the people of Iraq, particularly the children, an immediate end to all aspects of the embargo against Iraq should be demanded of the United States and the United Nations.

Adeeb Abed represents the Palestine Aid Society; Gavrielle Gemma co-coordinates the National Coalition to Stop U.S. Intervention in the Middle East. This report was given in New York on May 11, 1991.

Eyewitness Interviews

Bombing of Textile Factory on Outskirts of Babylon, Iraq

A clothing factory on the outskirts of Babylon was among the civilian factories destroyed. The plant was built by an Italian and English company, which means the allies knew exactly what this plant manufactured—shirts and pajamas. It was bombed three times. Mr. Hassan, the plant manager, describes the attack, which took place on January 19, 1991, at 12:00 noon.

"The workers were working. George Bush's planes came at noon while people were in the midst of work. They hit three places. The first hit was the spinning mill. Two women workers fell martyrs. The rest of the people panicked and began to run in all directions.

"The second hit was at the opposite end of the building, an area of preparation for weaving. The third hit was at the end of the plant, a storage area for raw material.

"Besides the two women killed, sixteen others were wounded, women and men. First they burned the raw material, then they damaged the machines. We need a lot of work to be done here and a lot of money to be spent, by foreign countries."

Q. *Are the materials and machines you need to rebuild prohibited under the U.S. boycott?*

A. Yes.

Q. *How many people are out of work now because of this bombing and the sanctions?*

A. Two-thousand-eight-hundred people are out of work. And they need their jobs very much. The factory needs to be functioning again very quickly.

Q. *How many women work in this plant?*

A. Four-hundred-fifty women.

Eyewitness Report:

The Bombing of Al-Ameriyah Shelter, Baghdad

Al-Ameriyah shelter and community center in Baghdad suffered a direct hit by two U.S. "smart bombs" on February 13, 1991. Smoke poured out of the shelter for days. The Bush administration claimed that it was a military command post. But neighbors explained to the Commission team that al-Ameriyah served as a community center for neighborhood youth. The entire area is residential. According to the Iraqi government, 400 were killed, but neighbors interviewed said some 1,500 lost their lives in the bombing, mostly women, youth, and children.

Public Shelter No. 25 in the Ameriyah section of suburban Baghdad was hit by two 2,000 pound laser-guided bombs designed to penetrate the reinforced roof and explode inside. U.S officials insisted that the bombing was not a mistake, that this shelter and some twenty-five others in Baghdad were on the target list from the beginning. Defense Secretary Cheney said, "Saddam might now be resorting to a practice of placing civilians in harm's way." Schwarzkopf told reporters, "there is no way, no way at all the United States would refrain from hitting all urban military targets, even for a brief time" (*New York Times*, February 15, 1991: A1.)

(Above) Banners outside of homes list family members killed in the al-Ameriyah shelter. In some school classes, half the students had been killed. The Commission's investigating team picked several houses and interviewed the survivors. Many lost entire families. Listed are the names of a man and a wife, their four children, and two grandchildren. (Below) Every day these women come to the shelter to pray for family members killed there, but whose bodies were incinerated by the heat and never found or so badly burned that they could not be identified. (Photos: Commission of Inquiry, April 2 & 4, 1991)

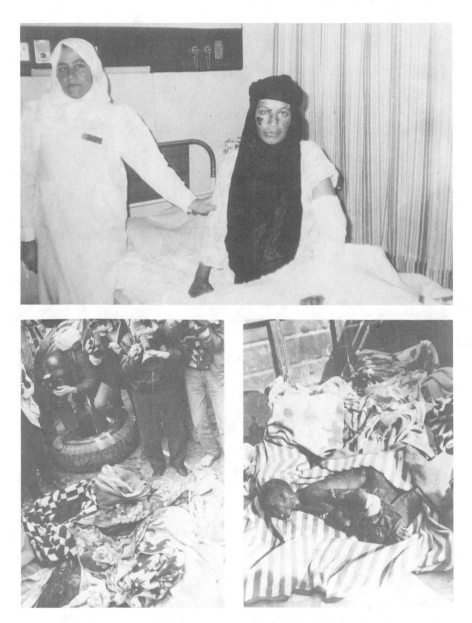

(Above) One of the eleven survivors of the U.S. bombing of the al-Ameriyah shelter. (Below left) Charred bodies and pieces of bodies recovered from the shelter. (Below right) A child burned to death. The Bush administration claimed the shelter was a military command post, but neighbors explained to the Commission's fact finding team that al-Ameriyah served as a community center for neighborhood youth. The entire area is residential. (Photos: Commission of Inquiry)

Eyewitness Interview:

Bus Driver in Amman, Jordan

The Pentagon said the targets of attacks were only military. The following testimony, however, reveals a deliberate air assault on a clear civilian target—a passenger bus in Kuwait. The bus was hit by rockets, then planes returned to strafe those fleeing the vehicles. A Palestinian bus driver was interviewed by the Commission April 2, 1991, in Amman, Jordan. He was traveling in a convoy of civilian vehicles, including other buses and cars, when the February 1, 1991 attack took place. Over all, some 200 civilians were killed.

"My name is Najib Toubasi. I am 47 years old. I drive a bus from Kuwait to Amman. On Feb. 1, 1991, at approximately 1:20 p.m., I took 57 passengers, all civilians, from Kuwait City.

"At 2:30 p.m. I was surprised by a hit to the rear of the bus. I had to stop and open the door. People were leaving the bus. Within a couple of minutes half the people were out of the bus. The area was called Mutlaa, about 20 kilometers from Kuwait [City]. There were other civilian vehicles, but no military vehicles on the road.

"I was surprised by another rocket which hit the center of the bus. People ran to the desert, 200 meters from the bus. A third rocket hit in the midst of the people. All of the people were obviously civilians.

"The bus burned. About twenty-five people were burned inside the bus. I saw some horrific scenes. I saw legs with no bodies. I was wounded in my right leg. I was holding onto a woman with my right hand and a child in my left hand. We were running across the desert. The woman got hit, and the child was screaming, 'I don't want to die! I don't want to die!'

"People were running away and the planes followed them and strafed them with machine guns.

"I saw some people screaming while they were on fire near the bus. It was possible for me to help some of them. It was a shock—standing, watching them in front of me. I helped some that were with me, close relatives of mine. Six persons came with me. I carried them to the hospital. There was another bus behind me. That driver took some of the injured, about 20. I went to Sabah Hospital in Kuwait. They placed the dead in the morgue. I took the child that was alive to her parents.

"I came back to the hospital where I underwent surgery and they removed the shrapnel from my leg.

"The next day I left the hospital and went to the Palestine Red Crescent.

They went with me to the site and photographed the bus and the bodies scattered around, bodies with no heads, burned bones inside the bus. Some bodies still had bullet holes from both sides from machine gun fire. They gathered the bones and put them in the crater that was created by the rocket. The crater was three meters away from the bus.

"I went back to Kuwait with the Palestine Red Crescent. They transferred me to Baghdad, and from there to the Jordanian Embassy, then to Amman where I stayed a week in the hospital."

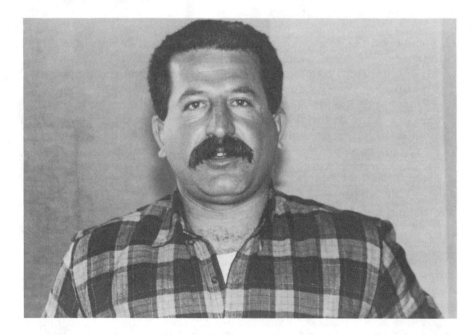

Najib Toubasi was driving a bus from Kuwait City to Basra in a convoy of other civilian vehicles. The convoy was bombed on February 9, 1991 by U.S. and allied forces. Passengers fled from bombed vehicles. The planes returned to shoot the fleeing passengers, including children. Out of fifty-seven passengers on Toubasi's bus, forty-two were killed. (Photo: Commission of Inquiry, April 2, 1991, Amman, Jordan)

Eyewitness Interview:

Palestinian Tortured in Kuwait

Excerpts from an interview with Omar Abdullah Abdullah, a Palestinian who was arrested in Kuwait and tortured there for ten days. In addition to telling Mr. Abdullah's story, this interview gives a feel for how the entire Palestinian community was treated when the U.S. military was in charge of Kuwait. The interview was conducted by the Commission's fact finding team in Hussein Refugee Camp, Amman, Jordan, March 31, 1991.

"My name is Omar Abdullah Abdullah. I am a Palestinian who carries a Jordanian passport."

Q: How long did you live in Kuwait?

A: I lived in Kuwait in an area called Kalabalshour for a year prior to the Iraqi entrance. I am an auto body repairman.

Q: Tell us what happened to you and how you were arrested.

A: After the Iraqi forces left Kuwait, a lot of the Kuwaiti civilians entered the neighborhoods and shot people. So we hid inside the houses. Many families were killed. After that, the regular army entered—the Kuwaitis, along with the Egyptian and Syrian army.

Q: Were there any Americans with this official Kuwaiti army?

A: There would be Kuwaitis, Saudis, Syrians, Egyptians, and the Americans following in a separate car. In the police stations, there are always Americans. There were American officers and soldiers in all the police stations where torture took place. Americans were present in the schools, where most of the torture took place.

The Kuwaitis, along with the Egyptian and Syrian armies, set up checkpoints on the streets. If you were a Palestinian or Jordanian national they would stop your car and search you. If you have Iraqi money, they took it and hit you. Specifically the Egyptians and the Syrians. They confiscated my car.

Then they came to the homes with loudspeakers saying, 'We captured the Kuwaiti resistance. Come out and things are safe.' And because I heard that things were safe and calm I left for work.

They started coming to my place of work, to the garage. They would ask me, 'Are you a Palestinian national carrying Jordanian papers?' I would say 'yes,' and they would take me to the [police] station. They would torture me for three or four hours, asking, 'Who do you know from the Iraqi army, who do you know from the Palestinian movement?' and I would tell them that I know nothing. I just go from home to work. That has happened to me two or three days. After that I stopped going to work.

The food ran out. They started to bring some food, distributing it only to the Kuwaitis, the Egyptians and the Syrians. They would tell us, 'Palestinians, go back to your home.' And we would ask them, 'Open the border for us so we can travel. I want to go to my country. Just open the road, open the borders.' This continued until the first day of Ramadan.

The last time they came to our house it was Ramadan. I was fasting [Moslems do not eat or drink in the daylight hours during the month of Ramadan]. They blindfolded me and took me to an area that I did not know. I recognized the area after I left it.

Q: *What's the name of the area?*

A: I found out later it was called al-Abali Station. They took me there and told me I was accused of knowing people. They didn't know exactly what they wanted to accuse me of. Sometimes they told me that I knew the PLO, sometimes that I knew Iraqi soldiers. They just took people for no reason. They started to come up with reasons before any interrogation.

They put me inside a room with a Kuwaiti first lieutenant who had a crowbar. He told me, 'You killed my brother, you killed my brother.' Then he hit me on the head. He busted my head wide open. He hit me on the back, on the legs. All the marks are still visible. I passed out because of the very severe blows with that crowbar.

Some of the other soldiers there said, 'Have mercy on him. You should at least get him treated because he will die from the hemorrhaging.' There was blood all over my head. He told them 'That's all right. Let him die. He's a Palestinian, a dog, let him die. He'll be just like the others before him.'

Then he hit me with an electrical cable. The American officer who was in charge came in. The Kuwaitis there apparently did not speak English. When the American officer came, they tried to hide me, and they spilled some water over the blood that was in the room. By that time I'd been bleeding for a full hour, and nobody bothered to look at me or give me first aid. From that I became anemic.

The American asked them [the Kuwaitis], 'Who are you torturing?' They said, 'We're not torturing anybody. We're just horsing around, playing with each other.' There were Kuwaitis and Saudis in the station.

The American said, 'No, there is somebody. Open the door to this room.' So they finally opened the door and he found me there bleeding. He did not come to my aid immediately despite the fact that he saw blood all over the room. He didn't try to give me first aid or to help me. He came in and started to interrogate me as well. He asked, 'Did you collaborate with the Iraqis or not?' I told him, 'Help me first, treat me, then I'll answer your questions.' He wanted to bring a camera and photograph me.

Then they brought in a Kuwaiti officer who was in charge of the area. The Kuwaiti colonel told me to tell the American officer that my head hit a wall and that, 'We didn't hit you.' I told him, 'If you take my head off, if you kill me, I'll still tell him the truth—that you're the ones who struck me.' He got upset with me, and started cursing Yassir Arafat and King Hussein.

But the American did not stay too long. He stayed with me for about a half hour. Then he left. It's a routine thing. He will come and then he will go, leaving you to the mercy of the Kuwaitis. The American officer told them that I must be taken to the hospital. They took me to the hospital. They apparently had an agreement with an Egyptian doctor there. The Egyptian doctor stitched my forehead without any anesthetics.

Q: *How many stitches were there?*

A: Twelve or fifteen. I told the Egyptian doctor, 'I can't see. I have been bleeding for two hours and I'm getting dizzy.' He told me, 'There is nothing wrong with you. You are fine.' He wrote this in my report.

He gave me some medication and told me to take it to stop the bleeding. I did not believe him. Later, when I got to Baghdad, I showed them the pills. They told me that the medication will make the blood thinner, and could make you bleed to death.

They [Kuwaitis] tied me with white plastic strips, real tight on my hands, and it stopped the circulation. They covered my eyes with a black blindfold. It was so tight that I felt it was going to go inside my eyes. They struck me in the car on the way back to the prison camp because I questioned the doctor.

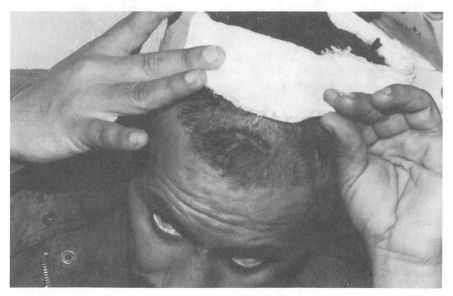

Omar Abdullah Abdullah, a Palestinian, shows Commission investigators a wound he received while he was in a Kuwaiti jail after U.S. troops established martial law in Kuwait. The wound was made with a crow bar. (Photo: Commission of Inquiry, March 1991, Hussein Refugee Camp, Amman Jordan)

When we got back to the prison camp I was told that those in charge lodged a complaint against me because I told the American I was hit by a crowbar and I did not fall against the wall. Since that time the American did not come back at all. He just disappeared. He abandoned me.

Q: *After you came back from the hospital, did you see the American officer in the prison?*

A: No. I did not see him at all. I heard that they [the Americans] had quarters below us, and they were aware of all that was taking place, and what was done to us. After I left, I saw the American vehicles, which were white.

When I was tied and blindfolded they made me get up, and pushed me to the left and right. My head would bump into various walls and into soldiers, who would strike me from different directions. I was tortured continuously.

I'm a Palestinian peaceful person. I was just working and, besides, the point is not what my government or representatives in the PLO have done, it is not my responsibility, I was in Kuwait just to make a living. But they kept on insisting that we carried out activities against the Kuwaitis, that we supported the Iraqis and that we attacked their women and looted their homes. I kept telling them that I was in Kuwait just to work and support my family.

They kicked us inside a room. Both my hands and legs were tied and I was blindfolded, so I landed on my head and I was bleeding profusely. In the same area with me were 38 Iraqi prisoners.

They tortured us with anything that you can imagine until 2:00 in the morning. They struck us with their boots and with sticks. They gave us electric shocks to the ears and other parts of the body. They hit me to the point where I could not feel any more. After 2 o'clock, they took us to interrogation.

After nine hours of torture, fasting all the time [for Ramadan] I begged them for a drink of water. They wouldn't give me any. The interrogator asked me, 'What's your situation?' I told him, 'I don't know, you brought me here, you know my situation.' They started hitting me. If you don't answer you're going to get hit, and if you answer, you're still going to get hit.

Those torturing us during the interrogation were both military and civilian. I was blindfolded, but I could see their feet, and the bottom of the white robe, the distasha, on the civilian.

The interrogator said, 'I'm sure that you know some people who are involved in the Palestinian movement, or Iraqis.' I told him, 'I don't know anything. The only thing I do is walk from the repair shop to the house, back and forth.'

Someone grabbed me and put my fingerprints on a piece of paper. I had no idea what he put my fingerprints on, and I asked him, 'Why did you put my fingerprints on this paper?' He said, 'You just sign this clean sheet of paper and we will decide what charges to put on it. This is a confession form.'

They took me back to the prison and I thought that there I would be able to relax, but the opposite actually happened. Every stage is more brutal and more difficult than the previous one.

Someone asked me, 'What are your charges,' I told him, 'I don't know.' He told me, 'You're a Palestinian dog, you're brothers of whores,' and kept cursing me. I couldn't respond to all these curses because it would bring more torture. They brought pictures of Yassir Arafat, they brought a Palestinian flag and asked me to step on it. I refused, saying, 'What does the Palestinian flag have to do with it? The PLO maybe supported Iraq, but this is a symbol, the national flag, and I will not step on it.'

When I refused the Kuwaiti officer took his hand and grabbed the stitches in my forehead and pulled them apart, tore them open with his hand. And I told him, 'If you tear me to pieces I will not step on the Palestinian flag.'

The Kuwaiti officer tells me, 'You supported Saddam Hussein.' Then one soldier started beating me for over a half hour and then he said to me, 'Why are you putting pictures of Saddam Hussein on cars in Jordan?' And I said 'What do I have to do with what happens in Amman, I'm here in Kuwait.' He was just taking out revenge in a vicious way. I really couldn't deal with it anymore. I was praying that they would just shoot me and get it over with. Another time a soldier came and struck me on the head with his rifle and said, 'You're a bunch of dogs, you plotted when Saddam came into Kuwait.' I told him, 'What do I have to do with it? I'm trying to make a living and that's all.' And other soldiers would come and start beating us.

Q: *How many Palestinians were in this camp besides you?*

A: About 20. I didn't know the total numbers in prison, but I know those who were in the same room and adjacent to me. We even heard women's voices nearby, but because we were in semi-isolation, we could not tell how many people were in the entire complex.

This vicious torture continued relentlessly for four or five days, day and night. We couldn't go to the bathroom, we had to urinate in our clothes. They were just reducing us to something less than human.

One guy came and asked me, 'Are you fasting?' I said, 'Yes.' He said, 'Well get up then and do your prayers. It's okay for you to pray.' As soon as I kneeled to pray he came from behind me, put his boot in my back and kicked me forward. My head struck the wall. They do this because they consider us less than honorable Arabs.

Every time somebody walked in, it was an opportunity for them to beat us up and torture us. They would bring rice with meat, and they would take the meat off the rice and say, 'You guys don't deserve this meat because you were helping the Iraqis and you don't deserve to eat meat.' They would take the meat and put it in the trash and give us just the plain rice. Then they would give us some dirty water to drink and very small amounts, and they would hit us on the kidneys and on the backbone.

Q: How long did this torture take place, and when were you released?

A: I was arrested on the first day of Ramadan and I was released on a Friday. I couldn't tell day from night. The night before my release I received intense and concentrated torture, and I felt that one of two things would happen. Either I would be released the next day or I would be killed.

There was another Palestinian young man who they tortured because they accused him of stealing a car. There were two witnesses who showed he bought and paid for the car. He even brought the Indian who he bought the car from. When the Indian told them that he sold the car to the Palestinian, to this young fellow by the name of Yassir, they [the Kuwaiti soldiers] told him to go and not come back, that they didn't need his testimony. They tortured Yassir until he died.

He received the most torture. They tied him up, both hands and legs, and blindfolded him. Two soldiers would carry him by the feet and lift him up and drop him on his head. They would just kick and beat him without paying any attention to where their blows fell.

Q: How were you released from the prison? Where did they take you? What did you do on the day of your release?

A: They let me out at 11:00 in the morning and I asked where they were taking me. I was really afraid that they would kill me because of the signature and thumb print that they took from me. I didn't know what I had signed, and I was afraid that maybe it was a confession that would result in my death. But they told me not to worry because they were taking me to another prison camp.

They did not tell me I was being released so that I would not ask for my passport or my money. They took me to an area called Jaharia. We were just four Palestinians and the rest were Iraqis. They were all civilians.

They put us on a bus, tied and blindfolded us, then drove for a short while. They took us to a place called Safwan [on the Iraqi border] where there was a Red Cross station. It was not there to receive us, it was there to receive the Iraqi opposition forces [forces opposed to Saddam Hussein].

I asked [the Kuwaitis] where is our money? They said, 'You have 4,000 Iraqi dinars,' but because it has the picture of Saddam on it they confiscated it. They took everything, including our sandals. The Red Cross was asked to receive us and sign a piece of paper saying we were released from Kuwait. The Red Cross refused to accept responsibility for us, saying we were bodies with almost no life. The Kuwaiti major said, 'Drop them a few yards behind the building. Let them go there.'

We walked around 22 kilometers on all kinds of fragments. Around us were unexploded shells. I couldn't walk. Two guys carried me. They helped me until we reached the town of Safwan, an Iraqi village. American troops were there.

I found some media people. They were French and American. I was able to read the names on their cameras—the channel numbers, stations and network names. They took pictures of me because my face was all swollen, my hands were swollen, my feet were swollen, the signs of cigarette burns were still on me. They took plenty of pictures, but I'm sure they're not going to be published in America because it's not in the interest of the government. Even the interviews conducted with me, I'm sure they will not be published because it's not in the interest of the American officers.

Q: How were you received by the Iraqis when you reached Safwan?

A: We were received very well by the Iraqis. They gave us some money. They had a food shortage, but they gave us their food because of our situation. They carried me to the government offices in spite of the rebellion and what was going on. The governor gave me documents that allowed me to travel. All of my documents were destroyed by the Kuwaitis. And they gave us medication.

The Kuwaitis destroyed our papers so that when the Iraqis would see us they would think that we were from the [Iraqi anti-Saddam] opposition, because the opposition does not have any documents. The Kuwaitis wanted us to be killed. But the Iraqis treated us well and gave us documents that we were able to travel on.

Eyewitness Interview:

Doctors in Baghdad Hospitals

Before the Gulf war, Iraq had one of the best health care systems in the Arab world, available to the entire population at a nominal cost. Now, due to the war and the sanctions, people are dying for want of the most basic medicines.

The following testimony was taken from doctors in Baghdad's Kindi Hospital and Saddam Hussein Pediatric Hospital. Kindi is a community hospital in a poor neighborhood of Baghdad. Saddam Hussein Pediatric, which treats children from all over Iraq, is renowned throughout the Middle East for its state-of-the-art equipment and its quality care.

This testimony deals with the effects of the embargo and the war: the shortage of key drugs and the lack of electrical power in these modern medical institutions. The doctors also describe the medical problems that are directly related to the embargo and the U.S. bombing of the civilian infrastructure needed to maintain the population.

Kindi Hospital, Baghdad

April 4, 1991—The Commission team was told that about half of the 1,000 patients brought to this hospital during the U.S. bombing died. A significant factor was the lack of electricity in the hospital. The electricity in Kindi Hospital was knocked out the night of January 16 – 17, 1991, the first night of bombing. When the interview was conducted, Kindi was using a backup generator, but only had enough power for surgery and emergency cases, and then only for half the day, due to fuel shortages.

"I'm Doctor Saad Sallal, working here as a resident, and a student in the Iraqi Board of Plastic Surgery, in the Department of Surgery."

Q: *What kind of medical problems did you see during the war? How were they dealt with?*

A: An increasing number of people died due to the lack of facilities and the lack of medicine. For example, there were many amputations of those with diabetes because there was no medication. Many of the heart patients also died due to lack of medication.

We need medicine for chronic diseases, and to replace some equipment that was destroyed due to the bombing. Most who came to the hospital were suffering from malnutrition, and again there were a lot of amputations due to the lack of medication for those who are chronically ill. This had a devastating effect on children and women, because some of them had a lower resistance.

Q: What effects have the sanctions had on medical care in this hospital?

A: We no longer have access to certain drugs we cannot manufacture in Iraq, especially drugs for chronic diseases like diabetes, hypertension and heart problems. These drugs are exported by American companies, by other Western companies, by Israeli companies and by others.

Patients in hypertensive crisis, diabetic crisis and with cardiac problems, especially acute problems, have died in this hospital because of these shortages, especially in the intensive care unit. We are especially suffering due to the electricity cutoff. Because we had no electricity, we lost the blood banks. We lost not less than 3,000 to 4,000 bags of blood needed for patients here, especially for surgical emergencies.

Q: This is April 4, 1991. The bombing stopped about three weeks ago. What problems do you see now?

A: Let's start with the children, who are at a critical time in their lives. They suffer from malnutrition and hygiene problems. Water that was not properly processed was given to the people.

You'll find less sanitation health problems with adults. With them, it's a matter of food preparation, and living without electricity. I am not poor. I am a doctor. In my house, my family has no water to wash their face or hands before eating. I have no electricity to study. I'm 36 years old, and I haven't enough electricity to shave. My family lives in an area that hasn't had electricity for three to four months. A few locations in Baghdad get electricity on and off, but not continuously.

Here in the hospital it is very difficult to even wash our hands. There is no way to sterilize or clean. We work in the operating theater under these conditions. Take, for instance, the dressing of skin grafts. We have to open the wound to look at it. But we cannot open the wounds in the wards, due to the unsanitary conditions. We have to bring the patients to the operating room just to have a look at the wound. Unfortunately, you [the Commission team] don't have enough time to see all the pus and infection we have in this hospital due to the low level of basic sanitation.

Later I'll take you to my locker and show you the same cap and mask I use continuously. Last month I found just one disposable mask. I have been using it ever since, working day and night with the same disposable mask.

Eyewitness Interview:

Dr. Talaat Talal, Saddam Pediatric Hospital, Baghdad

April 7, 1991—"We have no insulin. One of my neighbors came to me about 10 p.m., and said there was a 2-year-old child in my hospital, newly diagnosed and severely ill. One ampule of insulin would save her life. [doctor broke down crying here]. We looked all over the hospital and couldn't find any. I offered five liters of benzene [gasoline] to the man who brought the child in so that he could go to another hospital, Medical City. We got the insulin and the baby is well now. I am so happy. You have to understand my feelings, seeing patients dying for simple, simple, simple measures. Every corner of the world has insulin."

[The doctor took the Commission team on a tour of the hospital.] "Now we are seeing a baby with dehydration, a case of renal disease. She was referred from the city of Najaf, where there was a lack of hospital care. He needs a simple test for blood urea, potassium and sodium. Very simple tests that should be done in this big hospital. I sent for the results and here you can see [holds up lab report] the tests could not be done because the laboratories are not functioning due to lack of electricity."

Q: Is there any way of treating this child?

A: Sure. I will help. He's uremic, he's acidotic, his potassium is shooting up, in my clinical judgment. But we should have a lab report. What century are we in? What hospital are we in? Previously we had everything. We couldn't want to work better than we have in the last two years. He [the child] is miserable.

Q: How many children have been affected by the lack of medicine and lack of electricity. How many died?

A: There are a lot. Every day I come across many cases like this baby. Everything has been affected.

Q: Are you seeing examples of malnutrition, or problems as a result of the poor sanitation?

A: A lot of malnutrition. I have been a doctor for eight years in Iraq, I have not seen one case of kwashiorkor [a disease of severe protein malnutrition]. You won't believe it, but three days ago I saw a case of kwashiorkor. The mother had not fed the baby milk for six months, only sugar and water. Can you imagine?

[Moving to the next child] This baby weighs three kilograms [about 6.5 lbs., the weight of a newborn]. He's got gastroenteritis, diarrhea and vomiting caused by poor sanitation. He is marasmic as well [severe malnutrition—both protein and calories], and has feeding problems as well. I talked about the micro drip [special tubing that delivers intravenous fluids at the slower rate needed for babies and children], specially set for this baby.

In 24 hours we can collect 6,000 cubic centimeters of this fluid for this baby. You know this drip is for bigger persons, not for babies, because these big drops are equal to 15 small drops. And he receives the fluid so quick, 500 cc in about two hours. Now the micro drip is not working.

Previously we did not see such tension in the nursing staff. Look how many children are here. It is a very difficult job for the nurses. It could be the fault of the nurse or of the doctor if we don't have a device that we need, or we don't arrange for the patient to have a chart. There is even a lack of paper for the chart. Every aspect of our job is affected.

Q: What about masks, gloves, etc.?

A: We have a test we call the CSF [Cerebro-Spinal Fluid]. We take fluid from the spinal column for the diagnosis of meningitis, etc. Usually the test is done under sterile conditions, using gloves and anesthetic spirits for the area. Gloves? We don't have gloves. Imagine, we do the puncture [spinal tap] with just our hands. It is a tragedy. We save the life of a patient with meningitis, and then induce infection.

Q: Are there a lot of cases of marasmus now?

A: Marasmus, yes. [Marasmus is chronic total under-nutrition which produces general wasting away of body tissues and emaciation.]

Q: What about malnutrition? Prenatal care for pregnant women?

A: You know, we have progressed a lot in our country. Every woman, even in the rural areas, had pre-natal and post-natal care. We were providing tonics, folic acid supplements and vaccinations, prenatal and postnatal. We had reached a very high level. And now everything has changed.

Look at this child. She has severe asthma but we don't have the oxygen for this patient. We don't have enough oxygen, or a nebulizer. An asthmatic patient must have an inter-solution. This is a special device, not the inhaler, but by mask. In this hospital, which is a central hospital, the devices are not working. There is a lack of inter-solution. This patient is in very serious condition. She may run into respiratory failure at any time because we don't have the devices or the medication.

Q: What is happening with your operating facilities now?

A: It is working, but only for emergency cases, not for hernia or rectal collapse or hare lips. No elective surgery.

Q: How is the electricity in this hospital working?

A: There is a generator now.

Q: Is it on 24 hours a day?

A: Twenty-four hours now. But the summer is coming, and a generator in this facility cannot operate the central air conditioning. I can just imagine what will happen in the summer [Baghdad summer temperatures go over 100 degrees Fahrenheit.].

Q: What do you think will happen when the warm weather brings an increase in bacteria growth?

A: I don't know. This is winter, and we have all this gastroenteritis and severe asthma. What about the summer? We hope to improve our functioning by then.

[Continuing the tour] This patient has renal acidosis. We have previously diagnosed this baby, and for two years we were happy to give him Scholl Solution. A component of this solution is citric acid, sodium, potassium. The mother gives this fluid to the child at home. The dosage is determined by body weight. But his mother could not give him Scholl Solution because it was not present in the pharmacy. Now he is acidotic. He's not taking the medicine because it's not available.

In this country we have deficiencies of an enzyme in the blood. It is a hereditary sex-linked disease. In our country it is called favasin, because when a child eats fava beans it affects the blood. This child was dying. We gave him blood by the slide method, not by cross-match, the long method. I think he will be well. [Cross-matching is a method of matching blood from the recipient of the transfusion with the donor blood to make sure that it is compatible.]

Q: How was the blood supply affected?

A: There is a central blood bank here. We order a type of blood, we send it to the blood bank, and there is a donor. We kept it functioning during the war.

This is a very famous hospital because we are doing our best. We have been working for more than eighteen hours a day for the last year.

[Victims of the bombing did not come to this hospital.]

The children were not going to school. Now they are going to school, but they are crowded. I don't know about the sanitation in the schools.

Q: How do people pay for medical care here?

A: Anyone can enter this hospital. You just have to pay half a dinar to get a ticket and to be examined by a doctor. Every day you stay here you pay one dinar. This covers everything, including medication.

Q: At this point you don't have any oxygen?

A: No, no. The oxygen supply is zero. I just don't know what will happen if any severely affected child comes in now.

Q: How was the country supplied with oxygen tanks prior to the war?

A: There are special factories. They aren't working.

In our hospital there are twelve wards with intensive care, 300 beds, I think. I have a friend whose daughter had a car accident. He is my colleague, a doctor as well. He transferred the baby to the neurosurgical hospital at night. They have a small generator, but it doesn't supply enough electricity for the x-ray machine to work, or to bring up the one CAT Scan in that hospital. The baby was unconscious. Without the benefit of an x-ray, they performed an operation because they suspected there was bleeding in the brain. Imagine a neurosurgeon working without a simple x-ray or scan to see if there was bleeding? There was no bleeding, only brain injury.

Eyewitness Interview:

Widow of a Truck Driver in Amman, Jordan

Mrs. Zehda was interviewed by the Commission in East Amman, Jordan on March 30, 1991. Her husband was killed by U.S. and allied bombing of the highway from Amman to Baghdad. Mr. Zehda's trailer was empty. He was making a return trip after carrying refrigerated food to Iraq. The food items had been pre-approved by the UN.

Q: Could you please tell us what happened to your husband, and could you describe his work and the incident that took his life?

A: My husband was a driver on the Iraq-Amman highway, transporting foodstuffs. He went on a trip to Baghdad. On the way back, there was an air raid at the al-Rutbah area, that's the 106 kilometer mark heading back from Baghdad towards Amman. The air raid took place, and he was killed.

Q: How many years had he worked on this line?

A: He had been a driver on this line for 16 years.

Q: The foodstuff that he was carrying, was it approved by the UN at the border?

A: He had a permit from the United Nations observers at the border to carry it through.

Q: What was his destination?

A: To Mosul, Iraq.

Q: Was he by himself in the cab of the truck, or had he somebody with him?

A: He was driving along with another individual sitting beside him. The other person was burned totally, and there was nothing left of him except charred remains. My husband jumped out of the cab after the bombing, and then he ran about 25 meters from the truck. The planes came back and strafed him, and he was hit with machine gun fire.

We have nothing to do with this war. The driver had nothing to do with politics. He was carrying normal foodstuff. He was not a combatant, he had nothing to do with the war.

Q: How many children did he leave behind?

A: Seven children, four boys, three girls. The oldest, 14, the youngest, 4.

Mrs. Zeheda, who is Palestinian, was interviewed by the Commission's team in East Amman, Jordan. His truck was bombed by U.S. planes while he was returning from Baghdad. He ran out of the flaming truck, but the plane returned and killed him with gunfire. (Photo: Commission of Inquiry, March 30, 1991)

Crimes Against Egyptian and Palestinian Civilians in Iraq and Kuwait

Professor Mustafa El Bakri

In its recent war against Iraq, the United States attacked civilians and destroyed non-military installations, including, specifically, those projects that constitute the infrastructure of Iraq. There is a considerable and varied amount of evidence to establish this fact, of which part has been revealed and a large part remains unrevealed.

Salem Abdel Hamid, an Egyptian citizen from al-Minya Province, has given an account of some of the incidents that took place before his eyes in Basra. He states that from the beginning of their attacks Coalition forces targeted water storage tanks and power stations, with the intention of paralyzing the city's life and forcing its inhabitants to flee towards Iran. He further states that he saw with his own eyes scores of corpses of civilians who perished inside water and power stations. This Egyptian national, who has succeeded in returning to Egypt after the end of the Gulf War, has related a number of facts about the spread of epidemics and starvation in the city. He stressed that American forces deliberately directed devastating attacks against food-processing and medicine plants, thus deeply affecting the health of the population, hundreds of whom have fallen victim to the diseases that have spread as a result of the destruction of the sewage disposal plants in the city. More than sixty percent of the buildings in Basra were destroyed, and many people perished under the rubble.

In Baghdad, Omar Adnan, a 17-year old Egyptian citizen, in a statement to the Baghdad correspondent of the Associated Press, said that he had suffered severe burns as a result of the bombing of the al-Ameriyah Shelter. "I was asleep," he said, "when, all of a sudden, I felt intense heat . . . the bed sheets were burning. Soon after, I felt I was choking. I turned to touch my mother, but I found nothing but a piece of burnt-up flesh." He added that he was the only one to survive among the members of his family, which included his father and mother and their three daughters.

Alfred Roger, the Baghdad correspondent of the Spanish newspaper *El Mundo*, has reported that, at a hospital in the holy city of Najaf, he saw

an Iraqi child groaning with pain. In answer to questions, he said his name
was Ahmed Abdallah. He was with his family in front of their home when
"things" started to fall down. He did not know where his mother or father
were. The correspondent says that the child opened his big eyes while he
was twisting like one whose feet were caught in a trap. Shell fragments
had hit his left foot. Other fragments were embedded in his side, and both
of his feet were covered with blood.

In the tragedy of the al-Ameriyah shelter, which was deliberately hit
by an American pilot, hundreds of Iraqi women and children lost their lives.
Away from that shelter, there is hardly a part of Iraqi soil that has not
witnessed similar scenes of gory tragedy. Those criminal attacks made no
distinction between military personnel and civilians or between Iraqis and
non-Iraqis. Their aim was to destroy Iraq, all of Iraq. CNN correspondent
Peter Arnett has described the effects of the bombing by Coalition aircraft
of the town of Falluja, west of Baghdad. One of the sites destroyed was a
hotel where Egyptians were residing. The number of those killed is estimated
to range from fifty to one hundred thirty.

Samir al-Manshawi, an Egyptian citizen who was working in Iraq and
who is now residing in Aziz, a village in Qalleen Center in Kifr el Shaykh
Province, has stated that he was hit in the arm by shell fragments when
a residence where he lived with ten other Egyptians was bombed in air raids
on Baghdad. Four of the Egyptians were killed, including his cousin Abdel
Ghaffar al-Manshawi. Describing the events, Samir al-Manshawi said: "We
were transported by Iraqi Police to Medical City Hospital in Baghdad, where
I stayed for fifteen days. I assumed responsibility for receiving the remains
of the four who had been killed and completing the documentation needed
for their shipment to Egypt. I myself returned by the land road to Amman.
On the way from Baghdad to Amman, I saw on the roadside a bus which
had been burned by American aircraft. According to our Jordanian driver,
it was carrying ninety-two Egyptians to Amman airport. During my trip
to the Amman airport from the Iraqi border, which took six days on account
of continuous air raids, the car I was traveling in had often to turn off the
lights and hide for prolonged periods of time to avoid being bombed."

American crimes in the Gulf War are many, and they did not come
to an end with the end of the war but continued on more than one level.
Apart from imposing the economic embargo and starving out the Iraqi
population, many crimes were committed by American forces on Kuwaiti
territory after it was "liberated" from Iraqi forces. The Emirate of Kuwait
came under a purely American administration. The American ambassador
and the commander of the American forces in Kuwait assumed the administration of the Emirate for all practical purposes. During that time, and
with the support of United States forces, many crimes were committed
against Egyptians and other Arab communities living in Kuwait. As a result
of severe torture, five Egyptians died: they had been arrested, imprisoned

and then tortured. Another 300 were imprisoned and tortured without being charged with any real offense. These facts have been confirmed by the Egyptian Organization for Human Rights, through its representative who went to Kuwait after its "liberation" and disclosed the extent of the suffering being inflicted upon Egyptians and members of the other Arab communities there by militias of the Al-Sabah family acting in coordination with U.S. forces.

The Arab community that suffered the most from acts of repression and brutal treatment in Kuwait is the Palestinian community. They were accused of having supported the occupying forces, although a prominent Kuwaiti personality, Member of Parliament Khalid Sultan, has stated to the U.S. Information Agency that that was untrue. He said: "Let us be truthful: many Palestinians assisted us during that period. Some went as far as fighting alongside the Kuwaiti resistance. They took food to Kuwaiti officers. They carried packages and letters through Jordan to members of our families who were outside Kuwait."

The Palestinian Committee on Human Rights has prepared a report on massacres and acts of repression based upon available reports and testimony. These reports have affirmed that execution squads led by American and British officers of the Coalition forces have assumed the task of pursuing, tracking down and catching Palestinians selectively and deliberately throughout Kuwait with the help of Kuwaiti, Saudi Arabian and other Gulf military units specializing in such operations. They would hysterically raid, comb and invade city neighborhoods populated by Palestinians. They would lead away whole families, most often to U.S. Army camps, where special security and intelligence experts would screen the detainees on the basis of prepared lists they already possessed, then have them transferred to investigation centers and concentration camps established by the Coalition forces in various parts of Kuwait.

Information and testimony given by some Palestinians who had the good fortune to escape the looming danger of mass graves indicate that the course taken by investigations in those centers, which are run by American forces, had nothing to do with the familiar charges of collaboration with Iraqi authorities that were leveled against Palestinians. Rather, inquiries and interrogations—accompanied by threats of death and physical liquidation as well as brutal torture to extract information by any means whatsoever—focused on the relationship of these citizens with the Intifada and Palestinian organizational structures and institutions both in Palestine and in the Gulf and Arab Peninsula region.

According to that testimony, many Palestinian detainees were transported by helicopter to a U.S. base, from where they were taken to occupied Palestine and further investigated by the Israeli occupiers on charges of participation in the Intifada, providing it with financial support or conducting military operations against Israel.

The testimony published on March 26, 1991 in the Jordanian daily *Al Ra'y* by one of its senior editors, Mr. Sultan al-Hattab, on the basis of statements made by the Palestinian citizen Fuad, who had survived organized mass killings in Kuwait, will perhaps expose part of this hideous conspiracy launched by the Coalition forces against the Palestinian people in Kuwait. Similarly, the series of reports published by the British *Guardian* under the bylines of its correspondents Kate Evans and Simon Tysdale, although well within the limits of what is permitted to be published on the situation in Kuwait under Coalition forces, would make one's hair stand on end. This testimony discloses part of what the Palestinians have suffered. It speaks of atrocities, indiscriminate arrests and disappearances suffered by individual Palestinians in addition to inhumane acts to which they are collectively subjected in their areas of residence at the hands of the masked militias of the Kuwaiti authorities, who carry out their raids under the protection of U.S. forces and the supervision of officers of the U.S. Special Forces.

Tysdale has further confirmed that there is a unit of the U.S. Special Forces which oversees acts of mass repression and terrorization inflicted on Palestinians. Tysdale has pointed out that some of these American officers speak fluent Arabic, which makes it all the easier for them to carry out their horrible tasks. The same facts have also been confirmed by a correspondent of the British *Observer*, who has spoken bitterly of the torture of the innocent in Kuwait that takes place with the knowledge and under the very eyes of the U.S. forces.

In addition to press reports and reports by other information media, both written and visual, there are official statements by United States, French and British officials both inside and outside Kuwait as well as documented testimony gathered on the spot by representatives of Amnesty International, the International Committee of the Red Cross, such United Nations Agencies as the UNESCO and the UNHCR and various human rights organizations, the totality of which constitutes irrefutable and unambiguous evidence of the extent of the dangers faced by the Palestinians and the crimes inflicted on hundreds and hundreds of them: assassinations, direct and deliberate physical liquidation by shooting in the head at close range or by severe torture in concentration camps, including such procedures as the extraction of fingernails, burning by electricity and cigarette butts, disfigurement and the burning of bodies.

This criminal sadism has been carried to the point of burning a number of detainees alive by tying their hands and pouring gasoline on them as stated by citizen Fuad in his testimony to the Jordanian newspaper *Al Ra'y*.

These facts are further confirmed by the testimony of a member of the Kuwaiti Association for the Defense of Victims of War and Protection of Human Rights in Kuwait, an association which was formed after the entry into Kuwait of the Coalition forces, and whose goal, as stated by one of its most prominent founders, Dr. Ghanim An-Najjar, is to defend members of the Palestinian community and other Arabs in the face of the flagrant violation of their human rights by the Coalition forces and the now re-empowered Kuwaiti Security Services. In addition, the Association concerns itself with the conditions of prisoners of war as well as forcibly banished Bedouins. The Bedouins, who have been subjected to persecution and live under the continuing threat of expulsion, are in the same situation as the Palestinians and other Arabs, hundreds of whom have been dumped in the desert on the Iraqi-Kuwaiti border after being stripped of all their belongings. As testified by Bob Drogin, correspondent of the American newspaper the *Los Angeles Times*, they are left there in a state of total exhaustion brought about by the torture which they have undergone and they badly need hospitalization. The same newspaper also contained flagrant facts about the execution of Palestinians and other Arabs and the merciless, indiscriminate detention of women and children and old men.

Drogin quoted three individuals (a Palestinian, a Sudanese and an Algerian) to the effect that they had seen a Palestinian and two Sudanese youths breathing their last under beatings with rifle butts and pistols to which they had been subjected for three days in a cell packed with one hundred and nine other prisoners, including men over sixty years of age. At least three women in a neighboring cell were also subjected to beatings and torture, Drogin's witnesses told him.

Reports by French Reuters have spoken of no less than eighty un-identified corpses of individuals killed by shots in the head at close range and buried in mass graves in the Silinjat and Raqqa areas in southern Kuwait. Among them were the bodies of twelve young men fifteen to thirty years of age showing marks of horrible torture and mutilation. They were buried in the mass graves of Raqqa on Sunday, March 17, 1991. Paul Tyler, a British correspondent for Reuters News Service, has seen these graves with his own eyes.

Workers in Mubarak Hospital as well as a number of gravediggers have given shocking accounts about Palestinians who have been killed by being shot in the head at close range and who have then been buried secretly, or whose dead bodies were thrown in the streets of Hula, Khitan, Nuqra and Farwaniyah (all of which are low-income residential areas normally inhabited by Palestinians) with the intent of striking terror in the hearts of those among them who have remained outside the concentration camps and inducing them to leave the country.

According to official Palestinian reports, at least two-hundred and ten Palestinians, including women and children, were killed after Coalition forces entered Kuwait. Most of these Palestinians died under brutal, systematic torture or by being hanged or shot in the head. In addition, there are some 4,000 Palestinians whose fate or place of detention remains unknown. They include a number of Palestinian physicians who played a prominent humanitarian role in the hospitals of Kuwait during the war. The fate of hundreds of other Arab citizens (Jordanians, Egyptians, Sudanese, Iraqis, Moroccans and Yemenis) also remains unknown.

Another illustration of this situation is to be found in what happened to Mr. Ali Hassan (Abu Ayman), a prominent Palestinian of Kuwait. As is widely acknowledged in Kuwaiti circles, he has, over the decades, played a memorable role in the rise and prosperity of Kuwait. During the presence of the Iraqi forces in Kuwait, he also had an important role to play in forming people's and neighborhood committees to provide humanitarian and social care to the needy. Last week, masked armed groups, led by American officers, raided his house and attempted to assassinate him by opening fire on him, and he was hit by some of the bullets of this dark hatred. They then burned his house and its contents, room by room.

There has been some movement on the part of international and humanitarian organizations and large sectors of Western public opinion in the face of this state of affairs. Amnesty International, for example, on March 18, 1991, has called for putting a stop to these crimes and taking steps for a prompt and independent investigation thereof. On March 22, 1991, Mr. Andrew Whitley, director of the American organization Middle East Watch, released an urgent appeal for help in protecting the lives and rights of members of the Palestinian community in Kuwait. Even so, some aspects of these statements and the actions they call for have been used— rather, abused—by the Coalition powers to shirk responsibility for these crimes which are being committed in a programmed and systematic manner under the protection of their military forces and political authority. This brings to mind what happened when Israel invaded Lebanon and swept over Beirut, and how Israeli forces together with sectarian militias committed the Sabra and Shatila massacres of Palestinians in 1982 under the very eyes and within the hearing of the American, French, and other multi-lateral forces in exactly the same manner as is being repeated today in Kuwait in almost identical circumstances.

Of course the atrocities I have discussed here are only a fraction of what the United States forces have perpetrated with the support of other Coalition forces on Arab land. The massacres of civilians have not been committed for the sake of liberating Kuwait but to humiliate the Arab nation and make an example of Iraq for all those who wouldn't be warned. These are dirty aims in the implementation of which U.S. President Bush and his assistants have played the basic role. The record of the crimes I have mentioned should be sufficient cause to demand a full disclosure of the record of this criminal world leader and bring him to trial for these heinous crimes which should cover his face with shame. The victims of this dastardly war in their hundreds of thousands curse the American president from their graves and call on all people of conscience to pronounce their historic judgment against this man who has repudiated all legal and humane norms of behavior and enforced the law of the jungle so that he might become the sole arbiter in all relations between the peoples of the world.

Professor Bakri's testimony was presented on August 7, 1991, in Cairo, where the Egyptian branch of the Commission of Inquiry held a hearing on war crimes committed by the United States in Iraq and Kuwait. The hearing was the first in an Arab country and took place in spite of Egyptian President Mubarak's collaboration with Bush's war against the Iraqi people. (Egyptian soldiers suffered the highest casualties of any Coalition forces in the Gulf war.) Much of the testimony at the hearing focused on the experiences of Egyptian workers, who made up a large part of the labor force in the Gulf states and Iraq. The Egyptian Commission, which was convened by author and activist Dr. Sherif Hetata of Egypt's leading opposition party, comprised such well-known individuals as Dr. Nawal El Saadawi, an internationally acclaimed author and president of the Arab Women's Solidarity Association (whose Egyptian branch was forcibly closed by the Egyptian government in July); Dr. Latifa El Zayyat of Ain Shams University; former Foreign Minister Dr. Mohamed Ibrahim Kamel, now president of the Egyptian Human Rights Organization; Prof. Gamal El Ghitani, columnist for *Al Akbar* newspaper; former ambassadors Dr. Wafaa Hejazi and Dr. Bahiyeddin El Rashidi; and Lt. Gen. Mohamed Fawzi (ret.); among many others.

Speakers at the Cairo hearing, which was held in the meeting hall of the National Progressive Unionist Rally Party (Hizb al Tagammu), included Dr. Mohamed Abdel Fadhil, professor of economics at Cairo University, who spoke on the consequences of the war on the Iraqi people; Prof. Mustafa El Bakri, who spoke on the experiences of Egyptian workers in Kuwait and Iraq both during and after the war; Mr. Abdel Rahman Kheer of the Engineers Union, who spoke on the effect of the war on the already impoverished Egyptian working class; and Commission founder Mr. Ramsey Clark.

Waging War on Civilization

Fadwa El Guindi, Ph.D.

It was ironic to hear the former Prime Minister of Britain Margaret Thatcher ridiculing President Saddam Hussein and referring to Iraq as uncivilized—ironic because Europe was largely mired in barbarism when Baghdad was the world's most refined, most cosmopolitan center, the Baghdad of *1001 Nights* and *The Ruba'iyat*, the center of philosophical, scientific and literary achievements still remembered as the peak of high civilization, the pinnacle of Arab culture.

There is something barbarian about brutally bombing the world's cradle of civilization. It is cowardly to launch an unprecedented assault by high-tech weapons of destruction on a defenseless Third World country, and hypocritical on the part of the most powerful nation to do so in the name of civilization, in the name of order—a new world order—while it is destroying the birthplace of the world's truly first world order. It was in Mesopotamia that the world saw the earliest codes of law, forms of human government and other administrative advances, urban life, farming and writing, technical and scientific discoveries. Accompanying these gigantic achievements were lasting contributions to world art and literature.

Is there no sanctity for the sacred places of worship ancient and continuing—temples, churches and mosques? Is there no concern that this is the believed birthplace of the patriarch Abraham, the root of our heritage, that it is the home for extremely valuable human history, the guardian and keeper of knowledge about our history?

Many people probably connect Iraq and ancient Mesopotamia, but most people may not know how much we owe to Iraq's ancient civilizations. Mesopotamia was the world's birthplace of urban, literate civilization. Then again in the early Middle Ages, Islamic Baghdad was a seat of learning and a world capital at a time when most of Europe was peripheral and had been reduced to a near-barbarian condition. With reference to these two high civilizations, it was pointed out by anthropologist Robert McAdams of the Smithsonian Institution that there exists no comparable examples in history in which a country has produced two extended periods of comparable richness from entirely separate cultural traditions more than a thousand years apart.

A true new world order treasures its irreplaceable heritage, but with all this destruction, the U.S. will be remembered as a destroyer of antiquity. There was a treacherous deception by the media and military to present an image of Iraq to the American public and the world as if it were simply an empty desert with some oil wells, thus obscuring the direct and indirect threat posed to the extraordinary contributions of Mesopotamia that have elevated humankind above the beasts. "The archeological treasures in the museum in Baghdad are, in a very real sense, the property of all the peoples of the world," said David Stonach, professor of Near East archeology at the University of California at Berkeley. He said, "If it were suggested somehow that it was necessary to bomb Athens in a war, there would be a very large outcry from the scholars of the world that the Acropolis should not be put in such danger. It seems appropriate to me to point out the equal danger of our cultural patrimony in Iraq." Instead, neither front page coverage nor nightly newscasts give the people any hint that the Western world has any stake in Iraq beyond petrodollars.

Iraqi Contributions

Among the contributions of Mesopotamia to the world are: writing, the wheel, irrigation-agriculture, monumental architecture, organized religion, kingship, empire, social stratification, industrial production of goods and large-scale trade, law, administration, cities, schools, literature, poetry, medical, scientific and mathematical texts, geometry, astronomy, building bricks, wheeled transportation, and the first architectural ground-plans. Moreover, in addition to the ideological role that goddesses and women played in the mythical history, Ancient Mesopotamia produced the first poet known in history: a woman called Enheduanna, a high priestess, in 2,300 BC. We have to remember this when, as American women, we celebrate the literary or artistic contributions of Founding Mothers, of about one hundred years ago.

By about 2,000 BC schools, libraries, literature, epics, scientific documents, dictionaries, encyclopedias had already existed. Stone Age skeletons found in Shanidar Cave, in northern Iraq, show the earliest evidence of ritual burial. A 6,000 year old temple unearthed at Abu Shahrein, about 80 miles north of the Kuwaiti border, is the oldest religious structure known to us. Iraq, some scholars argue, even gave rise to the concept of the single god. Commerce, as well as religion, had its pioneering aspects in Iraq. Installment plan purchasing has been documented in clay tablets dated to 2,500 BC and found near the Iraqi fighter base at Jalibah.

Such achievements appear to have flowered first in "the fertile crescent" stretching along the mountains of Kurdistan to the Persian Gulf. According to Dr. Adams, they emerged due to the particular climatological and geographical features of Mesopotamia at that time. True it was a very fertile area, but such achievements were possible only if people were cooperating —some irrigating the plains, some as shepherds in the steppes; that is, they had a division of labor and role specialization. And that required and rewarded social organization—writing, the accumulation and transfer of knowledge, a stratified social structure and the like.

Less easily explainable and perhaps more wonderful, he says, is that "these advances were not just linear and utilitarian. They were accompanied by tremendous creative surges in areas like sculpture, carpentry, ceramics and architecture—the arts that evidence a flowering of the human spirit." This occurred from the emergence of the Sumerian civilization, about 3,000 BC, to the overthrow of the Old Babylonian empire about 1600 BC. "Such learning as the world had achieved up to that time was to be found in the scribal schools and libraries of what is now Iraq. They were teaching the Pythagorean theories (of geometry) a thousand years before Pythagoras."

In the 6th century BC, Iraq fell to the Persians, and two centuries later to the Greeks. The Greek conquest was short lived, and soon afterwards an indigenous dynasty, the Parthian, arose later, succeeded by a Sassanian dynasty, which remained until the advent of Islam.

With the coming of Islam and the Arab rule of the Abbasid Caliphs, 750 – 1,250 AD, Iraq once again became the world center of learning.

Appeal and Concern

Some voices of scholars and specialists showed concern and appealed for restraint, and stressed the scholarly, archeological, biblical, and artistic significance of Iraq and possible loss. In a letter to the editor published in the *Washington Post* on February 12, 1991, Dr. Robert Adams, Secretary, Smithsonian Institution, Washington D.C., and Prudence Harper, Curator of Ancient Near Eastern Art, Metropolitan Museum of Art, New York, referred to the intense and widespread human suffering denied by the use of the euphemism of "collateral damage." The immediacy of human suffering and environmental damage has forced into the background the uniquely rich and important history of the region that is today Iraq. The letter goes on to mention that the abandoned cities and villages of the last 8,000 or 9,000 years now take the form of *tells* or mounds that almost continuously blanket the country (hence very vulnerable). They cautioned that at risk from bombing are standing archeological monuments such as Samarra and the Arch of Ctesiphon. Of greatest concern are Iraq's museums, housing such treasures as Assyrian reliefs, royal tomb offerings from Ur and an unsurpassed wealth of clay tablets with early cuneiform writing— many still unstudied.

These remains constitute a priceless heritage of all humanity. Worried about damage to this heritage, some scholars appealed for restraint: "Recognizing that accident, miscalculation and uncertainty play a major part in every war, we can only solemnly urge that all parties to the hostilities take every possible measure to protect them and to avoid military operations in their immediate vicinity. Intentional crime or careless error leading to their destruction would almost equally darken the record of any nation or individual responsible. As specialists in the antiquities and history of Mesopotamia, we share with scholars in many countries, including Iraq, a special responsibility for this crucial segment of our common cultural heritage."

Dr. Robert Adams stressed that the situation "in no sense diminished either our sense of responsibility or of colleagueship . . . our collective inheritance of these creative accomplishments, and the meaning they still have for our lives, should not be forgotten even while this war is waged . . . [and] when hostilities cease, [it is hoped that we can] safeguard Iraq's antiquities and restore the amicable and productive atmosphere of international study of them under Iraqi supervision. Steps should be taken immediately to ensure that these needs will be adequately met."

In a call to preserve the cradle of civilization, Martha Sharp Joukowsky, president of the Archeological Institute of America and associate professor at the Center for Old World Archeology and Art at Brown University, raised the question: "What is being done to preserve the cultural heritage of Iraq?" Emphasizing both the biblical and archeological heritage, she pointed to the cultural importance of ancient Iraq (as it extended south to the Gulf) referring to the first eleven chapters of Genesis: "in the east," the land of "Shinar" [Sumer], in southern Iraq "Eden" was the name of a district in southern Sumer.

She mentioned how the account of Noah's flood bears striking similarities to a Babylonian legend of a great flood and added that according to Genesis, the first cities founded in Shinar after the flood were Babel (Babylon), Erech (Uruk), and Accad (Akkad), while the first cities in Assyria (northern Iraq) were said to be Nineveh and Calah. There are well-preserved remains of most of these cities in Iraq today. The "tower of Babel" was the great ziggurat, or temple tower, of Babylon. Though dismantled by Alexander the Great, its foundations are still preserved. Ur of the Chaldees in southern Iraq, the believed home of Abraham, has spectacular remains, especially its huge ziggurat.

On the outskirts of Baghdad are two ancient sites with well-preserved architecture: Aqar Quf, with its great ziggurat, and Ctesiphon, with the immense vault of its Sassanian palace. In the heart of Baghdad is the Iraq Museum, with the most important collection of Mesopotamian antiquities worldwide. Throughout Iraq are old and beautiful mosques, and in the north are some of the oldest Christian churches in the world.

The citadel town of Erbil, with its medieval city wall, high atop a mound that has been inhabited for thousands of years, is perhaps one of the most picturesque sites in northern Iraq. Virtually the whole country is an archeological site. The *Atlas of Archeological Sites in Iraq*, compiled by the Iraqi Department of Antiquities and Heritage, lists thousands of known sites, and many more yet to be identified.

Archeologists have had the time and resources to investigate only a small fraction of these sites, but even this limited sample continues to produce significant discoveries every year. Three of the world's oldest known villages have been explored in the north during the last few years. At Sippar, south of Baghdad, Iraqi archeologists recently discovered an extensive library with hundreds of clay tablets still arranged on shelves. These are still unread, unresearched, uninterpreted. An Assyrian palace was partially excavated by Iraqi archeologists at Nineveh this past spring.

The destruction of this material would leave a gap in human history impossible to fill. The risks that the Gulf war posed for the record of human development must not be minimized. Many sites, particularly those that are the sources for the earliest stage of civilization, could easily be obliterated without ever having been documented. Just like the deceptive assurances by the administration that Iraqi civilians were not targeted due to the precision of smart bombing, vague assurances were made by the military that cultural sites were not targeted. There is no evidence that any archeologists or scholars of Iraq were consulted prior to the war. Without consulting scholars and archeologists, the non-specialized cannot determine or identify such archeological remains.

Spectacular remains, such as the Parthian city of Hatra and the ziggurat at Ur of the Chaldees in southern Iraq, are visible and known monuments, but 90% of Mesopotamia is still below the ground, and valuable remains appear only in the form of mounds that the U.S. military cannot on their own appreciate. Remains below the ground may not seem significant to the present administration, but in fact the significance of such unknown sites is immeasurable and far-reaching.

According to Dr. Robert Adams, in brief remarks on television, he was asked by the Air Force to submit a map of the sites after the Allied bombing had ended and at the time of the so-called ground war phase. No specialists in the archeology and heritage of Iraq are known to have been consulted by American military planners prior to that. The few voices of concern went unheeded by the government, other voices were muted by their institutions or scholarly organizations and ignored by the media. Some institutions prevented scholars from making statements to the media. It is sad to realize that many of the scholars who commented on the war did so after the air war was over. They were silent through most of the devastation. The *San Francisco Chronicle* of March 6, 1991, published a story about the meeting of the American Oriental Society held in Berkeley at that time, during which a resolution proposed by some scholars expressed concern about the war and the damage to Iraq's valuable historical record. Shockingly, the Society voted against the resolution, using the pretext that such a resolution is political! I know of no resolution being proposed or action taken by any other national society of scholars.

Recent Discoveries

Months before the war, archeologists digging in Iraq reported to have uncovered the ruins of a huge temple to the Babylonian goddess of healing that they believe will produce new insights into the early practice of medicine. The discovery was made in 1990 at Nippur, the ancient religious center of Mesopotamia about sixty miles southeast of Baghdad. The ruins now being examined date from 1,600 BC to 1,200 BC, but they prove that beneath this layer previous structures stood on the same site, perhaps as early as 5,000 years ago in the time of the Sumerians. Dr. McGuire Gibson, an archeologist at the Oriental Institute of the University of Chicago, who is directing the excavations, said the size of the temple, which may prove to be as large as a football field, was a surprise and might mean that concerning down health and medicine played a more significant role in the people's lives than had previously been supposed. Many of the people who made pilgrimages to Nippur probably came to seek healing at the temple dedicated to the goddess Gula. Among the artifacts found at the site were small clay figurines of humans that were apparently left at the temple by ill people. One is holding his throat and another his stomach, gestures that Dr. Gibson said obviously referred to their ailments. "These figurines are telling the goddess where it hurts," he said. "We know from cuneiform tablets that the ancient Mesopotamians used figurines in a number of rituals, but we don't know much about their use in healing—I am reminded of figurine that are left in Mexican churches, even today, as reminders to the saints to help cure someone. I have a feeling that the figurines in the Gula temple are for much the same purpose." The temple's association with Gula was established by the presence of dog figurines, known to be central to the worship of the goddess, and by an inscription to Gula, dated at about 1,300 BC, that was found on a disk of lapis lazuli.

Further excavations which were scheduled to begin in January 1991 would have consisted of a search for a main chamber, where archeologists expect to find a statue of Gula, and for clay tablets to document in more detail how the temple fit in with Babylonian medicine, which was largely based on herbal treatments described in previously discovered clay cuneiform texts.

Previous temples discovered at Nippur have been rich lodes of Sumerian and Akkadian documents written on clay tablets. Some forms of herbal treatments may go back to the Stone Age, but historians of medicine say the Babylonians and the Egyptians were among the first people to develop a systematic practice of medicine. Their writings include instructions for specific recipes of herbs to treat certain conditions, from eye infections to diarrhea or constipation, and even to restore gray hair to a more youthful tint.

Dr. Robert D. Biggs, professor of Assyriology at the University of Chicago and specialist in Babylonian medicine, said the people also went to magicians to drive out the demons responsible for their afflictions. The discovery of medical texts in the temple, he said, could clarify the relationship between the herbalists and magicians and the place of the temple in their practices. Dr. Gibson said the Gula temple was probably the center of elaborate economic activity, with people bringing offerings to help in healing and buying clay figurines at the doorway.

Only two years ago, archeologists unearthed a previously unknown 4,000 year old city, Mashkan-shapir, mentioned in the writings of King Hammurabi. It is in Iraq that archeologists have found the earliest evidence of organized human society—more than a century older than comparable artifacts in Egypt and a thousand years before any found in China.

Bombing

But the full industrialized fury of a new world civilization (or is it called Order?) was turned on the very land that gave civilization birth. The *Los Angeles Times* of February 14, 1991, reported that the Bush administration accused Iraqi President Saddam Hussein of endangering one of the world's most precious archeological treasures by parking two warplanes near the ruins of an ancient temple in the historic city of Ur. Defense Secretary Richard Cheney said the Iraqi military command has placed the two Soviet-made MiG-21 fighter-bombers "right next to the pyramid" at Ur, a reference to the famous temple of Ur-Nammu, the king who reigned over the city-state about 2,100 BC. Defense Secretary Cheney's ignorance as to the difference between a pyramid and a ziggurat was evident. Also in another television appearance, Cheney incorrectly stated that "the pyramids of Iraq were older than the pyramids of Egypt." According to present evidence known to archeologists and anthropologists, the ziggurat of Iraq (indeed, not pyramids) appeared over 500 years after the pyramids of Giza. This is not the place to debate scholarly dating, but the evident ignorance of archeology by the military and the administration has posed a serious threat to human knowledge and to significant human history. Anthropologists and archeologists should have been consulted prior to decisions on war.

Instead, the only stated concern by the administration and the military was that civilization was an obstacle to their plans of destruction and that it was Iraq's fault that it was. Professor McGuire Gibson of the University of Chicago was worried that U.S. military planners were ignorant of Iraq's rich archeological legacy. He and other archeologists were explicit in their warning that all of Iraq is archeologically significant. They expressed concern that the archeological sites left by successive ancient civilizations that flourished in the area were at great risk during the bombing. Carpet bombing could wipe out 5,000 year old artifacts in five minutes—hundreds of thousands of sites in the form of mounds. There are also Iraq's museums housing irreplaceable records—some 100,000 cuneiform tablets in Baghdad museums have not been read.

Some 10,000 archeological sites in Iraq, out of possibly 500,000, exist among or near military targets. Basra, founded in 637, enjoys a strategic position close to the sea and the border with Iran, already ravaged in the eight years of war with Iran—a war that has been supported and supplied by the U.S. Mythical Babylon, which reached the height of its splendor during the reign of Hammurabi around 1,750 BC is only 6.2 miles from Iraq's Hilla chemical arsenal. The modern city of Mosul has undergone waves of allied air missions, because it contains missile ramps. It has not yet been confirmed whether the Nur ad-Din mosque, built in 1170, and its seventeen foot high minaret are still intact.

Experts have also worried about Nineveh, the third capital city of the Assyrians. This was surrounded with conventional weapons and chemical weapons plants. Nearby are seven and a half miles of wall that enclose Jonah's Hill, which is Jonah's burial place, where in 1990 a palace from the 7th century BC was discovered. Only slightly farther to the north is Khorsabad, the site of the best known of the Assyrian palaces. Also there is Nimrud, some twenty miles from Mosul, and its famous palaces, such as that of Ashurnasirpal II. Under restoration, Nimrud was recently the site of the discovery of untouched tombs of Assyrian queens and princesses and a tomb of the king's wife and her three ladies-in-waiting.

Ur was a Sumerian capital and is believed to be the birthplace of the biblical patriarch Abraham. Its temple, or ziggurat, is perhaps the most spectacular archeological relic in Mesopotamia, the area between the Tigris and Euphrates rivers known as the cradle of civilization. Ur may be the most significant city of Sumerian culture. It is close to the nuclear plant in the town of Nasiriya which has been bombed several times. Among other relics, Ur holds the royal tombs that have provided treasures for Iraqi and British museums. On the outskirts of Samarra, another target is a dam and a chemical weapons plant. Two buildings of great importance to the history of architecture also are there: the Aljama' mosque and the Abu Duluf mosque, one of them crowned with a great spiral minaret.

Cheney said the decision to park the planes by the temple shows that President Hussein should bear the blame for unintended destruction by allied bombers of civilian neighborhoods, cultural sites, and other non-military facilities. Speaking to the U.S. Chamber of Commerce, Cheney said the two MiGs were spotted by "satellite imagery" and blamed President Hussein for "using the archeologically significant facility to protect his military capabilities." The same *Los Angeles Times* story claimed that Near Eastern specialists confirmed that Hussein has placed military installations near ancient sites. Independent communication with archeologists led me to the fact that this statement was a misrepresentation and that the military bases had been built by the colonial British deliberately over archeological sites for defense purposes. It is not uncommon for developing nations to continue to use the colonial military bases.

Damage

It is still uncertain how much damage was inflicted on archeological and cultural sites in Iraq during the unprecedented, relentless allied bombing. It is significant to mention that the Iraqi government had requested from UNESCO that a group of scholars go to Iraq to assess damage, but that the UN sanctions committee had voted against it. There has been talk, according to the office of Dr. Robert Adams and observations by Professor McGuire, about a team of UNESCO observers to be dispatched to make an investigation of damage to cultural sites, but so far this has not happened.

It has been confirmed that the Iraqi Museum in Baghdad and the 900 year old church of St. Thomas in Mosul in northern Iraq were hit during the first five days of the bombing. Reports trickling out of Iraq suggest that allied bombers did strike in areas around important archeological and cultural sites. According to McGuire Gibson, professor of Mesopotamian archeology at the University of Chicago's Oriental Institute, these sites include Samarra, home of a 9th century mosque and minaret tower, the ancient city of Nineveh, in northern Iraq, and Ctesiphon, situated eighteen miles southeast of Baghdad. The famous hundred foot arch at Ctesiphon, the world's largest single span vault, a fragment of a 1,400 year old royal palace, is reported still standing but precariously, Gibson says. The arch, which has undergone considerable restoration over the last five decades, was violently shaken by shock waves during bombing raids and may be in danger of collapse.

In the *World Press Review* of April 1991, there are reports from the newsmagazine *Cambio 16* of Madrid of assaults on the Iraq Museum in Baghdad, on the Tigris River, and on some sacred cities, such as al-Kufa, on the west bank of the Euphrates where Ali, son-in-law and cousin of the Prophet Mohammad, made his home in the 7th century; Kerbala, the seat of Shi'a sacred shrines; and Najaf, where Ali was buried. Allied troops bombed Kirkuk, in northeastern Iraq, a city that has been inhabited since the second millennium before Christ. Kirkuk—an artificial hill formed by the superimposition of cities from different eras "is a living archeological document," says Spanish archeologist Joaquin Cordoba—a professor of Eastern history at the Autonomous University of Madrid. "The loss of the museum's artifacts would mean the loss of an irreplaceable resource for the preservation of Mesopotamian culture."

According to the *New York Times* of May 5, 1991, Iraq reported that priceless art works and artifacts, some of them Islamic but many dating back thousands of years to the ancient civilizations of Babylon, Nineveh and Ur, have been looted from Iraqi museums. Iraq's Director General of Antiquities, Dr. Muayad Said, suspects that these treasures may soon appear on the international art market in Europe and the States. Among the stolen arts in southern Iraq are illuminated Islamic manuscripts; gold and silver coins and jewelry; and statues, pottery and carvings in stone and ivory that were excavated from the ancient cities of Mesopotamia and Sumeria. These were reported stolen from the museums of Basra, Kufa and other southern cities. In northern Iraq from the museums of Kirkuk, Dohuk and others, similar ancient objects were missing. Also a local museum in the town of Nasiriya was looted.

Dr. Said reported the good news that they succeeded in preserving contents of the Iraqi National Museum in Baghdad, which housed one of the finest collections of ancient Sumerian and Mesopotamian art—these were removed and hidden, and the most famous pieces have survived, such as the 4,000 year old golden harp from ancient Ur, and the headdresses of golden myrtle leaves found in the Royal Tombs, and a strikingly realistic bronze head of King Sargon, who founded the Akkadian dynasty in Mesopotamia around the year 2,334 BC.

This is critical since it was reported that the National Museum building was damaged by nearby bomb explosions during the allied air raids, including a direct hit on the telephone exchange across the road, damaging windows. Other than broken windows, the main door of the museum was blown in and parts of the roof were destroyed. The safety of the artifacts mentioned above is due to Iraqi efforts and measures of precaution prior to bombing. Unfortunate for the world, however, some of the ancient Assyrian bas-relief carvings that were built into the museum's walls were cracked and shaken loose.

Furthermore, Dr. Said reported that several famous monuments suffered strain and damage from the effects of nearby bomb explosions, causing cracks in the walls and roofs of ancient buildings—including the Mustansiriya School, the university founded by the Abbasid Caliph al-Mustansir Billah in 1,226, which helped keep alive the learning of the ancient Greeks until it was rediscovered by Western Europe at the time of the Renaissance.

The nearby Abbasid Palace, built by the Caliph al-Nasser Lidnillah around the year 1,179, has also developed cracks and structural weaknesses.

The bombing of a nearby central bank building has caused flooding to develop in the basement of the Khan Murjan, the largest covered caravanserai in existence, serving as a marketplace, where Arab traders once gathered with their camels to prepare caravans across the desert, and where important goods were exchanged.

Outside Baghdad, bombing resulted in cracks and other damage in the walls of the Assyrian royal palace at Nimrud, usually known as the northwestern palace. At Ur the reconstructed stairway of the Great Ziggurat was also said to have been damaged. At Ctesiphon, about thirty miles south of Baghdad, the great third-century brick arch, the largest such structure in the world, was damaged by the blast from allied attacks supposedly on a nearby Iraqi nuclear installation and is in danger of collapse. "Bricks have started falling down from the top of the arch, and without urgent repairs, the whole thing could soon fall down."

In addition to the direct destruction, the economic embargo and military blockade of Iraq can only hasten the process of destruction of hundreds of archeological sites, because food shortages are driving Iraq to cultivate more land in places that could have been avoided under normal conditions. The situation will further be aggravated because the destruction of the infrastructure has caused a shortage of labor power and technology that is necessary for the Iraqi Antiquities Department to document the disappearing sites prior to emergency cultivation. In other words, even after the direct threat from the bombing, the inhumane sanctions against Iraq continue to cause direct destruction of antiquities and are a factor in obliterating a priceless record of human achievement.

Effect and Action

Iraq today is a demoralized nation with a demoralized people who are devastated by destruction and death and threatened by famine and disease. But also less stressed is the fact that Iraq is the culmination of this rich heritage and a guardian of its knowledge and evidence. The Iraqi people are proud of the archeological heritage, which stretches back to the time it was the center of the Islamic world in the Middle Ages, as well as to the ancient civilizations that flourished between the Tigris and Euphrates rivers at the dawn of history. Knowledge of these shining episodes may well be a strengthening and unifying element for the Iraqi people today. Consciousness of their rich past is part of the psychological makeup of their character. Iraqis are enriched by an identity that stretches deep in history and civilization. Other than the loss to the entire body of humanity, the destruction or the threat of destruction of such heritage shakes the fundamental sense of their identity—the very essence of who they are. Americans rightly deserve to be informed about Iraqi civilian casualties.

But scholars find it urgent that a full account be made of the steps and measures that have been taken or, as evident, not taken by the United States to protect our irreplaceable cultural patrimony.

Dr. Fadwa El Guindi is a well-known anthropologist with the El Nil Research Foundation in Los Angeles, California. This paper was presented at the Los Angeles Commission of Inquiry hearing on September 15, 1991.

The Attack on the Women's Peace Ship

E. Faye Williams

My testimony is the narrative of a sea voyage I began in early December 1990 prior to the start of the war the United States waged against Iraq. For nearly six weeks I was a "peace messenger" on a ship that sailed from Algeria in the Mediterranean Sea to Basra, Iraq, in the Gulf. Together with 200 women from around the world, I joined in an effort to prevent the United States from launching that war. Our immediate mission failed; war began on January 16, 1991, on the day after the voyage ended.

But the mission was a failure only in the narrowest sense. The women "messengers of peace" added to the growing cry of all the peoples of the earth: There must be, and there is, a better way than war. Each voice raised brings us closer to that day when even the most powerful military force will yield before a greater power, the power of people who will see through the lies and myths of our warrior leaders. On that day, we will no longer obey without question the command to kill other human beings just because someone above us tells us they are the enemy.

On December 3, 1990, I received an invitation to join an international delegation of women to travel by sea to Iraq. The voyage was to be a witness for peace in opposition to the impending war against that country. The invitation came from the President of the Union of Arab Women.

The plan was to launch a "Ship of Peace" to sail to various ports of call and collect food, medicine and letters for the children of Iraq. Discussions were to be organized on the trip to determine ways that women could work to advance world peace. Women from Arab countries were to be joined by women and children from other countries, including leading peace advocates in artistic, literary, and the political fields. The theme of the voyage was to be: "Food and Medicine—a Human Right for All."

The initiators of the venture issued a resolution stating the following:

"The message of the trip is purely humanitarian. It is a call for peace and love, a rejection of war, and an appeal for international solidarity and dialogue." Its purpose is "to achieve a global and lasting solution to the Middle East conflict and the crisis in the Gulf by peaceful means; the women seek to preserve world peace and security."

I responded to the invitation by saying, "I am pleased to have been invited to participate in this peace mission. I firmly believe women must speak out and take all possible action we can to support a peaceful resolution to the current Persian Gulf crisis, as well as to the question of Palestine."

After two days of hectic preparations, I departed for Tunisia on December 5, 1990. I boarded the ship "Ibn Khaldun" in the port of Tunis. However, during the voyage the women would refer to the ship as the "Ship of Peace" and ourselves as "peace messengers."

The Ship of Peace had begun its voyage from Algiers a few days earlier. The first part of the delegation had embarked with gifts of food and medicine to be taken to a hospital for children near Basra, Iraq. The Ship of Peace was scheduled to stop at ports in six countries, taking on additional groups of women from each country. Each group was to contribute food and medicine, adding to the previously collected gifts. The contingent of "peace messengers" would grow until there were approximately two hundred women on board. Three-quarters of the women were from Arab nations. The remainder were women from Sweden, Japan, Britain, Italy and Spain. Unfortunately, I was the only woman "peace messenger" from the United States. In addition, there were fifteen children as well as journalists and the ship's crew, making up a total of approximately three hundred people on board. One of the journalists was the only other woman from United States, Laurie Betlach from California, who covered the voyage for Pacifica News.

I originally expected to return to the United States by December 22, 1990, but did not return until after the United States had actually begun the war against Iraq. The ship encountered numerous delays caused by bad weather, political harassment at several ports, and finally a military attack on the ship by U.S. Marines.

From the port of Tunis, the ship proceeded to Tripoli, Libya, and then on to Port Said, Egypt, before entering the Suez Canal. There the ship was boarded and exhaustively searched by the Egyptian police. The ship's departure for passage through the Canal was held up until late at night, apparently to prevent contact with a group of Egyptian women who were supporters of the mission. After passing through the Canal and entering the Red Sea, the ship called at Port Sudan to pick up another group of women. The itinerary continued with two more stops in Yemen, Al-Hudayday and Aden, and then to Muscat in Oman.

After the vessel left Aden for Muscat it was joined and then followed by a fleet of U.S.-led Navy ships. On the day after Christmas, at five in the morning while the passengers were still sleeping, the Ship of Peace was passing the island of Masirah on the Omani coast. Suddenly, landing vessels approached the ship, surrounding her and forcing her to heave to at sea. Helicopters swarmed overhead dangling ropes above the deck. Contingents of U.S. Marines stormed aboard from the landing ships and dropped onto the deck, sliding down the ropes from the helicopters. They were firing their weapons over the heads of the women who had been awakened by the terrible commotion and noise. We had thrown on our clothing and had run up on deck where we began praying and singing.

Some of the women held their hands high while making the peace sign. Others held placards lettered with peace slogans. The Marines had their faces camouflaged in black so that it was possible for the women from other countries to mistake them for African Americans, which was extremely upsetting to me as an African American. The overwhelming majority of the Marines appeared to be white, with a small number of African Americans, and possibly a few men from other countries allied with the United States. Even though American flag insignia were worn by nearly all the Marines, it was otherwise impossible to identify anyone in the boarding party, as the men had their ranks, identification badges and other insignia covered or removed.

Without giving any orders or stating what we were to do, the Marines rushed about the ship kicking and beating the women with their rifle butts, all the while screaming obscenities. They fired electrical stun guns pressed against the women's bodies and fired tear gas at us. They also sought out the journalists and smashed much of their video and other recording equipment, and confiscated the rest. Approximately fifty women were injured in the melée. Many were crying hysterically.

The Marines then forced us to enter a narrow passageway in the interior of the ship and forced some of us to other decks. Several of the Marines had preceded us and turned off the ventilation system, making the interior of the ship suffocatingly hot. This chaos continued for two hours while the Marines tore the ship apart, ostensibly searching for weapons and other contraband. Finally a Coast Guard officer, who seemed to be the commander of the entire landing operation, appeared on the ship. It was just prior to his arrival, that some of the women knowing that I spoke English, asked me to speak to the Marines to ask that the ventilators be turned back on for the sake of the women being held inside, as well as the members of the crew being forcefully held in the engine room.

The Captain of the Ibn Khaldun, Emad Hassan, who had been handcuffed when the ship was first boarded, was being held on the bridge. Holding my hands above my head, I approached one of the Marines who brandished his weapon at me. I identified myself as a U.S. citizen and attempted to talk to him. In reply, the Marine swung his weapon and held it against the Captain's head, calling me obscene names. He threatened that if I said one more word, his next word would be a bullet in the Captain's head. He screamed at me to get out of his way and ordered me to tell the other women to be quiet. I sought to avoid provoking him further and urged the other women to be silent. They had continued their praying and singing in spite of their terror of the landing party.

The Coast Guard officer in command was an older man who seemed calmer and more rational than the younger Marines. I was able to approach him and ask him to get the ventilation turned back on, which he did. He then asked me to assist in gathering the injured together in the officer's lounge. There were many injuries among the women from the beatings, and much intentional damage to the ship. Some of the women were in shock from being terrorized by the landing operation or were sickened by exposure to the tear gas. Two of the women were pregnant and faced the possibility of miscarriage.

The commander even ordered some of the Marines to apologize to me for their previous behavior. However, the man who had threatened to shoot the Captain had continued to be abusive and threatening even after the commander had appeared, and had to be physically removed. Of course, it was clear that no arms were on board after the ship was ransacked, so there was no longer even a pretext for the violence of the landing party.

At this point, there were at least fifteen ships and aircraft carriers visible from the deck of the Ship of Peace, and it seemed possible that more naval ships were near, but out of sight. In addition, naval warplanes flew overhead and helicopters hovered close by.

The ostensible reason for the attack on the ship, that it was possibly carrying terrorist weapons as well as embargoed goods, was, as the Naval authorities knew full well, totally false. The authorities must have known that the ship had already been searched at Port Said by the Egyptian police, and no weapons had been found. In addition to a load of sugar, the ship carried various other food supplies for use by the passengers and crew. The remainder of the food was to be brought as gifts to Basra. The sugar which had been loaded in Tripoli was marked as originating in Cuba. The other food supplies included cooking oil, spaghetti, rice and boxes marked "sweets," which the Captain informed us contained dates.

As to violating the trade embargo, this charge was also false on two grounds. First, food and medicine were excluded from the embargo by the United Nations resolutions. In fact, to have included food and medicine in the resolution would have been a violation of international law. Second, the embargo was against commercial trade with Iraq, and the cargo of the Ship of Peace was being delivered as a gift. No commercial transaction was involved. On the day after the attack and boarding of our ship, newspaper articles quoted United States Navy spokespersons as making generalized statements that we were carrying contraband goods, but never mentioned what specific goods were in violation of the embargo.

Nevertheless, the Coast Guard officer who commanded the landing operation informed us that we would not be allowed to take the sugar to Iraq (probably because it was produced in Cuba, not because the cargo was contraband). He mentioned no other item. The commander then gave the women three choices: (1) return to Algiers, the origin of the voyage; (2) be taken by force to a destination chosen by him; or (3) voluntarily proceed under escort to the port of Al Fujeira, in the United Arab Emirates.

It did not take long for us to make a decision, as the final choice was obvious. To have returned to Algiers was out of the question. The Egyptians had charged the Ship of Peace a toll of $100,000, five times the normal fee for a ship of her size. The ship's water, food and fuel supplies were very low, and the Egyptians had also overcharged us for water at Port Said. Of the remaining two choices, going to Al Fujeira brought us closer to our original destination and was certainly preferable to some unknown port to be chosen by our captors.

Nevertheless, the Ship of Peace was not allowed to proceed. For the next eleven days we were held at anchor where we had been attacked and boarded—without any further orders or word from the armada that surrounded us. It was not until January 6, 1991, that we were again permitted to proceed, under escort to our next port. During those eleven days, at our request, two women who were ill were evacuated from the ship by the Navy and taken to a hospital. Other requests for medication for some of the less seriously ill women were ignored. We also requested additional water to replenish our increasingly depleted supply. Our captors were unsympathetic to these last requests and never responded.

On January 6, 1991, the Ship of Peace finally received orders to resume its voyage. We were informed that the ship would be taken to Muscat, Oman, instead of Al Fujeira. The Naval authorities then asked if we had permission to enter Muscat, which of course, we didn't. Muscat hadn't even been one of the options offered by our captors back on December 26. It was a rather bizarre question in any case, since we were under the total control of an imposing naval armada. We assumed that the detail of obtaining permission to land would be requested by and granted to our escort.

We finally arrived offshore from the port of Muscat, unable to enter the harbor because nobody had requested the required permission.

We met to discuss what to do and decided to contact any Arab ambassadors we could reach in Muscat. We managed to call ashore by radio telephone and did reach several ambassadors, who managed to obtain permission for the ship to enter the harbor. Eventually, an Omani police boat approached and five or six Arab ambassadors from various countries came abroad. The ambassadors were appalled by the condition of the ship, as well as the many injuries inflicted on the women. They were also extremely surprised at how many days we had been held. Apparently, the U.S. authorities had intentionally led them to believe that there were no passengers injured and had not mentioned our long detention at sea. They were then informed by the local U.S. Embassy that we could depart from Muscat only if we unloaded our entire cargo of sugar and retained only a reasonable amount of other food sufficient for use by the passengers and crew. The orders had mysteriously been changed and made more onerous since the first day of our captivity.

We discussed the problem with the Arab ambassadors and decided to offload the specified food gifts. The ambassadors guaranteed that the food would be delivered to Sudan, since it would be put to good use in that country which was suffering from famine.

The Ship of Peace, with permission to depart, sailed for Basra at around two o'clock in the afternoon of the 13th of January. We arrived in the evening of the next day. The war was to start approximately forty-eight hours later. The Iraqi government personnel were very concerned for the safety of the "peace messengers" and anxious that they leave Iraq before President Bush's deadline for starting the war. Still, several of the women on board the ship, who were physicians and nurses, told the Iraqi authorities that they would be willing to stay behind in case war broke out. They knew their skills would be needed. The Iraqis refused their offer, however, since they felt it would be too dangerous.

All the women were immediately flown to Baghdad that night, and then via Amman, Jordan, on to Tunis.

I arrived in Tunis, where I boarded a connecting flight back to the United States on January 16, 1991. The first bombs were already falling on Iraq before I landed in Washington, D.C.

E. Faye Williams is Staff Counsel for the House Committee on the District of Columbia and an aide to U.S. Representative Mervyn Dymally (D.-CA). She has twice run for congress in her home district of Alexandria, Louisiana, where she narrowly lost after an intense sabotage campaign by the national Republican Party. This testimony was presented at the New York Commission hearing, and Ms. Williams has authored a book, *Peace Terrorist* on her experiences during the Gulf War.

The Truth Behind Economic Sanctions:
A Report on the Embargo of
Food and Medicines to Iraq

Eric Hoskins, MD

Resolution 661, passed by the United Nations Security Council on August 6, 1990, states that the following items are exempt from the economic embargo of Iraq:

supplies intended strictly for medical purposes, and, in humanitarian circumstances, foodstuffs.

Resolution 661 also calls for the establishment of a Sanctions Committee (called the Committee of the Security Council) to clarify and implement the terms of the Sanctions Resolution. One month later, on September 13, 1990, Resolution 666 was passed by the Security Council, further defining (and limiting) the conditions under which food and medicine would be permitted to enter Iraq. Since August 1990, the international community has been led to believe that economic sanctions did not include an embargo on food or medicine. Furthermore, the public was told that Iraqi civilians would continue to have access to these essential commodities. However, nothing could be further from the truth. The truth is that Iraqi civilians have been dying of starvation and disease in the thousands. They are dying because of lack of basic food and medicine—the same food and medicine that the United Nations claims the civilian population has always had access to.

It is likely that sanctions have resulted in more suffering and death of the civilian population of Iraq than even the war itself. The true and lasting war against the Iraqi people has been the war waged by economic sanctions. The continued imposition of punitive sanctions will, with certainty, lead to widespread epidemics (including cholera), hunger, and death. A blatant violation of fundamental human rights, sanctions have made their presence felt in a number of ways.

1. Medicines

It has been estimated by international experts that, since August 1990, less than one-thirtieth of Iraq's medicine requirements were being met. Historically, Iraq imports more than $500 million worth of medicines each year (one of the highest per capita rates in the Middle East). All medicines —including medicated milk for infants with diarrhea, vaccines, drugs for chronic diseases (diabetes, asthma, angina, tuberculosis), anesthetics for surgery, and antibiotics—have been found to be in short supply and this shortage is well-documented by independent international observers since late 1990.

Medical supplies—syringes, intravenous fluids, spare parts for incubators, X-ray equipment, surgical supplies—either ran out or are in short supply. Now, with the country's infrastructure destroyed, most health facilities have no electricity, no running water, no emergency transport, patients and staff are unable to find transport to reach health facilities, and food and medicine for patients is either unavailable or in short supply. Despite access to health care being a fundamental human right, the following methods were used to effectively prevent medicine from entering Iraq. All these methods are still being used against Iraq today.

a) It is illegal for the government of Iraq to purchase and import any medicines or medical equipment.

b) Many pharmaceutical companies refuse to sell or are being pressured not to sell medicines to Iraq following the August embargo.

c) All medicines purchased or manufactured in the United States require a special license from the U.S. Treasury Department before export to Iraq. This is true for any humanitarian aid sent to Iraq and results in many delays and refusals.

d) More than fifty separate consignments of medicines and thousands of tons of infant formula and milk powder were purchased by the government of Iraq prior to August 1990. Governments of the countries where these consignments are being held still refuse to forward them to Iraq.

e) Only those items which the Security Council has deemed "supplies intended strictly for medical purposes" are allowed under the sanction's restrictions. All materials, spare parts, transport, and other para-medical items essential for the operation of a health care system are still prohibited—except on a time-consuming and unreliable case-by-case basis involving application to the Security Council.

Following two extensive health assessments carried out in Iraq by Gulf Peace Team health and relief experts during March and April 1991, it is clear that the health care system in Iraq is almost totally non-functioning.

The Simpler Truth

The Gulf Peace Team carried out an extensive health assessment in Iraq over a four-week period ending April 24, 1991. Health experts visited fourteen towns, including Basra, Nasiriyah, Najaf, Kerbala, Baghdad, Kirkuk, Sulaimaniyah, Erbil, Mosul, Dohuk and al Amadiyah.

The team's findings include:

1. In all parts of the country, critical shortages of clean drinking water have led to epidemic levels of gastroenteritis (infectious diarrhea). Thousands have died. Already at this early date over fifty cases of cholera have been confirmed by laboratory diagnosis. The true number could be one hundred times this figure since, in most parts of Iraq, hospital laboratories have been shut down due to lack of electricity and reagents—making diagnosis impossible. In Nasiriyah Pediatric Hospital, ninety-eight percent of admissions are children with diarrhea. Infants as young as two months old are admitted badly malnourished and dying from diarrheal disease. A lack of infant formula and contaminated water are responsible. Now these babies, in hospital, are given only an intravenous drip of fluid since doctors have no drugs with which to treat the diarrhea, and no medicated milk (the drug of choice for diarrhea) with which to feed them.

2. Hospitals have been reduced to mere reservoirs of infection since most medicines are in short supply, laboratories cannot function, operating theaters have no supplies, and basic services (including food, water and electricity) are unavailable. In Kirkuk Hospital, an old man lay dying at the entrance to the emergency ward. Suffering from a potentially fatal exacerbation of his chronic high blood pressure, there were no medicines to give him. Inside, the 400-bed hospital's only physician explained how she had just completed an emergency cesarian section, "with flies swarming over the incision because operating room windows had been shattered during bomb blasts" and sanctions will not allow their replacement.

3. Food throughout the country is prohibitively expensive and generally in scarce supply. Agricultural production has been halted due to a lack of inputs (fertilizers, seeds, fuel and spare parts) all prohibited under the sanctions resolutions. Between August 1990 and January 1991, food prices had gone up by as much as 1,000%.

For the first time in history, a government has been prohibited from purchasing and importing food and medicine for its own people. Despite clear indications that a humanitarian emergency existed within Iraq, from August 6, 1990 to March 1991 no food whatsoever was allowed to enter Iraq (from any source) according to the provision of sanctions Resolutions 661 and 666. It is patently obvious that thousands of innocent Iraqi civilians (mostly children) are dying of disease and starvation. They are dying because the international community has withdrawn from them their fundamental human right to food and medical care. It is a dreadful lie when governments and individuals claim that food and medicine are getting through in adequate amounts to the Iraqi people. We must decide who the coalition forces fought this war against. We must also decide whether it is worth sacrificing the lives of thousands more innocent victims to achieve the removal of Saddam Hussein. And finally, we must show equal compassion to all innocent victims of this war regardless of their locality.

It is the opinion of the health assessment team that most of the current civilian ill-health and suffering (mostly of children) is a direct result of both the war and especially the continued imposition of punitive sanctions against Iraq. These sanctions violate not only of the Geneva Conventions and Protocols but also the Universal Declaration of Human Rights and every other United Nations resolution and convention concerned with human rights. The situation with regards to foodstuffs is even more worrisome.

2. Foodstuffs

The text of Resolution 661 referring to the importation of foodstuffs states that the embargo does not include,

in humanitarian circumstances, foodstuffs.

Resolution 666 passed on September 13, 1990, issues a clarification that no food will be allowed into Iraq from any source until such time as a humanitarian emergency requiring the importation of food into Iraq is declared by the Security Council of the United Nations. Such a declaration requires a report issued from the Secretary-General's office and based on a United Nations mission to Iraq, recommending the declaration of a humanitarian emergency.

The Security Council must then go on to ask the Secretary-General to "seek urgently, and on a continuing basis, information . . . on the availability of food in Iraq." However, no such information was gathered until February 16, 1991, when the first United Nations mission (a UNICEF/WHO medical convoy from Teheran) entered Iraq to assess the humanitarian situation. Despite clear indications that a humanitarian emergency existed within Iraq, from August 6, 1990 to March 3, 1991, no food was allowed to enter Iraq (from any source) according to the provisions of sanctions Resolutions 661 and 666. In early March, after considerable pressure by humanitarian organizations and non-aligned governments, a humanitarian emergency was finally declared by the United Nations Security Council and food was allowed into Iraq subject to the following stringent conditions:

a) all foodstuffs should be provided through the United Nations in cooperation with the International Committee of the Red Cross or other appropriate humanitarian agencies,

b) Iraq would continue not to be allowed to purchase or distribute
its own foodstuffs.

Up until this point in time, only two humanitarian agencies had been
declared "appropriate" by the Sanctions Committee of the Security
Council—the United Nations itself and the International Committee of
the Red Cross. For all anticipated shipments of food, candidate humanitarian
agencies would have to submit in advance to the Sanctions Committee
a detailed application requesting approval to import and distribute specific
food items. The truth is that this is a mechanism guaranteed to obstruct
the movement of even small quantities of food, since many agencies either
had no knowledge of the application procedure required, had no access to
the Sanctions Committee in New York, were unable to draw up detailed
lists weeks in advance of predicted convoys, or were unlikely to gain
approval as "acceptable" to the security Council.

More to the point, Iraq historically imports more than seventy percent
of its foodstuffs. As a result of war, agricultural production had ground to
a halt (due to lack of seeds, fertilizers, spare parts and fuel for irrigation
pumps, etc.). This meant that Iraq had become almost totally dependent
on food obtained from abroad. With a population of 18 million persons,
Iraq's daily food requirements (of grain only) amount to approximately
10,000 metric tons per day. From August 1990 to April 1991, the total
amount of food provided by the international community was less than
10,000 metric tons— enough for only a single day's ration for the Iraqi
people. Distribution of this token amount of food has been limited to
hospitals and orphanages with no general ration distribution using these
foodstuffs.

Not only is the international community entirely incapable of
responding to Iraq's food requirements, it seems totally unwilling to try.
Of the $178 million requested by the United Nations for humanitarian relief
within Iraq, less than twenty percent has been forthcoming. Meanwhile,
aid continues to pour in for Kurdish refugees in Turkey. While in urgent
need of such aid, the 1-2 million Kurdish refugees share this need with over
17 million other Iraqis living in emergency conditions throughout the
country. It is clear that until such time as the United Nations and the
international community end the punitive sanctions against Iraq and allow
them to import food and medicine for themselves, conditions within Iraq
will continue to deteriorate. Starvation is already apparent in some parts
of Iraq; it is only a matter of time before widespread famine (as predicted
by the United Nations itself) sets in.

3. Recommendations

Until the government of Iraq is able to begin purchasing and importing medicines, undoubtedly Iraqi civilians will continue to suffer. In light of this urgent situation, the following recommendations need to be implemented immediately:

a) End all punitive sanctions against Iraq. Conditions under which the sanctions resolutions were applied (that is, the Iraqi invasion of Kuwait) no longer exist. Furthermore, it has become clear in recent days, and publicly stated, that even if Iraq complies with all terms of the cease-fire agreement, sanctions will not be loosened (let alone withdrawn) until such time as Saddam Hussein is removed from power. This blatant use of food, disease, and human lives as weapons for interfering with the internal politics of a country is both offensive and illegal.

b) Negotiate the release of Iraqi government assets currently frozen in overseas accounts to be used for the purchase of essential humanitarian commodities.

c) Allow Iraq to export commodities (including petroleum) for the purchase of food and medicine for the civilian population.

d) Release consignments of food and medicines currently being held in ports and along borders around the world.

e) Urgently implement the bilateral agreement signed between the United Nations and the Iraqi government regarding humanitarian assistance to affected groups.

f) Urgently implement a massive humanitarian relief effort to supply food and medicine to the civilian population of Iraq, both within Iraq and in neighboring countries.

In the concluding paragraph of his report, United Nations special representative Martti Ahtisaari states that "the Iraqi people may soon face a further imminent catastrophe, which could include epidemic and famine, if massive life-supporting needs are not rapidly met." Without an immediate and unqualified lifting of the punitive economic sanctions against Iraq and the Iraqi people, conditions will continue to deteriorate, thousands upon thousands of innocent civilians will perish, and the responsibility for the continuing despair of so many Iraqi women, men and children will rest on our shoulders and on our conscience.

Dr. Eric Hoskins was the Medical Coordinator for the Gulf Peace Team which was based in Amman and London. He is a specialist in public health and disaster relief. This report is based on travels in Iraq during March and April 1991. His testimony was presented at the Belgian Commission of Inquiry held in Brussels between June 13th and 15th 1991.

Part Four:

The New World Order

The New World Order—
What It Is and How to Fight It

Monica Moorehead

All of the international hearings will seek to uncover the truth as to the extent war crimes were committed before, during, and after the bombing of Iraq and Kuwait by the U.S. and its allies. The Commission intends to expose this truth to the world, and especially in this country, the United States, where all the war atrocities committed have been hidden in a sea of nauseating flag-waving and yellow ribbons.

There are, however, many bits and pieces confirming the nature of this war that we have been cognizant of for some time. Some of what we already know includes: the loss of anywhere between 125,000 and 300,000 Iraqi lives and that the intensity of the destruction of Iraq has left it at the level of a country in a "preindustrial age."

Bush and his Pentagon war-planners said that this war, which was really a mass slaughter, was justified in order to rid Iraq and the Arabian Peninsula of "a madman, a tyrant, and a demon" in the form of Saddam Hussein. Bush implied that without actually saying so that removing him by any means necessary, including assassination, would bring democracy and stability to the Iraqi people and to the region. This is the impression they gave to us day in and day out. But doesn't this sound like the same old song-and-dance that we were inundated with when it came to removing General Noriega from Panama or Muammar Qaddafi in Libya? Didn't the U.S. government portray these two leaders as the most evil men on the face of the earth right before they began the bombing? What this amounts to is decimating these countries as the only way to eradicate these leaders who didn't go along with the game plan. Isn't this the real meaning of Bush's New World Order?

What helped to give impetus to this new geopolitical development was the unprecedented accommodation of the Gorbachev leadership in the Soviet Union, and, to a lesser degree, the Chinese leadership, to the U.S. and its allies, especially during the war against Iraq. This shift in the relationship of forces has given Bush the green light to economically and militarily strangle, invade and destroy whole countries and regions with impunity. In other words, the end of the so-called Cold War has not led to some dreamy, wonderful and more passive world. On the contrary, Soviet "new thinking," which is their desire to end the U.S. – Soviet confrontation, has only emboldened the Pentagon to believe that it can go anywhere, bomb anything, and destroy any country without the threat of retaliation.

The fact that the U.S. can turn the United Nations, a body supposedly committed to peace, into an instrument of war through threats and bribery is another example of this New World Order. Who will be the next victims of this insidious scheme? Will it be Cuba? Or North Korea? Or Haiti? The U.S. already feels emboldened enough with its military victory over Iraq to up the ante with increasing threats against Cuba and North Korea. The anti-war movement must not be caught off guard. It must stand firm to defend the sovereignty of these countries and any other country that dares to stand up to the bullying of the U.S. and its allies.

There is another side to this New World Order scandal and that is the war being carried out at home. The U.S. military used phosphorous bombs, cluster bombs, napalm and other weapons of mass destruction against Iraq, but at home, this war has taken on another, different character. The kinds of weapons that we've had to endure are unemployment, homelessness, drug addiction, decay in inner cities, assaults on health care, racism, sexism, anti-lesbian and anti-gay bigotry, union-busting, and cuts in education. This is the kind of freedom and democracy that we've been subjected to, while at the same time an entire country is being decimated and a region terrorized.

There should be no doubt in anyone's mind that this war against Iraq was fought to help safeguard and promote super-profits, not only for the big oil monopolies but for other corporate and banking interests. Bush was banking on this war to bring the economy up from the depths of this recession, which is really a polite word for a depression. But it didn't happen. Just the opposite happened. Instead of saving this economy, the war has just depressed the situation even further.

We see every day in the business section of the newspapers that the growing militarization of the civilian economy has become a burden, not an asset. This economic crisis has been put on our backs. Just take New York City, for example. Mayor David Dinkins gave a talk in early May 1991 saying that all New Yorkers have to pull together; that we have to tighten our belts; that we have to swallow the closings of thirty-two community centers and drug rehabilitation centers; the layoffs of at least 20,000 city workers; a 25% cut in street lights; the closing of the Central Park Zoo; the elimination of infant mortality prevention programs; and other many other cuts in programs the government was established to administrate. The cuts amount to a criminal neglect of governmental responsibility. New York Governor Mario Cuomo is echoing the same response statewide. The same can be heard in Connecticut, New Jersey, and all over the United

States. Is it any wonder that the City University of New York students, the majority Black and Latino, occupied the buildings to protest the increases in tuition? These increases will bar them from getting a decent education.

What about the tens of thousands of city and service workers who protested against the New York City budget cuts on April 30, 1991? We know that sometime in the not too distant future these same underpaid workers, including the undocumented and the unemployed, will not only march on Wall Street but they will occupy Wall Street.

If these budget cuts and layoffs weren't enough, the war-makers actually celebrated their massacre with a war parade right here in New York City. Can you imagine a war parade, a parade to celebrate the mass slaughter of Iraqi people, a parade to honor the engineers of mass killing like Powell and Schwarzkopf and Cheney. Just as importantly, it was a parade to divert attention away from the economic crisis and the rising racism in this city.

This parade should have been canceled. What did any American have to celebrate? More budget cuts? More assaults on our living standards? For Dinkins and Cuomo, the local bosses, and the big real estate developers, this parade was timely, for it helped to dilute any mass anger and frustration that people were—and are—feeling now more than ever.

I want to end by saying that just as the war in the Middle East goes through various phases, so does the struggle here. By holding this Commission hearing, we are in essence putting unbridled U.S. militarism on trial for crimes against humanity and crimes against peace. We are showing that it can be done and it must be done in the midst of rabid political reaction. But we cannot forget the crimes against humanity that go on every day in this country. From the police shooting of a Salvadoran man in Washington, D.C., which sparked an heroic rebellion in Washington on May 5, 1991, to the utter decay of our cities, the rulers of this country have the same old answers to their crisis: more cutbacks, more layoffs, and more racism.

But if they don't have the answers, we certainly do, and that is to continue to organize the workers of all nationalities, the students, lesbians and gay men, women, the seniors and disabled into a mighty movement that will put an end once and for all to imperialist war, poverty, and unemployment.

Monica Moorehead is a Co-coordinator of the National Coalition to Stop U.S. Intervention in the Middle East. She presented this report on May 11, 1991 at the New York Commission hearing.

The Demonization of Saddam Hussein—
A Violation of the
UN Convention Against Racism

Esmeralda Brown

"Saddam Hussein does not share our view of the sanctity of life."
—Marlin Fitzwater, White House Press spokesperson

While peoples in European-dominated countries and the United States, which have traditionally operated on foreign policies rooted in the doctrine of Manifest Destiny and superiority based on racial, language, religious and cultural differentiation, celebrate the mass destruction of the nation of Iraq, the rest of the world is somber, saddened and reflective.

As part of this reflective process, and instead of folding our tents because U.S. soldiers have come back home from the scene of massacre, we have gathered here today as peoples of conscience to make sure that the peoples of the United States, as was also done with the Nuremberg Trials and Bertrand Russell Tribunals, remember and learn from the crimes committed against humanity by the government of the United States of America.

As part of this effort, I have explored the racial implications of these war crimes, and the extent to which those implications are violations of international conventions. Any policy of demonization as a tool and mechanism of international aggression is contrary to the international convention on the elimination of all forms of racial discrimination, adopted by the General Assembly of the United Nations in Resolution 2106A of December 21, 1965. The charter of the United Nations is based on the principles of the dignity and equality inherent in all human beings. All member states, including the United States, have pledged themselves to take joint and separate action in cooperation with the organization for the achievement of one of the purposes of the United Nations, which is to promote and encourage universal respect for an observance of human rights, and fundamental freedoms for all without distinction as to race, sex, language or religion.

Demonization is an incitement of discrimination whose purpose is to create an irrational hatred of an individual or nation in order to make it easier to invade that nation, or to utilize mass destruction techniques against the peoples of that nation.

When analyzing demonization activity to date, in each instance race, ethnic origin, religious differences and racial superiority have been tied in with a large dose of negative disinformation to generate hatred. That is in contradiction to the findings in the resolutions of the convention on the elimination of all forms of discrimination that states,

> *Convinced* that any doctrine of superiority based on racial differentiation is scientifically false, morally condemnable, socially unjust and dangerous, and that there is no justification for racial discrimination, in theory or in practice, anywhere,
> *Reaffirming* that discrimination between human beings on the grounds of race, color or ethnic origin is an obstacle to friendly and peaceful relations among nations, and is capable of disturbing peace and security among peoples, and the harmony of persons living side by side, even within one and the same state.
> *Convinced* that the existence of racial barriers is repugnant to the ideals of any society. . . .

The resolution then goes on to define what is meant by "racial discrimination":

> 1. In this Convention, the term 'racial discrimination' shall mean any distinction, exclusion, restriction or preference based on race, color, descent or national or ethnic origin which has the purpose or effect of nullifying or impairing the recognition, enjoyment or exercise on an equal footing of human rights and fundamental freedoms in the political, economic, social, cultural or any other field of public life. (Part I, Article 1)[1]

The demonization of Qaddafi in Libya was accompanied with a parallel negative stereotype of Arabs and the people of the Middle East, as terrorists. This was further utilized in the demonization of Saddam Hussein, who President Bush and the U.S. media also called a "Hitler."

In the case of Noriega, it was carefully whispered that he was part Black and Indian and was surrounded by Blacks and Indian thugs who were intimidating those beautiful, defenseless white Panamanians. The narco-trafficker charges were added as the massive negative disinformation ingredient long after the racial demonization had been completed. In fact, what they neglected to say is that it was and continues to be the white Panamanian oligarchy who controlls the narco-traffic money laundering with the U.S. banking interests.

In the case of Cuba, there is a conspiracy that is racial also. The latest step of demonization campaign is now against Fidel Castro and the Cuban Revolution. I use the term "step of demonization" because this is a continuation of thirty-two years of economic, military and political aggression, and demonization of Fidel and the Cuban Revolution. They try to imply that the white Cubans in Miami and New Jersey, who were the former oligarchy and oppressors in Cuba, were representatives of the majority of the Cuban people. Policy makers of the U.S. have simply hidden from the North American people the fact that the majority of Cuban people are Blacks and Mestizos, and also the fact that the Cuban people in Cuba are not intimidated or repressed in Cuba but instead participated in the liberation of Cuba from the white oligarchy now residing in the United States.

The people of Cuba want to be left alone to determine their own destiny without interference, without the constant threat of U.S. invasion, a U.S. founded on and motivated by the doctrine of superiority based on racial differences. We've got to be very clear about that.

In each instance previously mentioned, religious differences were also utilized to encourage hatred. In the case of Qaddafi and Saddam, the non-Christian, non-Jewish and Moslem nature of their religion was exploited. In the case of Noriega, it was alleged that he practiced Santoria, which was only mentioned to accentuate religious differences and foment hatred. Much is made of the fact that many of the supporters of the Cuban Revolution practiced Santoria, which is an African religion, and that the Santoria priests of Cuba have blessed and protected Fidel. That might be true. They complete this conspiracy by falsely charging that the Cuban government is opposed to Christianity.

In closing, I am presenting to this very important Commission of Inquiry a request that in your process of investigating the war crimes committed against the people of Iraq, that you include investigatory work and documentation around the racist character of the demonization campaign that has permitted the North American people to sanction and celebrate with parades this successful utilization of mass destruction weapons on the people of Iraq, as they did with the people of Panama, and also the people of Grenada.

This Commission of Inquiry is very important because it is only through efforts by organizations such as this that we will be able to combat disinformation, demonization, and through education raise the level of consciousness of the North American people to the level where they can resist current and future demonization through the press, through campaigns, through aggressions, and resist the massacring of other peoples in the Third World.

I have just returned from a trip throughout Latin America and the Caribbean, and I ended up of course in my own country, Panama. I can tell you what the bombing has meant for my people. For the first time, human beings were burned with lasers. I have never in my life seen the bodies of human beings with their skin just burned and boiled and swollen an inch high. This is what the people of the world need to know. The conspiracy of silence needs to be broken.

We need to say to the people of the United States that they need to struggle against the embargo placed on Iraq. The embargo means the starvation of a people into submission, either you submit or accede to be bombed. The people of Panama were bombed because they did not accede.

I would like to close by saying that we have a responsibility for humanity, we have a responsibility to charge the warmongers in Washington with war crimes against humanity.

Notes

1. *Yearbook of the United Nations, 1965* (New York: Columbia University Press, 1967).

Esmeralda Brown is a Panamanian and a member of the Women's Workshop in the Americas. Her report was delivered at the New York Commission hearing.

The Impact of the Gulf War on Women and Children

Nawal El Saadawi, MD

I was in the United States in February and March of 1991, participating in a tour and speaking about the effects of the war in our region. When I went back to Egypt and turned on the television, I found a celebration of the war exactly like I had seen on CNN in the United States. We, the opposition in Egypt, felt a lot of despair because the government supported the war and sent troops. We were silenced then, and we continue to be silenced. In Egypt, we don't even have the little democracy you have here.

But when I went to my village and I found that my relatives, the women, were grieving for their sons who died in Iraq, in Kuwait, in Saudi Arabia—in the war. So, I represent the people of Egypt—not the government—I represent the opposition that is silenced. The people in Algeria, Tunisia, the Sudan, in Morocco, Libya, and Tunis demonstrated against the war. There are millions of women and men in the Arab world who were against the war and who demonstrated. But they were the silent majority. Their voice never reached the United States, much less the leaders of the government. They were ignored totally by the media.

I think that the major crime was against truth. The big lie of George Bush, the U.S. coalition, and its allies was propagated through the media. A lot of people believed it. Bush and others spoke about human rights and the liberation of Kuwait. Kuwait is not liberated. Kuwait is now the 51st state of the United States. They spoke about democracy and against the dictatorship of Saddam Hussein, yet they are protecting the most vicious dictatorships in the Arab world: King Fahd of Saudi Arabia and the El Sabah family in Kuwait in the Gulf states.

This war is a war against the poor. It's a war against us women, children, and against the men who do the fighting. This war is going to continue. If Saddam Hussein vanishes, the leaders of the United States and the former colonial powers in France and England will create another Saddam Hussein against which they can wage wars as a pretext for continuing the colonization of resource rich areas of the world. The military-industrial machine cannot survive without wars. They profit from war. They need it to sell their weapons, to test new weapons, to control the world. Only the U.S. and Israel have nuclear power in the region, power to kill the Palestinians and all the other people who are resisting for justice and freedom. So the war will continue. That's why I'm speaking out now. Because we need international solidarity.

I am here to speak about the effect of the Gulf war on women and children. War usually impacts more on the poor and the weak and has a greater effect on women and children. You have heard that most of the people who suffered in Iraq and in the Gulf war were women and children. That's why women are a big force against war. War is created by this class, the patriarchal system, the system that's dominated by men and a ruling class, in the state and in the family. That's why women suffer most.

The war has had a very negative effect on us women in the Arab world— on Iraqi women, Kuwaiti women, Saudi Arabian women, Egyptian women, Algerian women and women all over the region. This was colonial war waged by the stronger, richer countries like the U.S. and Britain, with financial backing from Japan and Germany. Basically it was the imperialist countries against their former colonies fighting to deprive us of our resources, our oil, our money. The war was not waged to create a new world order but to preserve the old colonial order. We women are made poorer by the war. This is the feminization of poverty.

They try to deceive us in our region. They tell us that they are developing us. The war is military and then economic. After the military war, the World Bank came into Egypt and for the first time the Egyptian government submitted to all of its conditions. The result is to make the poor poorer and the rich richer.

One of the basic reasons for the war was to strengthen the domination of the dollar over the world and to decrease the value of our money, which is now almost useless. The conditions imposed by the World Bank make poor nations and women suffer the most since the conditions are imposed only to insure that our countries will continue to borrow more and more money and repay the debts with their high interest rates. The World Bank is the new form of transferring wealth from poorer nations to wealthy ones. Inflation increases, high prices increase, and unemployment increases—all in order to repay loans our government made in order to buy weapons or the industrial products of the United States and other industrial powers.

Whenever there is unemployment, women are the first to be driven from the labor force. Now they say women should go back home and not have jobs. Then sometimes they say, "Well, that's religion, that's Islam, God said you stay at home." They say this in order to hide the unemployment and the economic crisis. Our debt is increasing. In Egypt now, the interest on the debt itself is more than the debt itself. So we are drowning in debt. This is the vicious circle of the so-called U.S. development of the Third World. It's a false development. Here in the U.S. you call it "loan sharking." Egypt is a fertile land, we have the Nile Valley. But we are forced to produce what we do not eat and eat what we do not produce. That's i imperialism. That's colonialism. They do all that under the name of development, democracy, human rights, and women's rights. You heard George Bush.

An American journalist came to me in Egypt and said, "You have been working for forty years for the liberation of Arab women, and now you must be happy because George Bush is telling Sheik al-Sabah in Kuwait that he should give Kuwaiti women the vote." I said, George Bush is going to give Kuwaiti women the vote? This is ridiculous. How can a foreign occupier, a foreign invader bring democracy to women? It's impossible. This is the Big Lie meant to deceive women.

The colonial powers say they are coming to give women the vote, to develop us, to give us loans, to give us some funds. But all these financial institutions, the so-called World Bank, and International Monetary Fund, are colonial institutions. They deceive the Third World, but the people are not deceived. It's our governments, our allies who benefit, not the people.

I would like to give you some statistics on the wealth of the sheiks in the Gulf countries. This war took place to protect those people. The ruling family in Kuwait has $100 billion in Britain alone. Sabah alone has $50 billion himself. King Fahd has $18 billion in U.S. banks. The ruling class in Saudi Arabia has $680 billion in Western banks. There are six Gulf states: Kuwait, Saudi Arabia, the Emirates, Bahrain, Oman and Qatar. Those six countries were created by the British colonial powers. There are only 10 million people in all six countries, yet they have $850 billion in Western banks. They invest only seven percent of this money in the Arab countries, and for luxury goods, never for serious development.

There are 190 million people in the Arab world. They have a debt of $208 billion. Starvation is the biggest killer of our children. You see, that's the situation. U.S. troops hurried in to protect those sheiks. They are protecting the petrodollar and their own allies in the Arab countries, rulers who oppress us. They are responsible for the poverty, hunger, unemployment, and diseases suffered by millions of women, men and children in the Arab countries. They impose the dictatorships, where the people are unable to express themselves.

And now, with Saudi Arabia taking over, we have so-called Islamic fundamentalism. Many people here in the west think that the U.S. invasion of the Arab world will create a war against fundamentalism. This is not true. In fact, in Saudi Arabia fanatic fundamentalist Islamic groups are supported by U.S. troops. We are now facing most vicious Islamic fundamentalist groups supported by Saudi Arabia in all our region. This has a negative affect on women. More women are veiled, more women are compelled to stay home in the name of God and Islam.

So that's how we live, and we expect to have more and more problems. But our hope is that with each crisis, something happens that will bring the poor and women out. And there is a positive element along with all the negative military, economic and social effects. Saudi Arabian women demonstrated to have the right to drive cars. All of them were dismissed from the work. Their husbands were put in jail, but still they are resisting. People in Egypt are resisting. The Arab Women's Solidarity Organization started the resistance after the war began. We traveled to Baghdad and to Geneva and here, and elsewhere, and we fought against this war. So with each crisis there is an awakening of the Arab women and men in our region.

That's our hope, and our hope also is this: unity between the progressive people in our region, and you here, progressive people in the West. We need a world front. It's no more an East-West, or a North-South division. We need another division. We need the progressive people in the world, men and women, to unite, and to come together and fight against this new imperialist order. I am participating in this Commission of Inquiry because I believe in you. You are the Third World here in the First World. We in the Arab world, men and women, and the poor, and you here, we must to fight together against this new colonial period.

Dr. Nawal El Saadawi is a prominent author and convener of the Egyptian Commission of Inquiry. She is president and founder of the of Arab Women's Solidarity Association, a pan-Arab group with over 2,000 members. She spoke at the New York Commission hearing on May 11, 1991.

The Continuing War and the Kurds

Ali Azad

As an Iranian who was one of the millions who successfully battled the Shah's tyranny, I've learned from our forerunners in the struggle for social and political justice in the Middle East. The most important lesson is that the struggle against imperialist domination of the region can accomplish nothing meaningful unless it also fights for the right of self-determination of the oppressed nationalities. With one fist, you have to punch the imperialist reaction; with the other, the racist foundation of the oppressor nation.

For the better part of this century, Iraqi, Iranian, Syrian and Kurdish anti-fascists and freedom fighters have been integrated. Many have been in the forefront of the Kurdish people's struggle. Thousands have been executed, and many are languishing in the prisons of these regimes, most notably in Turkey. The bond between the Kurdish and non-Kurdish movements of the Middle East is strong and unchallengeable. On some occasions this bond has been betrayed, mainly as a result of imperialist manipulation. This has been only an aberration, and not the norm.

In 1990-91, the Bush administration policies in the Persian Gulf and the invasion of Iraq resulted in two immediate catastrophic calamities: first, the genocide and economic suffocation of the Iraqi people; second, the painful and horrific exodus of the Kurdish people of northern Iraq resulting in thousands of deaths and injuries.

The first of these two equally barbaric crimes was conducted under the guise of liberating Kuwait. However, the findings and expositions of many groups, and the anti-war demonstrations of millions of people of the international community, have shown the deception of this policy. The second crime, the atrocious situation of the Iraqi Kurds, has been concealed in a more sophisticated shroud of lies and demagoguery. The role of the U.S. in the past and at present is one of an enemy of the Kurdish struggle for self-determination. It is not, as the Bush administration wants us to believe, that of a friend.

In order to understand the Kurdish movement against national oppression and racism, one must look back to decades of U.S.-British treachery against the Kurdish people. One of the first manifestations of Kurdish self-rule was the establishment of the Republic of Mahabad. Archie Roosevelt, who served as U.S. assistant military attaché in Teheran from March 1946 to February 1947, wrote in an article published in the Middle East Journal in July 1947, "The dream of the Kurdish nation and the nationalists, an independent Kurdistan, was realized on a miniature scale in Iran from December 1945 to December 1946. The origin of this little Kurdish republic, its brief and stormy history, and its sudden collapse is one of the most illuminating stories of the contemporary Middle East."

On December 15, 1946, the Iranian Army, trained and armed by the U.S., entered Mahabad, crushing any resistance, and established the Shah's fascist occupation. Subsequently, the leaders of the Mahabad Republic, most outstanding among them Qazi Mohammed, who was one of the most legendary leaders of the Kurdish movement, were hanged in the town's main square. The question that Archie Roosevelt, the CIA man, does not answer, is how the Iranian army was able to launch such a massive and successful military attack against the Kurdish nationalists as early as 1946. The destruction of the Republic of Mahabad was carried out on the orders of U.S. President Harry Truman and under the leadership of General H. Norman Schwarzkopf, father of Desert Storm commander General H. Norman Schwarzkopf.

Perhaps one of the most illuminating chapters of U.S. involvement occurred between 1973 and 1975, at the time that U.S. supremacy in Iran through the puppet government of Mohammad Reza Pahlavi was unchallengeable and the status of the Kurdish minority was bleak. Between 1973 and 1975, the government of the Shah, which was fearful of echoes of Iraq's 1958 anti-imperialist revolution, armed and trained the Iraqi Kurdish forces to destabilize Iraq while at the same time suppressing the Iranian Kurds. This policy ended after the 1975 Algiers Pact between Iran and Iraq.

Turkish Kurdistan has the largest population of Kurds. Some twelve to fifteen million Kurds live in Turkey. This number is not exact, since there has never been an official census of Kurds in Turkey because the fascist government does not recognize the Kurds as a nation and instead refers to the Kurds as "mountain Turks."

Until the beginning of 1991, speaking in the Kurdish language in Turkey was a crime punishable by law. Turkish lawyers trying to communicate in Kurdish with clients who could not speak in Turkish were in turn locked up. The famous author of Kurdish history, Kendal, in a book called *A Country, Kurds, and Kurdistan Rights*, points out that "Illiteracy continues to be a major curse in Turkish Kurdistan, where, after half a century under a 'democratic' and secular regime, 72% of people over six years of age still can't read or write." Even today, most Kurdish villages have no primary school. Where there is one, a single teacher is responsible for teaching

Turkish to five classes. In all of the Kurdish areas inside Turkey, as of 1979, there were only fifty secondary schools, and only one university at Asram. In Kurdistan of Turkey, there is one doctor per 10,000 people.

The Turkish government is the only NATO member in Asia. The fascist government receives $800 million in military aid from the U.S., and constitutes one of the cornerstones of U.S. policy in the Middle East. U.S. bases in Turkey were used systematically during the Gulf War to bomb the Iraqi infrastructure. In brief, an independent observer of the Kurdish political scene can easily see that the U.S. government is no friend of the Kurdish people and has always helped to crush any manifestation of the Kurdish struggle for democracy and justice, be it in Iran, Iraq or Turkey.

But now in the aftermath of the Gulf War, President Bush and the American media are overflowing with concern for Kurdish people. As of May 11, 1991, more than 10,000 U.S. military personnel are occupying northern Iraq, supposedly to defend the Kurdish refugees from the wrath of Saddam Hussein. The question is, what during the spring of 1991 has caused the change of heart on the part of the Bush administration? Even a school child can see through this sham.

Northern Iraq is home to one of the richest oil fields in the Middle East, at Kirkuk, and the only one left unharmed after the U.S. invasion of Iraq. The history of U.S. military involvement shows—just like in Grenada and Panama—that every military action has been carried out under the guise of humanitarianism. But the true aim has always been to secure a base for exploitation of the natural resources of that region and the establishment of military bases.

The current chapter of the struggle of the Iraqi Kurdish people for self-determination and democracy is one of the most difficult ones, paved with treacherous obstacles. Iraqi Kurds, who have been systematically suppressed under the government of Saddam Hussein, a government which in part was strengthened and solidified as a result of military purchases from the U.S. and its allies, are being told that the U.S. and Britain are their saviors and that's who they have to rely on for salvation. This is one of the biggest shams ever concocted by the White House.

The bulk of the Kurdish refugees of one million have left for Iranian cities and towns. However, the bulk of U.S. aid to refugees has been concentrated on the Turkish borders. The disregard of the Kurds by the Bush administration is best illustrated by his answer to a reporter's question: "Why aren't you sending aid to the Kurds in Iran?" Bush replied, "You've got to be a realist. I mean, the Iranians have strained relations with the United States of America." This statement by itself has to be an eye opener for all those misinformed and misled who had hope in the White House generosity.

The U.S. occupation of Iraqi Kurdistan is not going to bring freedom and democracy and justice to the Kurdish people, the goals that the Kurdish masses for almost a century have been fighting for. At best it can yield a puppet fascist government like so many others that the U.S. has installed around the world: the Shah, Pinochet, Zia in Pakistan, just to name a few, with the aim of suppressing the struggle of neighboring Kurds in Turkey and Iran, and furthermore to threaten the nationalist movements in the Middle East and the whole region.

The only way out is solidarity of the Kurdish people and their movement, with the people and movement of the entire Middle East: Arab, Iranian, Turkish, Turkeman, Baluchi and many others, in a united front for the liberation of the entire Middle East from the yoke of the Wall Street bankers and Pentagon.

Ali Azad is the former coordinator of the Iran-Iraq Anti-War Committee, United States. He spoke at the New York Commission hearing.

Government Attacks and Violence Against Arab People

Neal Saad

Let me state on behalf of the Arab-American Community Center and the Committee for a Democratic Palestine our appreciation for inviting us to share with you certain aspects of our experience as Arab-Americans during the Gulf crisis.

These have been hard and difficult times for Arab-Americans here in the USA. Since the beginning of the Gulf crisis, the FBI has carried out a systematic policy of harassment and intimidation against our community, in order to create an atmosphere of fear within the Arab community. And they aimed to stop us from expressing our opinions and our opposition to U.S. policy and U.S. intervention in the Gulf. They thought that by harassing us, intimidating us, that the Arab-American community would not participate in the anti-war movement that was growing from August 2nd on. And they selected us as potential terrorists because of the simple fact that we are of Arab background. That was the official reason they gave when the FBI first came out and expressed confidence that it would be visiting 200 Arab-Americans here in the U.S. who would be considered potential terrorists.

We, as Arab-Americans, have been victims of Zionist terrorism. Many of you remember the death of an Arab-American on the West Coast, Alex Odeh, who was a representative of the Arab-American Anti-Discrimination Committee. Although our history shows that there was no evidence that Arab-Americans have participated in any type of terrorism here in the USA, the FBI insisted on carrying out this policy of intimidation and harassment. We have submitted documents to the Commission that were written by the Center for Constitutional Rights that document all of the cases here in the U.S. of this type of harassment.

The harassment and intimidation took various forms. One, Arab-Americans were visited in their homes in the early hours of the morning or in the late evening. Two, Arab-Americans were visited in their stores.

Three, they stopped Arab-Americans in the streets, in airports and public places. And four, they attempted to hire informers in our communities.

An FBI agent would visit, and would knock at the door, say at six o'clock in the morning. He would introduce himself as an FBI agent. He would then state that he is there in order to protect the community from any types of terrorism, and that he wanted to ask certain questions. These questions basically were related to the person's political view, for example: "Are you a supporter of the PLO? Do you support U.S. policy in the Middle East? Do you know of any terrorists? What takes place in the community centers?"

Certain members of our community experienced the FBI questioning in the early hours of the morning. They would knock on your door. You would open the door and here you would wake up. Your family was inside and here was the FBI asking you questions about terrorism. Can you imagine the impact that it has on someone who is a normal member of the community? Most of these people have children in the house. What kind of vibration does this send into the community? The FBI made the message clear, because the visits were fairly open.

Beyond the home visits, we had various members of our community visited in their stores. We have a case here in New York in which the FBI went to an Iraqi Arab's store and asked for him. They introduced themselves as the FBI. They took him. They didn't tell him why they were taking him. They had no warrant for arrest or anything. They brought him to Manhattan. He spent four hours, and no reason was given why that Iraqi-American was taken.

They would stop us in the streets and at airports. And all of you know about Pan American Airlines. Pan Am made a decision not to allow Arab Americans to fly in their planes. In the streets, for example, we have certain experiences where policemen for one reason or another were stopping Arab-Americans. Once the policeman stopped someone for a traffic ticket, he found out this person was an Arab-American. For example, his name showed it on the driver's license. Then the policeman would give him another ticket and said, "This is for Saddam Hussein."

Another important aspect of intimidation is the attempt by FBI agents to hire informants in our communities. There were a few cases in which they would look for those in our community who had certain legal problems. They would then approach that person and suggest that they would make things easier for him—sort of making a deal with that individual in the community. Although his legal problems might be minor, the FBI would try to use them to pressure that individual to become an informant for the FBI. And we had various cases where we were also in contact with the Center for Constitutional Rights.

This type of policy had a direct effect on the social level. Many of you saw the different cases where mosques were burned, and stores that were owned by Arabs were burned. Homes of Arabs were being attacked. These kinds of attacks basically originated in a policy by the U.S. government and were encouraged by it.

Regardless of this attempt by the FBI to suppress us and to keep us from expressing our view and our opposition to the U.S. policy in the Gulf, we Arab-Americans were an essential part of the anti-war movement. We did not allow this FBI harassment to affect us in any way, and we also effectively became involved and became part of the leadership of the anti-war movement.

Neal Saad is a member of the Committee for a Democratic Palestine and the Director of the Arab-American Community Center, New York. He spoke at the New York Commission hearing.

The Gulf War: A Crime Against
the Peoples of Africa and Asia

Karen Talbot

I would like to read into evidence some statistics on the immediate impact of just the sanctions against Iraq on many countries.

Thousands of Indians, Bangladeshis, Pakistanis, Filippinos and Sri Lankans who had been working in Iraq and Kuwait were forced to return to conditions of unemployment and poverty in their countries. According to Saul Landau of the Institute for Policy Studies in Washington, the Indian economy shrank by $2 billion from August through January. That was before the war started. This was a result of the loss of remittances from the 170,000 Indians who worked in the Persian Gulf region up to August 1990.

The Philippine government estimated a drop of between $293 to $438 million in worker remittances as a result of the Mideast war. The British Overseas Development Institute recorded that some forty countries, all in the south, lost over $12 billion as a result of the war. Such countries as Jordan, Yemen and Sri Lanka lost up to 25.3 percent of their gross national product. And then of course there were the countries that reported to the Security Council their losses. There were twenty-one countries, among which were Djibouti, India, Jordan, Lebanon, Seychelles, Sri Lanka, Sudan, Syria, Tunisia, Mauritania, Pakistan, Philippines, Uruguay, Vietnam, Yemen and two or three formerly socialist countries of Eastern Europe. They lost a total of $30 billion in just a short period of time. When some efforts were made to help these countries on the part of the United Nations Security Council, the U.S. blocked any help to Yemen, Sudan and Jordan.

The peoples of these countries are suffering as a result of the external debt and the extraction of tremendous amounts of natural resources, especially in the nations of Latin America, Asia, and Africa. The imposition of structural adjustment policies by the U.S.-controlled International Monetary Fund (IMF) and World Bank is part of the continuing plunder of these countries. The net result is a flow of wealth from the poorer nations to the richer, developed nations. And this will now be aggravated because the United States is flexing its muscles and feeling much stronger and will push harder for structural adjustment policies without any other nation daring to raise a voice of opposition.

For the record, the April 2, 1991, issue of *New York Newsday* reports that the U.S. military commander in the Middle East, General Norman Schwarzkopf, visited Bahrain last week, shortly after disclosing that the U.S. wants to establish a military headquarters in an unspecified Middle East country. U.S. sources have identified Bahrain as that likely site. Bahrain will explore for oil this year under a contract with a Texas company whose directors include George W. Bush, son of the president. Bahrain has provided docking, refueling, and other facilities for U.S. and European navy ships since World War II. During the recent war with Iraq, Bahrain's new air base was used by U.S. and British squadrons. The United States sold Bahrain twelve F-16 fighter jets in 1987 during the Iran-Iraq war after Vice-President George Bush visited Bahrain to reaffirm U.S. support for its defense.

And one could go on about the super-profits being made as a result of this war. An article in the *San Francisco Chronicle* on March 3, 1991, revealed that defense contractors in the United States are likely to enjoy fatter order books as a result of the allied victory over Iraq. As the U.S. military pummeled Saddam Hussein's army in Iraq and Kuwait, it also was showing off—advertising, literally—the latest high-tech American weapons to attentive foreign buyers. And that article goes on to enumerate the contracts that are in the making.

James Grant, Executive Director of the UN Children's Fund, said that hundreds of thousands of children could die as a result of this war. And Dr. Jacques Labasse, a French specialist in infectious diseases and a member of the medical delegation to Baghdad, said, "What is happening now in Iraq has never been observed before at such a scale." The epidemics and disease will not be confined to the borders of Iraq but will surely spread to other parts of the region and beyond.

The peoples of the Third World are also facing, more than ever, the threat of a military attack against them, such as was waged against Iraq. They are very fearful about the continuing and intensifying destabilization efforts against them. And as far as the threat to the Third World countries from U.S. military attacks, we need only to turn to the official U.S. government strategy, which was revealed by the press in August 1990. The keystone of this strategy is a massive, rapid deployment and permanent establishment of U.S. forces, particularly in Third World areas where there is a perceived threat to U.S. interests, unrest, drug trafficking, and terrorism.

Karen Talbot is the Director of the International Center for Peace and Justice. She testified at the New York Commission hearing.

Yemen: A Victim of the Bribery and Corruption of the UN

Abdel Hameed Noaman

As a Yemeni living in the United States, I have a conscientious obligation to the innocent workers of Yemen who were displaced from the Arabian peninsula—the Kingdom of Saudi Arabia. The Republic of Yemen took a neutral stand on the Iraq-Kuwait conflict in both the United Nations and the Arab League. According to the official Yemeni interpretation, this stand was taken to enable Yemen to pursue a peaceful solution to the conflict. This interpretation was conveyed to U.S. Secretary of State James Baker by Yemen's representative to the U.N., Mohammad Al-Ashtal, in the Security Council meeting on November 29, 1990, at 3:00 p.m.

The Yemeni government did not condone the Iraqi invasion of Kuwait — they condemned it. But they did not support the unjust economic embargo against Iraq. At that time, the government of Saudi Arabia was dissatisfied with the Yemeni position, and its reaction was to ruin the lives of 900,000 Yemeni workers. These workers were helpless, politically restrained and, due to their emigration and absence from their homeland, had no influence on the policy of their government. The Saudi government's actions persecuted the Yemeni workers living in Saudi Arabia. These inequities are listed below:

1. The Saudi government has forced the Yemeni workers and entrepreneurs to sell their belongings and businesses at prices lower than the accustomed market price. In consequence, these Yemeni immigrants also had to helplessly abandon compensation and ownership rights that they had acquired over decades. They did this without complaint. As their tradition dictates, they left their fate to God.

2. Before their departure, the Yemeni immigrants were interrogated and harassed by the Saudi officials, police officers, reactionary citizens. Soldiers at the Saudi-Yemeni border pushed people through at gun point. The Yemeni immigrant's pride was marred before the eyes of the world. Adolescents and children heard name calling and slurs against their families made by the Saudis. In the month of September 1990 alone, 140,000 workers

including thirteen pregnant women were dumped in the desert under the supervision and mercy of his majesty King Fahd ibn-Abel Aziz al-Saud.

As of November 1990 Yemen was already in debt for $7 billion. An additional $2 billion in remittances from workers in Saudi Arabia is gone with the wind, and so are the remittances from workers in Iraq and Kuwait. The annual grants provided by Iraq and Kuwait in support of the Yemeni budget have ended. Of course, some $95 million in aid from Iraq is gone. Another $17 million in foreign exchange from tourism has likewise vanished. The $370 million in loans from both the Arab Fund for Economic and Social Development and the Kuwait Fund for Arab Economic Development were also aborted.

Abdel Hameed Noaman is a member of the General Association of Yemeni Immigrants in the United States. He spoke at the New York Commission hearing.

The Expulsion of Guest Workers and the Impact on Africa

Dr. M. A. Samad-Matias

The Gulf crisis also affected two to three million so-called guest workers, whom we might more readily call exploited migrant workers. They came into the Gulf region and have been working there for several decades, building its infrastructure, cleaning its homes, digging its ditches, and in some cases, performing in a professional capacity. They came from the Middle East, North Africa, the Eastern Horn of Africa, Sahelian countries and Asia. Just about all of them were tossed out of Saudi Arabia, Kuwait and Iraq after August 1990 by this crisis. Many of them lost their lives. Those who survived lost everything else.

Many have disappeared and are still missing. Many lost their health or are incapacitated. Others left whatever properties or savings they may have had in Kuwait, Saudi Arabia, or Iraq. In most cases, they were forced to leave with nothing but what they were wearing on their backs. They were forced out, in some cases, into refugee camps or refugee ships. Some are still in those camps, mostly in Jordan. Some of the ships remind us of ships during World War II which went from port to port and were not allowed to dock.

Many came from countries such as Sudan, Ethiopia, and Somalia—countries which in themselves are in a state of war and chaos, a condition overshadowed by this Gulf War. I should say that the wars in those countries are also escalated by the same forces that were involved in the Gulf War, powerful nations which make money out of selling them arms, tanks and so on, and playing one group against the other.

Less than five percent of the guest workers were allowed to stay in the Gulf countries. Some of them stayed in the parts of Iraq later taken over by the U.S. In Kuwait, after the U.S. took over, Palestinians, Jordanians, Sudanese were beaten and tortured, some were castrated, some had their eyes gouged out because they were accused of having collaborated with the Iraqi occupation.

There were people who are working with contracts in Saudi Arabia and in Kuwait. These countries list them as having permission to be in those countries as long as they're working for their master. Master! They have no rights whatsoever in those countries. Like most of the people of Kuwait and Saudi Arabia, they were exploited. They have even less rights. Some of them were born and raised in those countries. Some of them have two and three generations born there but they still have no rights whatsoever. That means they are stateless now.

I was in the Eastern Horn of Africa last August when this began. Of course there was some confusion because, after all, the people there are exposed to the same misinformation on the BBC and CNN that we are. So they pictured the invasion of Kuwait as something just horrible. But after a very short time most people there began to see through the disinformation. They saw that the same forces that exploited them in their countries and as guest workers were now saying that Iraq must be invaded. The people clearly began to see that this is just the latest in a whole string of historical invasions by various imperialist countries, especially the United States, to take over any resources, any strategic locations, and to kill anyone who got in the way. I saw much clearer understanding in East Africa, and in Latin America, where I was in December, in Cuba, about this question, than we have here in the U.S. Here the people are very confused about the true nature of this war.

Why do you think these people from Africa and the Middle East would go to Kuwait or would go to Saudi Arabia, if they're such horrible countries? Because despite the exploitation by the corrupt imperial rulers in those countries, their economies are much greater than the less developed countries the workers come from. The workers have very little choice. Most work for eleven months and go home for one month. Women in particular were even more exploited than most men. Women are mostly domestic servants and subject to the usual whims of their boss, their master. Many of them, especially the Jamaicans, the Filipinos, some of the East Africans might have gotten pregnant after being raped. They have no rights. If there's any problem, they're just deported with nothing.

To give you an example of how many people from these countries were there. From Egypt, in Kuwait were 215,000 people. In Iraq there were 900,000 Egyptians. I don't have the figures for Saudi Arabia for the Egyptians. North African Arabs were 130,000 in Kuwait and 22,000 in Iraq. Africans from the Eastern Horn of Africa were 15,000 in Kuwait and 33,000 in Iraq. A total estimate for the number of people from Africa in both countries who were displaced by this crisis would be 375,000 in Kuwait and 1,555,000 in Iraq.

Iraq, despite its shortcomings, was one of the most developed countries of this region. It had also one of the best infrastructures, one of the best facilities for health care and for education that sent thousands of people, not just Iraqis, abroad to study. The guest workers did not want to leave Iraq, but when Iraq was embargoed and attacked the people from all the other countries that I've mentioned and others were subject to the same situation that affected the Iraqis. So there were Iraqis there and many, many others who had been given work there for years, where they were much less exploited than their brothers and sisters in Kuwait and Saudi Arabia.

To quote from an International Monetary Fund report: "Sixty-five nations of the world were negatively affected and impacted by the crisis. And Sub-Saharan African countries being the poorest, were among the worst affected. They had about a $4 billion loss due to and as a direct result of this war." What did that come from? Rising oil costs placed a burden of $2.7 billion on these countries. Additional losses came from the loss of exports and imports, the cancellation of international contracts, transportation, tourism, and the absence of expatriate remittances coming from these guest workers who were expelled or displaced.

The oil-importing African nations were especially vulnerable, such as Liberia, Sierra Leone, Somalia, Sudan, Burkina Faso, Mali, Niger, Zambia, Senegal, Mozambique, Chad, and Ethiopia. Also, other countries in Latin America, such as Cuba, imported oil from Iraq.

In most of the Latin American and African nations that I'm familiar with, if anyone had been confused about the hypocrisy of this United States or its allies, this should have woken them up. If anyone forgot the double standards used against people of color in this country and abroad, this should have been something to open their eyes. If anyone forgot Grenada, Santo Domingo, or Panama, Vietnam, Palestine, this should be something, once again, that made them remember. In some cases, the reaction may be fatalism and fundamentalism. But in many other cases, it is a greater resolve, a greater unity, against imperialism.

Despite the media, the majority of African, Arab, Latin American, Caribbean, and Asian people now understand, whether they're "educated" or not, that the U.S. and its allies were not invading Iraq to restore democracy or to protect anyone's independence. The average person I spoke to when I was abroad in Africa and in the Caribbean, unlike most of the misinformed people in the United States, understood clearly that this was a racist, machistic, classist, North American-European dominated outburst of greed and violence to completely dominate the world.

Dr. M. A. Samad-Matias is Professor of African and Caribbean Studies at the City University of New York. She spoke at the New York Commission hearings.

Palestine and the Gulf War

Houda Gazalwin

Before I start my remarks, allow me to share with you some of the experiences as to what happened in occupied Palestine during the Gulf War and after it. I lived there through this crisis and I am reporting from first-hand experience.

The Israeli authorities have used the situation in the Gulf and the concentration of the media on what is happening there in order to crack down on the Palestinian population in the occupied territories and prevent what little media coverage there was from taking place. They imposed a curfew on all of the West Bank and Gaza. The curfew was total with the exception of Jerusalem, which they considered to be an Israeli territory, and they forbade anybody that carried West Bank or Gaza papers from traveling anywhere through Jerusalem, thereby dividing the country. Whoever violated this order would face a prison sentence of three months and a very heavy fine.

Thus the Israeli government was able to divide the various sections and separate them, because Jerusalem represented the link between all the various sections of the country. During the curfew there were many instances where they would attack people in their homes, and they would beat up women, children. Young men especially would be arrested under the excuse that they violated the curfew.

Their objective was to empty the Palestinian neighborhoods of the young men and women, therefore limiting the resistance activities. The plan was carried to a point where the Israeli prison system was unable to accommodate all the Palestinian prisoners, and many of them would be left in police stations and holding areas, handcuffed and naked. As for the curfew, it would be lifted for 1-2 hours in some areas per week. However, in the north of Palestine, it went for over thirty days without the curfew being lifted for even one hour for people to have the opportunity to buy and to attend to their daily needs. This curfew lasted for the duration of the War until after Iraq left Kuwait and the bombing had ceased.

The curfew was lifted from some of the villages during the day. However, it continues at night in all parts of the West Bank and Gaza. The

Palestinian people lived through very hard economic conditions, and this was intensified due to the Israeli order not allowing Palestinian workers to travel inside Israel for their work without receiving permits which are good for one day only. Any Palestinian worker who had a relative who was imprisoned in the Israeli prison system would be denied the daily work permit that he needed. Therefore, that limited the numbers of those who can seek work to a very small percentage of the Palestinian work force. This was in addition to the economic hardship and was produced as a result of the Gulf crisis because many of the Palestinians have family members who were supporting them and who lived in Kuwait and the Gulf states. All that support has stopped as a direct result of the war. We find many Palestinians who are unable to find their daily subsistence, and especially in the Gaza Strip, where the largest percentage of Palestinian workers live. This has been added to the Israeli oppression.

However, in spite of all these hardships, the Palestinian Intifada will not stop, not for one moment. The people were suffering from the repression of the occupation before the war, and that oppression produced the revolution that is insisting on achieving the rights of the Palestinian people and their right to be represented by the Palestine Liberation Organization as their sole legitimate representative. This was clear after the recent visit by U.S. Secretary of State James Baker, which represents the continuation of the U.S. conspiracy to impose its hegemony on the area by appearing to solve the Palestinian issue. The Palestinian people were aware and realized that this meeting with the Palestinians of the West Bank was nothing more than an attempt to gain time for Israel and to divide the Palestinian people between the Palestinians inside the occupied territories and the Palestine Liberation Organization outside. The Palestinian people expressed their dissatisfaction and their rejection of the James Baker mission by holding a general strike for three consecutive days and intensifying the demonstrations and the resistance in all areas—saying to James Baker that their only representative is the Palestine Liberation Organization.

Palestinian women's organizations have held many sit-ins and demonstrations in front of UN institutions and UN offices rejecting the James Baker solution and insisting that the only solution for the Palestinians is an international conference with the participation of the Palestine Liberation Organization on equal footing with all the concerned parties. Our people in the occupied territories are steadfast and they will not be affected by all the repression that the Israeli authorities inflict on them, and our working people seek only the food, bread, and milk for their children in order to continue the struggle.

It is important to show our support through activities such as this to the Palestinian people, and any other forms of support that we can extend to the Palestinians in the occupied territories in order that they will be able to continue resisting and confronting the occupying forces. With regard to the Palestinian community in Kuwait, I wish only to add that I would like to appeal to the peace movement all over the world, the anti-American imperialist movement, to launch a campaign with the objective of exposing what is happening to Palestinians in Kuwait—from oppression and torture to the killing of our Palestinians in Kuwait. World exposure of these crimes will serve as a form of pressure on the government of Kuwait and the American government to ensure the safety of our children and our women, our elders, those peaceful people who are living in Kuwait and now are threatened by the hands of the criminals, the Sabah family, and the criminal George Bush.

Houda Gazalwin is from the Federation of Palestinian Women Work Committees in Palestine on the West Bank. This article was translated by Adeeb Abed. She spoke at the New York Commission hearing.

The Harsh Government
Prosecution of Military Resisters

William Kunstler

Of all the protesters against the war, the ones who risk the most, I think, are those Marine, Air Force, and Army reservists who said, "No," and thus subjected themselves to courts martial at Camp Lejeune (North Carolina) and Quantico (Virginia). And I think they've been severely misunderstood by many of the people who say, "Well, you joined the military and here's a war. How is it that you can say, 'I'm not going to participate.' You shouldn't have joined if that was your feeling."

A lot of people who enlisted in the military did so at the age of seventeen; they usually were Third World people who couldn't get an education or a job unless they joined the military, which explains why so many people in the military are Third World people. You saw them on your screens during the so-called Persian Gulf War. A lot of the people took their chances, like twenty-two Marines at LeJeune who said, "We're not going to go."

They then applied for what is called conscientious objector status. Now a conscientious objector (CO), the military says, is a person who has, "a firm, fixed and sincere objection to participating in war in any form or the bearing of arms by reason of religion or training." All the services have a provision that a true conscientious objector must be honorably discharged from the military or given non-combatant duties. I remember when I was bayoneted during World War II. My nurse was Lew Ayres, the actor, who was a conscientious objector and who was given non-combatant status and who I think was responsible for keeping them from cutting off my left arm. But in any event, that's what the military says.

Once a soldier submits an application for CO status, the military is required to provide duties that don't conflict with his or her stated beliefs until they can have some sort of a hearing. And he must be, or she must be, immediately removed from combatant status until the application is decided. Now a soldier or a reservist who seeks CO status must demonstrate an opposition to all wars, not a particular war. Frequently, the investigator for the military will say, "You don't want to go to Saudi Arabia, but wouldn't you fight Hitler if Hitler were around? Or wouldn't you fight against apartheid in South Africa?" These are loaded questions. But no applicant is required to be a time traveller or to pretend that he is someone else living in a different place. You don't need hypotheticals. And you shouldn't need hypotheticals to give you conscientious objector status.

A conscientious objector doesn't have to be a pacifist. Indeed, few really are. A conscientious objector must say, "I will not participate in war." And whether they would act in self-defense or defense of home and family and personal decisions are legally irrelevant to CO status. All you need, theoretically, at least, is that you must have some religious training or belief that war is immoral. But this doesn't mean and shouldn't mean any particular faith, any special creed, or even a belief in God. A belief that life is sacred, that war is immoral constitutes a legally sufficient religious belief and the training is merely life experience that gives rise to the belief, not formal instruction in any particular religion.

Everybody that enlists in the Army, Navy, or Air Force must certify in the application that they are not conscientious objectors. It's a condition of acceptance. But many people are only seventeen or eighteen when they sign that statement, and then they begin to change their view. They begin to understand that what they thought as teenagers—that the military was a good way to get a job or an education—was shortsighted. They never gave thought to what it would be like to kill someone, what it would be like to engage in precision bombing or non-precision bombing, what it would be like to take a knife on the end of a gun and slip it into someone's intestines.

They took an opportunity in a country that doesn't give Third World people much of an opportunity unless they're willing to fight and die for it in the military. So they entered the military. They signed the condition and then they began to get religion in the sense that they began to understand that they are conscientious objectors. That understanding grows from a gradual disaffection with war as a form of human endeavor. It can arise as suddenly as the war itself. And this is especially true of reservists who are not on active duty and who enlisted as teenagers.

However, in this country where conscientious objectors have a long and honorable history, they are being subjected to courts martial. They are going to be given substantial penalties. They're going to go to the brig or to some military prison. They are going to be stripped of their pay and allowances. They are going to be branded with a dishonorable or less than honorable discharge. These people are the bravest of young people, because it takes guts to say, "I am not going to go," particularly when the country is reeking with patriotism.

So I and Ronald Kuby and Steve Somerstein and the other lawyers are representing the various COs in the military, at Quantico, at Lejeune, in the Air Force with Airman Jean Baptiste, and others. We feel privileged to represent these people and we know that they are making much more of a sacrifice than someone who stands on a picket line in New York City, even though those people do honorable work. The COs are really risking a lot of time in jail, and the destruction, essentially, of their lives, because faced with a dishonorable or less than honorable discharge, it's going to be very difficult to get employment. They're going to be branded by the Schwarzkopfs of the world as traitors, cowards, and all the other phrases they use.

But I tell you, in the history of the United States, people like this deserve the highest praise, the highest support. They take the greatest risk and in this instance they have demonstrated that the CO status in our country is an honorable thing. One of the highest aspirations of any free society is the triumph of the individual conscience and freedom of belief over the mass hysteria of the lemmings who rush over the cliff, carrying their American flags with them and their yellow buntings. My hat's off to them. I hope yours is, too.

William Kunstler is a civil rights attorney with a long record of defending those who in conscience cannot support U.S. government policies. He spoke at the New York Commission hearing.

The Old World Order
and the Causes of the Gulf War

Tony Benn

I have just come from the War Office—the Ministry of Defense, they call it now—where a small delegation of people presented a petition with 5,000 signatures in support of Vic Williams, a young soldier who would not fight in the Gulf. There were many brave soldiers in the United States and Britain who took a stand against the war because they knew in their hearts what this Tribunal is establishing in public: that the Gulf War was wrong. They are now paying the price for their stand.

The importance of the War Crimes Tribunal is that it provides us all with an opportunity to look back at the horrors of the Gulf War and to see through the smoke-screen which said it would pave the way for a new world order that would safeguard peace, democracy, and human rights under the United Nations. This Tribunal is not a search for individual scapegoats upon whom all the blame for the slaughter of innocent people can be heaped but an effort to remind us of the grave moral responsibility that lies upon all those in politics, in the media, in the military, and in the general public that went along with this war.

To be effective, we have to look back at the causes of the war, the conduct of the war, and the consequences of the war in order to reduce the likelihood of a repetition in the future. To start with the causes of the Gulf War, you have to go many centuries back into history, for over many centuries the West has tried to dominate the Middle East in its own strategic and economic interest. Sometimes wars were made in the name of religion, as during the Crusades. I learned when I was in Algiers, from a former foreign minister, that during the Crusades European arms manufacturers supplied weapons both to King Richard and to Saladin, so the military-industrial complex always gains out of that type of conflict. If you go back into the nineteenth century, it was the British who tried to establish themselves in the Middle East to dominate it in their own interest, and even the word "jingoism" goes back to the middle of the nineteenth century when Queen

Victoria sent an army to prevent the Russians from advancing into the Middle East and somebody wrote a little rhyme which goes, "we don't want to fight, but by jingo if we do, we've got the men, we've got the ships, we've got the money, too."

This new world order is a throwback to the old days of imperialism. After the first world war when the Turkish empire was defeated, the Kurds were promised their own homeland, Kurdistan, and that promise was later denied by Britain because Turkey was seen as a bastion of strength against the new power of the Soviet Union. Turkey is the home of the largest number of Kurds, and the formation of any Kurdistan will require large territorial concessions from Turkey. In the period between the wars, the British occupied Iraq. In the 1920s it was a British officer, wing commander Harris, who used mustard gas against rebels in Iraq, the very same man who later in the second world war was responsible for the total destruction of Dresden. It was Britain that created Kuwait as a separate state to guarantee oil supply for this country. In 1958 it was a British Foreign Secretary, Selwyn Lloyd, who wrote to John Foster Dulles, the American Secretary of State, saying that we, the British, are thinking of taking over Kuwait and making it into a British colony. Dulles wrote back and said, what very good idea.

When we look at the history of the Gulf War, it is riddled with hypocrisy on the part of western leaders. Nothing was done when Turkey moved into Cyprus; nothing was done when Israel moved into the occupied territories or Lebanon, nothing was done at the time of the Bay of Pigs or when the United States occupied Grenada (a British commonwealth nation), and nothing was done when the United States invaded Panama—nothing was done under the United Nation's Charter. What has happened in this case is that U.S. leaders decided that Saddam Hussein, whom they had supported consistently when he had his war with Iran, had become too strong for American interests and so they decided to destroy him. I do not believe that Iraq's invasion of Kuwait, which I totally opposed, was the real reason for the war. You just have to look at how the war was conducted to see that the liberation of Kuwait was not its main purpose. Clearly, the destruction of Iraq was the sole underlying purpose of the war. Kuwait was only the pretext.

During the occupation of Kuwait by Iraqi forces, I travelled to Baghdad to express my opposition to Saddam Hussein. I had three hours with him arguing about the occupation, and the one thing he said to me time and time again—which I didn't believe it the moment but I do believe it now— was that even if he withdraw his forces from Kuwait the United States would destroy Iraq. I believe he was right, at least in that analysis of the situation that confronted him concerning the causes of the American build up to war and the American intentions. The war against Iraq was really about the determination of the United States to control the Middle East and the oil there, and to assert its military ascendancy over its client states,

Now let me turn from the causes of the war to the conduct of the war. The conduct reveals all the ruthlessness of which modern military machines are capable, especially in the destruction of lives, even of innocent children, during and after the war. The destruction of the economic infrastructure of Iraq was designed to cripple that country for a generation or more and was to be a warning to others not to challenge the power of the United States of America. I was listening late on the night that the war began, and I heard the broadcast on CNN and the BBC from Baghdad when that horrific bombing occurred. What was being portrayed to us was a high-tech precision attack upon a war machine. It was no such thing. It was the indiscriminate destruction of Iraq for purposes that were clear in the minds of President Bush with the support of Margaret Thatcher and Prime Minister Major. The price in human suffering was quite unjustified and was bound to be condemned. The effect of the bombing was to leave that country in ruins. Ramsey Clark went to Iraq during the war and made a film showing the kinds of destruction that were not shown on television. What he showed is that thousands of innocent people were killed or injured and made homeless. Refugees were rising into millions, and the revenues of countries which had nationals working in Iraq and sending wages back home have been lost.

The consequences of the war are truly horrific in terms of human and ecological destruction. The double standards that have been peddled by governments and the media have also corrupted the morality that such a war was supposed to uphold. Undoubtedly, this corruption of public morality will pave the way for another attack on Libya and the destruction of Cuba, if the Americans can get away with it. I was one of those who demonstrated at the huge meeting in London just after the bombing of Libya. I was at Fairford when we had a big demonstration against the Gulf war as as that meeting ended with churchmen, nuns, and peace activists, the B-52s headed off for Iraq to destroy the cities. And as we left, the American servicemen and their wives and families and local people threw eggs at us as we walked away from that airbase. We have a responsibility in Britain for allowing the bases that the U.S. has in this country to be used to oppress other people in other parts of the world.

There is a need for a new world order, but do not be misled. The new world order of President Bush goes back to the world order of 1900 when three white men dominated the world: the King of England, the Kaiser of Germany, and the Czar of Russia. They ran the world and they were all the grandsons of Queen Victoria and you never heard anything about human rights when Queen Victoria's grandsons were oppressing the third world. Now we are seeing a return to that type of imperialism. As a little boy of six, I met Mr. Ghandi when he came to London in 1931. My father knew him and took me to see him. One of the journalists said to Mr. Ghandi, "what do you think of civilization in Britain?" Ghandi said, "I think it would be a very good idea." I think his comment is something we should remember because Ghandi's non-violent movement of offering resistance to oppression without bloodshed played a large part in the liberation of the Indian sub-continent from British imperialism.

We need a new world order that converts the world's resources from weapons of war to the means of development, to protect the planet from destruction, not just the pollution of chemicals but the destruction of the planet as we see in war. We need a new world order to establish and maintain the rights of human beings, men and women, to live with their children at peace in a world that now has enough to support all of us. This means the people of the world have got to unite to gain democratic control of the United Nations and prevent it from ever again being used by one super-power to protect its own economic and military interests at the expense of the lives of those who live in the third world. We have some history of partial gains in democracy in the world: the American revolution, some of the great struggles for democracy in Britain, or the overturning of apartheid in South Africa by the determination of the black people. We want democratic control of the United Nations. We want a popularly elected General Assembly. We want the people of the world to choose their own representatives at the UN and we want the General Assembly to have the power to overturn the veto one member of the Security Council by a vote so American cannot enslave the UN and bribe its members into assenting to the kind of war we have just witnessed.

I believe that task will require us to consolidate the gains we made in the peace movement during the war. Ramsey Clark and his staff have established this marvelous international Tribunal. During the course of the work I tried to do against the war, I received letters of support from Nelson Mandela, Julius Nyere, Rajiv Ghandi, Ron Dellums, and people all over the world who share the aspirations that bring us to this Tribunal to expose the war crimes of the American leadership. We have to build on that. We have to create a world movement powerful enough to stop the abuse of power for humanity could be destroyed by the splitting of the atom. Only by the uniting of the human race can we establish sufficient power to prevent that from happening and to guarantee to future generation the rights we though we had won when the set up the United Nations.

Tony Benn is a leading member of the British Labor Party and a member of Parliament. This paper was presented at the London Commission of Inquiry held at the Turkish/Kurdish Hall on December 1, 1991. Some 1,200 people listened to the analyses and testimony of twenty presenters.

Appendix A:

International Law

Protocol 1
Additional to the Geneva Conventions, 1977

PART IV: CIVILIAN POPULATION

Section I: General Protection Against Effects of Hostilities

Chapter I: Basic Rule and Field of Application

Article 48: Basic Rule

In order to ensure respect for and protection of the civilian population and civilian objects, the Parties to the conflict shall at all times distinguish between the civilian population and combatants and between civilian objects and military objectives and accordingly shall direct their operations only against military objectives.

Article 49: Definition of Attacks and Scope of Application

1. "Attacks" means acts of violence against the adversary, whether in offense or in defense.

2. The provisions of this Protocol with respect to attacks apply to all attacks in whatever territory conducted, including the national territory belonging to a Party to the conflict but under the control of an adverse Party.

3. The provisions of this Section apply to any land, air or sea warfare which may affect the civilian population, individual civilians or civilian objects on land. They further apply to all attacks from the sea or from the air against objectives on land but do not otherwise affect the rules of international law applicable in armed conflict at sea or in the air.

4. The provisions of this Section are additional to the rules concerning humanitarian protection contained in the Fourth Convention, particularly in Part II thereof, and in other international agreements binding upon the High Contracting Parties, as well as to other rules of international law relating to the protection of civilians and civilian objects on land, at sea or in the air against the effects of hostilities.

Chapter II: Civilians and Civilian Population

Article 50: Definition of Civilians and Civilian Population

1. A civilian is any person who does not belong to one of the categories of persons referred to in Article 4 A (1), (I), (3) and (6) of the Third Convention and in Article 43 of this Protocol. In case of doubt whether a person is a civilian, that person shall be considered to be a civilian.

2. The civilian population comprises all persons who are civilians.

3. The presence within the civilian population of individuals who do not come within the definition of civilians does not deprive the population of its civilian character.

Article 51: Protection of the Civilian Population

1. The civilian population and individual civilians shall enjoy general protection against dangers arising from military operations. To give effect to this protection, the following rules, which are additional to other applicable rules of international law, shall be observed in all circumstances.

2. The civilian population as such, as well as individual civilians, shall not be the object of attack. Acts or threats of violence the primary purpose of which is to spread terror among the civilian population are prohibited.

3. Civilians shall enjoy the protection afforded by this Section, unless and for such time as they take a direct part in hostilities.

4. Indiscriminate attacks are prohibited. Indiscriminate attacks are:

(a) those which are not directed at a specific military objective;
(b) those which employ a method or means of combat which cannot be directed at a specific military objective; or
c) those which employ a method or means of combat the effects of which cannot be limited as required by this Protocol; and consequently, in each such case, are of a nature to strike military objectives and civilians or civilian objects without distinction.

5. Among others, the following types of attacks are to be considered as indiscriminate:

(a) an attack by bombardment by any methods or means which treats as a single military objective a number of clearly separated and distinct military objectives located in a city, town, village or other area containing a similar concentration of civilians or civilian objects; and
(b) an attack which may be expected to cause incidental loss of civilian life, injury to civilians, damage to civilian objects, or a combination thereof, which would be excessive in

relation to the concrete and direct military advantage anticipated.

6. Attacks against the civilian population or civilians by way of reprisals are prohibited.

7. The presence or movements of the civilian population or individual civilians shall not be used to render certain points or areas immune from military operations, in particular in attempts to shield military objectives from attacks or to shield, favor or impede military operations. The Parties to the conflict shall not direct the movement of the civilian population or individual civilians in order to attempt to shield military objectives from attacks or to shield military operations.

8. Any violation of these prohibitions shall not release the Parties to the conflict from their legal obligations with respect to the civilian population and civilians, including the obligation to take the precautionary measures provided for in Article 57.

Chapter III: Civilian Objects

Article 52: General Protection of Civilian Objects

1. Civilian objects shall not be the object of attack or of reprisals. Civilian objects are all objects which are not military objectives as defined in paragraph 2.

2. Attacks shall be limited strictly to military objectives. In so far as objects are concerned, military objectives are limited to those objects which by their nature, location, purpose or use make an effective contribution to military action and whose total or partial destruction, capture or neutralization, in the circumstances ruling at the time, offers a definite military advantage.

3. In case of doubt whether an object which is normally dedicated to civilian purposes, such as a place of worship, a house or other dwelling or a school, is being used to make an effective contribution to military action, it shall be presumed not to be so used. Article 53 Protection of cultural objects and of places of worship without prejudice to the provisions of the Hague Convention for the Protection of Cultural Property in the Event of Armed Conflict of 14 May 1954, and of other relevant international instruments, it is prohibited:

    (a) to commit any acts of hostility directed against the historic monuments, works of art or places of worship which constitute the cultural or spiritual heritage of peoples;
    (b) to use such objects in support of the military effort;
    (c) to make such objects the object of reprisals.

Article 54: Protection of Objects Indispensable to the Survival of the Civilian Population

1. Starvation of civilians as a method of warfare is prohibited.

2. It is prohibited to attack, destroy, remove or render useless objects indispensable to the survival of the civilian population, such as foodstuffs, agricultural areas for the production of foodstuffs, crops, livestock, drinking water installations and supplies and irrigation works, for the specific purpose of denying them for their sustenance value to the civilian population or to the adverse Party, whatever the motive, whether in order to starve out civilians, to cause them to move away, or for any other motive.

3. The prohibitions in paragraph 2 shall not apply to such of the objects covered by it as are used by an adverse Party:

> (a) as sustenance solely for the members of its armed forces; or
> (b) if not as sustenance, then in direct support of military action, provided, however, that in no event shall actions against these objects be taken which may be expected to leave the civilian population with such inadequate food or water as to cause its starvation or force its movement.

4. These objects shall not be made the object of reprisals.

5. In recognition of the vital requirements of any Party to the conflict in the defense of its national territory against invasion, derogation from the prohibitions contained in paragraph 2 may be made by a Party to the conflict within such territory under its own control where required by imperative military necessity.

Article 55: Protection of the Natural Environment

1. Care shall be taken in warfare to protect the natural environment against widespread, long-term and severe damage. This protection includes a prohibition of the use of methods or means of warfare which are intended or may be expected to cause such damage to the natural environment and thereby to prejudice the health or survival of the population.

2. Attacks against the natural environment by way of reprisals are prohibited.

Article 56: Protection of Works and Installations Containing Dangerous Forces

1. Works or installations containing dangerous forces, namely dams, dikes and nuclear electrical generating stations, shall not be made the object of attack, even where these objects are military objectives, if such attack may cause the release of dangerous forces and consequent severe losses among the civilian population. Other military objectives located at or in the vicinity of these works or installations shall not be made the object of attack if such attack may cause the release of dangerous forces from the

works or installations and consequent severe losses among the civilian population.

2. The special protection against attack provided by paragraph I shall cease:

(a) for a dam or a dike only if it is used for other than its normal function and in regular, significant and direct support of military operations and if such attack is the only feasible way to terminate such support;

(b) for a nuclear electrical generating station only if it provides electric power in regular, significant and direct support of military operations and if such attack is the only feasible way to terminate such support;

(c) for other military objectives located at or in the vicinity of these works or installations only if they are used in regular, significant and direct support of military operations and if such attack is the only feasible way to terminate such support.

3. In all cases, the civilian population and individual civilians shall remain entitled to all the protection accorded them by international law, including the protection of the precautionary measures provided for in Article 57. If the protection ceases and any of the works, installations or military objectives mentioned in paragraph 1 is attacked, all practical precautions shall be taken to avoid the release of the dangerous forces.

4. It is prohibited to make any of the works, installations or military objectives mentioned in paragraph 1 the object of reprisals.

5. The Parties to the conflict shall endeavor to avoid locating any military objectives in the vicinity of the works or installations mentioned in paragraph 1. Nevertheless, installations erected for the sole purpose of defending the protected works or installations from attack are permissible and shall not themselves be made the object of attack, provided that they are not used in hostilities except for defensive actions necessary to respond to attacks against the protected works or installations and that their armament is limited to weapons capable only of repelling hostile action against the protected works or installations.

6. The High Contracting Parties and the Parties to the conflict are urged to conclude further agreements among themselves to provide additional protection for objects containing dangerous forces.

7. In order to facilitate the identification of the objects protected by this Article, the Parties to the conflict may mark them with a special sign consisting of a group of three bright orange circles placed on the same axis, as specified in Article 16 of Annex I to this Protocol. The absence of such marking in no way relieves any Party to the conflict of its obligations under this Article.

Chapter IV: Precautionary Measures

Article 57: Precautions in Attack

1. In the conduct of military operations, constant care shall be taken to spare the civilian population, civilians and civilian objects.

2. With respect to attacks, the following precautions shall be taken:

(a) those who plan or decide upon an attack shall:

(i) do everything feasible to verify that the objectives to be attacked are neither civilians nor civilian objects and are not subject to special protection but are military objectives within the meaning of paragraph 2 of Article 52 and that it is not prohibited by the provisions of this Protocol to attack them;

(ii) take all feasible precautions in the choice of means and methods of attack with a view to avoiding, and in any event to minimizing, incidental loss of civilian life, injury to civilians and damage to civilian objects;

(iii) refrain from deciding to launch any attack which may be expected to cause incidental loss of civilian life, injury to civilians, damage to civilian objects, or a combination thereof, which would be excessive in relation to the concrete and direct military advantage anticipated;

(b) an attack shall be canceled or suspended if it becomes apparent that the objective is not a military one or is subject to special protection or that the attack may be expected to cause incidental loss of civilian life, injury to civilians, damage to civilian objects, or a combination thereof, which would be excessive in relation to the concrete and direct military advantage anticipated;

(c) effective advance warning shall be given of attacks which may affect the civilian population, unless circumstances do not permit.

3. When a choice is possible between several military objectives for obtaining a similar military advantage, the objective to be selected shall be that the attack on which may be expected to cause the least danger to civilian lives and to civilian objects.

4. In the conduct of military operations at sea or in the air, each Party to the conflict shall, in conformity with its rights and duties under the rules of international law applicable in armed conflict, take all reasonable precautions to avoid losses of civilian lives and damage to civilian objects.

5. No provision of this article may be construed as authorizing any attacks against the civilian population, civilians or civilian objects.

Principles of the Nuremberg Tribunal, 1950

No. 82

Principles of International Law Recognized in the Charter of the Nuremberg Tribunal and in the Judgment of the Tribunal. Adopted by the International Law Commission of the United Nations, 1950.

Introductory note: Under General Assembly Resolution 177 (II), paragraph (a), the International Law Commission was directed to "formulate the principles of international law recognized in the Charter of the Nuremberg Tribunal and in the judgment of the Tribunal." In the course of the consideration of this subject, the question arose as to whether or not the Commission should ascertain to what extent the principles contained in the Charter and judgment constituted principles of international law. The conclusion was that since the Nuremberg Principles had been affirmed by the General Assembly, the task entrusted to the Commission was not to express any appreciation of these principles as principles of international law but merely to formulate them. The text below was adopted by the Commission at its second session. The Report of the Commission also contains commentaries on the principles (see *Yearbook of the International Law Commission*, 1950, Vol. II, pp. 374-378).

Authentic text: English

Text published in *Report of the International Law Commission Covering its Second Session, 5 June – 29 July 1950*, Document A/1316, pp. 11-14.

Principle I
    Any person who commits an act which constitutes a crime under international law is responsible therefor and liable to punishment.

Principle II
    The fact that internal law does not impose a penalty for an act which constitutes a crime under international law does not relieve the person who committed the act from responsibility under international law.

Principle III

The fact that a person who committed an act which constitutes a crime under international law acted as Head of State or responsible Government official does not relieve him from responsibility under international law.

Principle IV

The fact that a person acted pursuant to order of his Government or of a superior does not relieve him from responsibility under international law, provided a moral choice was in fact possible to him.

Principle V

Any person charged with a crime under international law has the right to a fair trial on the facts and law.

Principle VI

The crimes hereinafter set out are punishable as crimes under international law:
(a) Crimes against peace:

> (i) Planning, preparation, initiation or waging of a war of aggression or a war in violation of international treaties, agreements or assurances;
> (ii) Participation in a common plan or conspiracy for the accomplishment of any of the acts mentioned under (i).

(b) War crimes:
Violations of the laws or customs of war which include, but are not limited to, murder, ill-treatment or deportation to slave-labor or for any other purpose of civilian population of or in occupied territory, murder or ill-treatment of prisoners of war, of persons on the seas, killing of hostages, plunder of public or private property, wanton destruction of cities, towns, or villages, or devastation not justified by military necessity.
(c) Crimes against humanity:
Murder, extermination, enslavement, deportation and other inhuman acts done against any civilian population, or persecutions on political, racial or religious grounds, when such acts are done or such persecutions are carried on in execution of or in connection with any crime against peace or any war crime.

Principle VII

Complicity in the commission of a crime against peace, a war crime, or a crime against humanity as set forth in Principles VI is a crime under international law.

The Charter of
The United Nations

WE THE PEOPLE OF THE UNITED NATIONS DETERMINED

to save succeeding generations from the scourge of war, which twice in our lifetime has brought untold sorrow to mankind, and

to reaffirm faith in fundamental human rights, in the dignity and worth of the human person, in the equal rights of men and women, and of nations large and small, and

to establish conditions under which justice and respect for the obligations arising from treaties and other sources of international law can be maintained, and

to promote social progress and better standards of life in larger freedom. . . .

Article 2

The Organization and its Members, in pursuit of the Purposes stated in Article 1, shall act in accordance with the following Principles.

1. The Organization is based on the principle of the sovereign equality of all its members. . . .

3. All Members shall settle their international disputes by peaceful means in such a manner that international peace and security, and justice, are not endangered.

4. All Members shall refrain in their international relations from the threat or use of force against the territorial integrity or political independence of any state, or in any other manner inconsistent with the Purposes of the United Nations.

Chapter VI: Pacific Settlement of Disputes

Article 33

1. The parties to any dispute, the continuance of which is likely to endanger the maintenance of international peace and security, shall, first of all, seek a solution by negotiation, enquiry, mediation, conciliation, arbitration, judicial settlement, resort to regional agencies or arrangements, or other peaceful means of their own choice.

2. The Security Council shall, when it deems necessary, call upon the parties to settle their disputes by such means.

Appendix B:

Backgrounds

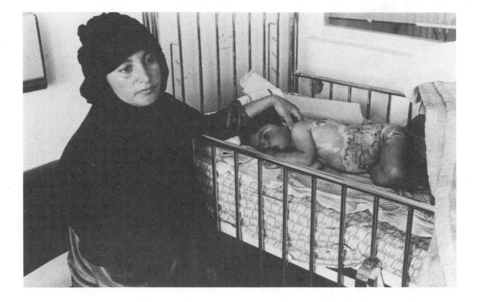

An Iraqi mother tending her badly burned child in Saddam Hussein Pediatric Hospital. Before the embargo and war, Iraq had one of the best health care systems in the entire Middle East. The war has virtually destroyed that system. Many Iraqis believe that the U.S. intended to destroy their civilization (see p. 113, above). The Harvard Team Report estimated that about 170,000 children would die within a year of the end of the war from the destruction of the civilian infrastructure. The continuing sanctions and reparation demands make rebuilding the health care system and infrastructure impossible. (Photo: Rick Rheinhardt)

Announcement of the Formation of a Commission of Inquiry into U.S. War Crimes and an International War Crimes Tribunal

The undersigned announce the formation of a Commission of Inquiry into U.S. War Crimes which will assemble evidence and testimony for a forthcoming international War Crimes Tribunal.

Even before the beginning of such an investigation, there is abundant *prima facie* evidence to support the allegation of war crimes. By rough estimate, 125,000 – 300,000 Iraqi people have been systematically slaughtered by a U.S.-led coalition of military forces using the most advanced technology. Millions in the region have been made homeless, subjected to hunger, threatened with epidemic, and forced into exile and refugee status.

The U.S. Air Force between January 16 and February 27 carried out the most sophisticated and violent air assault in history against a virtually defenseless people. A deliberate policy of bombing civilians and civilian life-sustaining facilities has resulted in the destruction of the Iraqi economy and urban infrastructure.

According to a report released on March 20 by an investigating team commissioned by the UN Secretary General himself, as a result of the bombing, "Iraq has, for some time to come, been relegated to a pre-industrial age," its economic infrastructure having suffered "near-apocalyptic" destruction. As the hot summer months approach, the casualties threaten to soar due to famine and epidemic.

The sanctions prohibiting food and medicine, plus interference with relief efforts, compound these life-threatening problems.

An immense number of the deaths and casualties were inflicted on Iraqi troops and civilians in retreat from Kuwait after Iraq had already agreed to the U.S. demands.

Kuwaiti royal troops accompanied by U.S. Special Forces are now carrying out systematic harassment, arrest, deportations and torture against Palestinians and other non-Kuwaitis.

The U.S. military still has 200,000 soldiers in Iraq and has established bases in Kuwait, Saudi Arabia, Oman, Qatar, Bahrain, and the United Arab Emirates, in addition to a nuclear naval armada in the Persian Gulf. The Pentagon has announced plans for a permanent, dominant presence in the area.

All this implies a "New World Order" based on the use and threat of U.S. military force to dominate the region's peoples and fabulous resources, with the aim of allocating the wealth among the rich countries at the expense of the poor nations. Such a global scheme could cost billions of lives.

For the sake of the future of humankind, it is imperative that the truth be known about the motivations, planning, execution and effect of these crimes against peace and humanity.

The Commission of Inquiry will assist the coordination of evidentiary hearings throughout the United States to accumulate evidence of U.S. crimes against peace, war crimes, crimes against humanity, and related crimes. It will coordinate with similar hearings conducted by committees in Africa, Asia, Europe, the Pacific and the Americas.

The first hearing will be in New York City in May. It is anticipated that additional hearings will be arranged in Toronto, Amman, Paris, London, Belgium, Algiers, Sydney and other sites under the auspices of cooperating organizations over a period of six months.

An International War Crimes Tribunal comprised of independent international figures will meet, review the evidence assembled by the Commission of Inquiry and render its judgment in early 1992 during the anniversary of the destruction of Iraq.

March 26, 1991

Algeria
Ahmed Ben Bella, former Pres. of
    Algeria; leader, Algerian
    Independence War
Nabil Bouaita, General Secretary,
    International Conference of Algiers
    on the Gulf Crisis
Amar Bentoumi, General Secretary,
    International Association of
    Democratic Lawyers

Argentina
Jorge Alberto Kreyness, Co-President,
    Consejo Argentino de la Paz

Australia
Human Rights & Civil Liberties Watch
    Committee

Bangladesh
Ali Aksad, General Secretary,
    Bangladesh Peace Council

Belgium
Prof. Rigaux, Catholic Univ. of Louvain

Coordination de Soutien aux Peuples du
    Tiers Monde

Botswana
Motsamai K. Mpha, P.M.S., President,
    Independence Party

Britain
Bill Bowring, President, Haldane Society
    of Socialist Lawyers
Keith Bennet, Political Editor, *Asian
    Times*
Hussein Hussein, President, General
    Union of Palestinian Students
John Pilger, Journalist

Canada
David Jacobs, Attorney, International
    Law
John Philpot, Association of American
    Jurists

Costa Rica
Codehuca, Human Rights Commission,
    San Jose

Egypt
Dr. Nawal El Saadawi, Author, Pres.,
   Arab Women's Solidarity Association
Mohamed Ibrahim Kamel, Ex-Foreign
   Minister of Egypt, Pres., Egyptian
   Organization for Human Rights
Dr. Sherif Hetata, Central Committee,
   Arab Progressive Unionist Party

France
Julian Dray, Member of Parliament
SOS Racisme
Resisters Inside the Army

Germany
Pastor Konrad Lubbert
Military Counseling Network
Gesellschaft Kultur des Friedens

Hong Kong
Asian Students Association

India
Har-dev Singh, All Democratic Lawyers
   Association
All India Peace and Solidarity
   Organization
V.R. Krishna Iyer, Former Chief Justice
   of India
Hanan Mollah, Member of Parliament

Italy
Father Ernesto Balducci
Giorgio Nebbia, Member of Parliament
Marinella Correggia, Gruppo
   Parlamentare Verde
Walter Peruzzi, Intellectuals Against the
   War, Milan

Japan
Civil Suit of Plaintiffs and Attorneys
   Against War
Japanese Lawyers International
   Solidarity Organization

Jordan
Bassam Haddadin, Member of
   Parliament, Jordanian Peoples
   Democratic Party*
Adeeb Hawatmeh, Executive
   Committee, Lawyers Union*

Malaysia
Fan Yew Teng, Author, former Member
   of Parliament
Dr. Chandra Muzaffar, President,
   ALIRAN social reform movement
Maria Chin Abdullah, President, All

Women's Action Society
Dr. Syed Husin Ali, President,
   Malaysian People's Party
Third World Resurgence Magazine

Mozambique
Julio Goncales Praga, Secretary General,
   Friendship & Solidarity with the
   People

Norway
Campaign for Peace in the Middle East

New Zealand
Sonja Davies, Member of Parliament
Gerald O'Brien, President, New Zealand
   Council for World Peace
Ron Smith, Chair, Campaign for
   Nuclear Disarmament, Wellington

Pakistan
Sheikh Mohamed Rashid, Former
   Deputy Prime Minister
Mohamed Hassan Sidiqi, Editor,
   Menatkar Magazine

Philippines
Nelia Sancho, Chairperson, BAYAN
GABRIELLA Women's Network of the
   Philippines

Sweden
Hans-Goran Franck, Member of
   Parliament
Action Group for Peace in the Middle
   East
Bishop Lars Carlzoh, Former Bishop of
   Stockholm
John Takman, M.D., Former Member of
   Parliament

Tunisia
Ne Abderrazak Kilani, Young Arab
   Lawyers Association

Turkey
Dr. Haluk Gerger
Doga Perincek, Chairman, Socialist
   Party

United States
Ramsey Clark
Professor George Wald, Nobel Laureate*
Bishop Thomas J. Gumbleton, Detroit*
Mary Kaufman, Attorney, Nuremberg
   Tribunal, 1949*
Casey Kasem, Radio Personality
Kris Kristofferson, Actor, Musician

Elias Guerrero, M.D., ACT-UP

E. Faye Williams, Staff Counsel, U.S.
Rep. Mervyn Dymally

Carlton Goodlett, M.D., Ph.D.,
Publisher, Former Head of National
Newspaper Publishers Association

Michael Ratner, Attorney, Center For
Constitutional Rights, filed lawsuit
with Congress members on
constitutionality of Gulf War

Lucius Walker, Exec. Dir., Interreligious
Foundation For Community
Organization

Rev. Dorsey Blake, Pres., Ecumenical
Peace Institute, Dir. Center for
Urban Black Studies, Berkeley

Anan Ameri, Palestine Aid Society*

Philip Agee, Author, former CIA Officer

Howard Zinn, Author and Historian

Harold Pinter, Playwright

Nasser Aruri, Author, Professor, SE
Massachusetts University

Francis A. Boyle, Prof. of International
Law, University of Illinois

Wilhelm Joseph, U.N. Rep., National
Conference of Black Lawyers

Michio Kaku, Prof. of Nuclear Physics,
City University of New York

Ronald Kuby, Attorney, Representing
Camp Lejeune Military Resisters

Frances "Sissy" Farenthold, Attorney,
former Candidate for Governor of
Texas

Prof. Ward Morehouse, Pres. Council on
International Public Affairs*

Deborah Jackson, V.P., American
Association of Jurists

Karen Talbot, Director, International
Center For Peace and Justice

Kate Millet, Author

Bob Schwartz, Dir., Disarm/Plowshares

Dr. Suzanne Ross, NGO Rep., Clergy
and Laity Concerned*

Gerry Condon, Exec. Dir., Veterans
Peace Action Teams

Neal Saad, Committee For a Democratic
Palestine

Committee of Artists United for Truth

Morris Kight, Commissioner on Human
Relations, Los Angeles

International Indian Treaty Council, San
Francisco

Prof. Dennis Brutus, S. African Exile,
former political prisoner

Prof. Robert Merrill, Dir., Institute for
Advanced Cultural Studies

United Labor Action Newsletter

Guardian Newsweekly

African American Coalition Against
U.S. Intervention

Latinos Coalition to Stop U.S.
Intervention

Young Koreans United

Committee Against Repression in Haiti

Independent Commission of Inquiry on
the U.S. Invasion of Panama

African Caribbean Resource Center

Puerto Rican Affirmation Committee,
New York

Plowshares Peace Center, Virginia

---

* For identification purposes only

[Text of Ramsey Clark's Report on the civilian impact of the war to UN
Secretary General Javier Pérez de Cuéllar following his trip to Iraq, Feb. 2 – 8,
1991, during the U.S. bombing of Iraq.]

February 12, 1991

Secretary-General Javier Perez de Cuellar
The Secretariat
United Nations Plaza
New York, NY 10017

Dear Mr. Secretary General:

During the period February 2 to February 8, 1991 I traveled in Iraq
to assess the damage to civilian life there resulting from the bombing and
the embargo, including civilian deaths, injuries, illness and destruction
and damage to civilian property. I was accompanied by an experienced camera
team that has filmed war and its destructiveness in many countries
including Afghanistan, Angola, Cambodia, El Salvador, Nicaragua, the
Philippines and Vietnam. Their film documents most of the damage I mention
in this letter and some I do not. In our party was an Iraqi-American guide
and translator who has family in Baghdad and Basra and is personally
familiar with those cities and many other areas of Iraq. He had last
visited Baghdad, Basra and Kuwait City in December 1990.

We traveled over 2,000 miles in seven days to view damage, learn of
casualties, discuss the effects of the bombing with government officials,
public health and safety agency staffs and private families and
individuals. We had cooperation from the government of Iraq including
Ministers, Governors, health and medical officials and civil defense
personnel. The bombing in all parts of Iraq made travel difficult,
requiring caution for bomb craters and damage to highways and roads and
making night driving especially hazardous.

The damage to residential areas and civilian structures, facilities
and utilities was extensive everywhere we went. Every city and town we
visited or that was reported to us had no municipal water, electricity or
telephone service. Parts of Baghdad had limited delivery of impure water
for an hour a day.

The effect of damage to municipal water systems on health and safety
is tremendous. The Minister of Health considered potable water for human
consumption the single greatest health need in the country. Tens of
thousands are known to suffer diarrhea and stomach disorders. There are
believed to be hundreds of thousands of unreported cases. Several thousands
are believed to have died.

There is no electric lighting in the cities, towns and countryside in
daytime or the long winter nights, except for a few interior spaces like
hospital emergency rooms where gasoline generators are available. The
meaning of this is brought home most painfully in the hospitals at night.

In the hospitals, there is no heat, no clean water except limited
quantities for drinking supplied in bottles, no electric light in wards and

hospital rooms, and inadequate medicine, even for pain alleviation, in the face of a great increase in critically and severely injured persons. Doctors we talked with in four hospitals are deeply concerned over the absence or shortage of needed medicine and sanitary supplies. Surgeons and medics treating wounds cannot keep their hands clean or gloved, and work in the cold, in poor light with greatly increased numbers of patients in unrelieved pain. Seven hospitals are reported closed by bomb damage. Many if not most have had windows shattered.

Schools are closed. Homes are cold. Candles are the principal lighting. Telephone communication does not exist. Transportation is extremely limited. Gasoline is scarce. Roads and bridges are bombing targets. There is no television. Radio reception is limited to battery powered radios which can receive short-wave signals, a few transmissions from Iraq stations or nearby foreign stations. According to the Ministry of Health, hospital officials and the Red Crescent, there is a substantial increase in falls, home accidents, stress, nervous disorders, shock, heart attack, miscarriage and premature births and infant mortality. Nightly air raids, the sounds of sirens, anti-aircraft fire and the explosion of bombs have placed a great strain on the society as a whole, but particularly on children and individuals with nervous system or heart disorders.

Dr. Ibrahem Al Noore has been head of the Red Crescent and Red Cross of Iraq for ten years. He is a pediatrician by training who interned at Children's Hospital in London, later headed Children Hospital in Baghdad and served in the Ministry of Health for some years, rising to Deputy Minister. Dr. Noore estimates that there have been 3,000 infant deaths since November 1, 1990 in excess of the normal rate, attributable solely to the shortage of infant milk formula and medicines. Only 14 tons of baby formula have been received during that period. Prior monthly national consumption was approximately 2,500 tons.

One of the early targets of U.S. bombing was the infant and baby milk processing facility in Baghdad. No Iraqi with whom we talked assumed this was a coincidence. The U.S. claim that the plant manufactured chemical warfare material is false. A French company built it. The twenty or more people whom we interviewed, who operated it, who visited it before its destruction and who have examined it since without ill effect all say it was a plant processing infant and baby milk formula. In a lengthy and unrestricted examination of the plant, we saw no evidence to the contrary.

In all areas we visited and all other areas reported to us, municipal water processing plants, pumping stations and even reservoirs have been bombed. Electric generators have been destroyed. Refineries and oil and gasoline storage facilities and filling stations have been attacked. Telephone exchange buildings, TV and radio stations, and some radio telephone relay stations and towers, have been damaged or destroyed. Many highways, roads, bridges, bus stations, schools, mosques and churches, cultural sites, and hospitals have been damaged. Government buildings including Executive Offices of the President, the Foreign Ministry, Defense Ministry, Ministry for Industry and Justice Ministry have been destroyed or damaged.

Ambassadors of member states should ask themselves if their capitals, major cities and towns were similarly destroyed and damaged by such bombing, would they consider the targets to be permissible under the International Laws of Armed Conflict. Imagine the reaction if water, electricity, telephones, gasoline, heating and air conditioning, TV and radio were denied to Lima and Arequipa, Lagos and Ibadan, Washington and Chicago, Paris and Marseilles, New Delhi and Calcutta, to Canberra and Sydney, while civilians were bombed in their homes, business, shops, markets, schools, churches, hospitals, public places, and roadways.

How can destruction of municipal electricity for Mosul, the telephone system for the people of Baghdad, the municipal water supplies for Basra, or shooting defenseless public buses and private cars on the road to Jordan and elsewhere possibly be justified as necessary to drive Iraq from Kuwait? If it can be so justified, then the United Nations has authorized the destruction of all civilian life of a whole nation.

The effect of the bombing, if continued, will be the destruction of much of the physical and economic basis for life in Iraq. The purpose of the bombing can only be explained rationally as the destruction of Iraq as a viable state for a generation or more. Will the United Nations be a party to this lawless violence?

I will briefly describe destruction to residential areas in some of the cities and towns we visited. In Basra Governor Abdullah Adjram described the bombing as of February 6 as worse than during the Iran-Iraq war. We carefully probed five residential areas that had been bombed.

1. A middle class residential area was heavily damaged at 9:30 p.m. on January 31. Twenty-eight persons were reported killed, 56 were injured, 20 homes and six shops were destroyed.

2. On January 22, an upper middle class residential neighborhood was shattered by three bombs destroying or extensively damaging more than 15 homes and reportedly injuring 40 persons, but without any deaths.

3. On January 24, an upper middle class neighborhood was bombed, killing eight, injuring 26 and destroying three homes and damaging many others.

4. On February 4, described by officials as the heaviest bombing of Basra to February 6, at 2:35 a.m., 14 persons were killed, 46 injured and 128 apartments and homes destroyed or damaged together with an adjacent Pepsi Cola bottling plant and offices across a wide avenue. The area devastated was three blocks deep on both sides of streets. At least fifteen cars were visible, crushed in garages. Small anti-personnel bombs were alleged to have fallen here and we saw what appeared to be one that did not explode embedded in rubble. We were shown the shell of a "mother" bomb which carries the small fragmentation bombs.

5. On January 28, about eighteen units in a very large low cost public housing project were destroyed or severely damaged, killing 46 and injuring 70. The nearby high school was damaged by a direct hit on a corner. The elementary school across the street was damaged.

On the evening of February 5 at 8:30 p.m. while our small group was dining alone by candlelight in the Sheraton Basra, three large bomb blasts broke glass in the room. We went upstairs to the roof. From there I saw one bomb fall into the Shaat-Al-Arab beyond the Teaching Hospital to the South throwing a column of water high into the air; another bomb hit near the Shaat. As agreed upon earlier, civil defense officials came to take us to the blast sites. They were 1.2 km down the street near the Shatt Al Arab. I had walked by the area about 6:30 p.m.

We found two buildings destroyed. It is an apartment and residential home area. One was a family club, the other a night club. If either had been open scores of people would have been killed. Palm trees were sheared off and shrapnel, rocks, dirt and glass covered the street for several hundred feet. We were unable to enter the buildings that night.

We returned the next morning and were told both buildings were empty at the time by the owners who were looking at the damage. The teaching hospital, about 150 yards distant, which had been closed for a week following earlier bombing, was without windows. It apparently received no new damage. As with all the other civilian damage we saw we could find no evidence of any military presence in the area. Here, there was no utility or facility that are frequent, if illegal, targets either. There were only homes, apartments and a few shops, grocery stores and other businesses found in residential areas, plus two small bridges connecting the hospital to the mainland.

We were informed by a variety of sources including visual observation during extensive driving in Basra, that many other residential properties had been hit and that the five areas we filmed were a minor fraction of the civilian damage that had occurred.

At the central market where more than 1,000 shops and vendors sell fruits, vegetables, fish, meat, foodstuffs and other items, a bomb leaving a huge crater had demolished a building with a grocery store and other shops and damaged an entry area to the market at about 4:00 p.m. It reportedly killed eight persons and injured 40.

We examined the rubble of a Sunni Moslem Mosque, Al Makal, where a family of 12 had taken sanctuary. The minaret remained standing. Ten bodies were found under the rubble and identified by a family member who had returned from his military post when informed of the tragedy. The dead included his wife and four young children.

In Diwaniya, a smaller town, we examined the same types of civilian damage we witnessed elsewhere and that was reported everywhere. In the town center, apparently seeking to destroy the radio telephone relay equipment in the post office, bombing had damaged the tower and the office. We saw many similar, or identical relay towers in the region that had not been attacked. Adjacent to the Post Office on the central circle of the city, three small hotels of 30 to 50 rooms were destroyed together with a host of shops, cafes, and offices including those of doctors and lawyers. We were told 12 people were killed and 35 injured. More damage could be seen across the circle among business and apartment buildings from one or more bombs that fell there.

Near the outskirts of town, four more-or-less contiguous residential areas had been bombed. Twenty-three persons were reported killed and 75 injured. Two schools were badly damaged. There was no water, electricity or telephone service. A water irrigation station was destroyed. Other damage was witnessed while driving around the town. On the outskirts an oil tank was on fire, one of more than a dozen we saw burning during our travels.

Baghdad has been more accessible to foreign observation than Basra and other places in Iraq. It will only be highlighted. We examined extensive damage on a main street in the blocks next to and across the street from the Ministry of Justice which had all its windows on one side blasted out. I know that area as a busy poor commercial residential area from walking through it on the way to the National Museum and visiting the Justice Ministry. A large supermarket, eight other stores and six or eight houses were destroyed or badly damaged. Across the street, one bomb hit on the sidewalk and another was a direct hit on housing behind the street front properties. Six shops, a restaurant and several other stores plus 9 or 10 homes were destroyed, or badly damaged. We could not get an agreed account of casualties from the 40 or 50 people standing around the damage. Some said as many as 30 died and many more were injured.

We visited a residential area where several homes were destroyed on February 7. Six persons in one family were killed in an expensive home and several others in adjacent properties. One 500 lb. bomb had failed to explode and the tail was seen above the thick concrete roof when a member of our team first drove by. When we returned, the bomb had been removed. Our camera team visited the hospital where the injured were taken later that afternoon. The critically injured father from the home where the bomb failed to explode was there. This was one of four hospitals treating persons injured in bombings that we visited.

A bus station was hit by a bomb and the stained glass in a nearby mosque shattered. We were unable to learn if any one was killed though 40-50 people were at the station near midnight when we drove by on our arrival.

We saw five different damaged telephone exchanges while driving around Baghdad and many destroyed and damaged government and private buildings. Bridges in Baghdad were a frequent target though damage to them was minimal when we left. The bridges are not a legitimate military target. Even Defense Ministry buildings are occupied by non-combatants. The telephone exchanges run by civilians are overwhelmingly processing non-military calls. The military has the most extensive independent communications capacity in the country. These are not legitimate targets and the effort to bomb them necessarily takes civilian lives.

Damage in Basra appeared to be considerably more extensive than in Baghdad and the actual bombing there was much more intensive than at any time we were in Baghdad. There were civilian deaths every night we were in Baghdad.

Visits to the towns of Hilla, Najaf and Nasseriya by press corps representatives and our crew found civilian casualties in residential areas of each, damages to a medical clinic, 12 deaths in one family, and 46 deaths in one night of bombing in one town. A small town was bombed a few minutes before we passed through on our drive back from Basra. We saw no military presence there. Smoke could be seen from three fires.

Over the 2,000 miles of highways, roads and streets we traveled, we saw scores, probably several hundred, destroyed vehicles. There were oil tank trucks, tractor trailers, lorries, pickup trucks, a public bus, a mini-bus, a taxicab and many private cars destroyed by aerial bombardment and strafing. Some were damaged when they ran into bomb craters in the highways or road damage caused by bombs and strafing. We found no evidence of military equipment or supplies in the vehicles. Along the roads we saw several oil refinery fires and numerous gasoline stations destroyed. One road repair camp had been bombed on the road to Amman.

As with the city streets in residential, industrial and commercial areas where we witnessed damage, we did not see a single damaged or destroyed military vehicle, tank, armored car, personnel carrier or other military equipment, or evidence of any having been removed. We saw scores of oil tank cars driving between Iraq and Jordan and parked in Jordan, as well as five or six that were destroyed by planes on the highway. We saw no evidence of any arms or military materiel on or around the destroyed and burned out tank trucks, or those not hit.

No one in the press corps or among the civilians we encountered reported to us that they had seen any evidence of the presence of military vehicles having been hit on the highways or having been in the vicinity of civilian property, or private vehicles hit before, during or after an aerial strike. We saw no evidence of any military presence in the areas of damage described in this letter.

It is preposterous to claim military equipment is being placed in residential areas to escape attack. Residential areas are regularly attacked. The claim reveals a policy of striking residential areas, because it purports to establish a justification for doing so. If there had been military vehicles in the civilian areas we examined, or on the roads and highways we traveled when bombing occurred, it is inconceivable that among all that debris we would not find some fragments of military vehicles, material, equipment or clothing. Not only did pinpoint precision fail to hit military targets in civilian areas, they were not collaterally damaged in the attacks on civilian life. Had they been present they would have been hit.

The government of Iraq has vastly understated civilian casualties in Iraq. This is not an uncommon phenomenon for governments in wartime.

The inescapable and tragic fact is thousands of civilians have been killed in the bombings. The bombings are conducted with this knowledge.

Dr. Noore, with more than four decades in medical service and ten years as head of Red Crescent, estimates 6,000 to 7,000 civilians deaths, and many thousands of injuries from bombings. Red Crescent vehicles transport medicine and medical supplies into Iraq from Jordan and Iran. They make deliveries as often as two to three times a week to some cities and hospitals but regularly to hospitals throughout the country. These contacts and hospital requests for medicines and supplies along with the relationships established over the years provide a solid base for his opinion.

He adds to the toll thousands of deaths from failure to obtain adequate supplies of infant formula and medicine, from contaminated water and from increased death rates from stress, heart attacks and similar causes.

While I applaud your recent initiative in designating a U.N. mission to Baghdad to carry medical supplies and ascertain the health needs of the Iraqi people, I urge you to seek major funding now or release of Iraqi funds for supplying 2,500 tons of infant and baby milk formula, greatly needed medicines and sanitation supplies, municipal water system restoration and water purification.

The bombing constitutes the most grievous violation of international law. It is intended to destroy the civilian life and economy of Iraq. It is not necessary, meaningful or permissible as a means of driving Iraq from Kuwait.

No UN resolution authorizes any military assault on Iraq, except as is necessary to drive Iraqi forces from Kuwait. The bombing that has occurred throughout Iraq is the clearest violation of international law and norms for armed conflict, including the Hague and Geneva Conventions and the Nuremberg Charter. It is uncivilized, brutal and racist by any moral standard. With few if any exceptions we witnessed, the destruction is not conceivably within the language or contemplation of Security Council Resolution 678/44.

I urge you to immediately notify the Member States of the General Assembly and the Security Council of the information herein provided. I urge you to ask for the creation of an investigative body to examine the effect of U.S. bombing of Iraq on the civilian life of the country. Most urgent, I ask you to do everything within your power to stop the bombing of cities, civilian population, public utilities, public highways, bridges and all other civilian areas and facilities in Iraq, and elsewhere. If there is no cease fire, bombing must be limited to military targets in Kuwait, concentrations of military forces in Iraq near the border of Kuwait, operational military air fields or identified Scud launching sites or mobile missile launchers in Iraq. If a cease fire is not achieved, the immediate cessation of this lawless bombing of civilian and non combatants is essential.

The use of highly sophisticated military technology with mass destructive capacity by rich nations against an essentially defenseless civilian population of a poor nation is one of the great tragedies of our time. United States annual military expenditures alone are four times the gross national product of Iraq. The scourge of war will never end if the United Nations tolerates this assault on life. The United Nations must not be an accessory to war crimes.

We have 6-7 hours of video tape of much of the damage to civilian life and property described above. It includes painful hospital interviews with children, women and men injured in these assaults. The tape was not reviewed or in any way examined by anyone in Iraq before we left, and the actual filming was largely unobserved by any Iraqi official. This footage is being edited. I will send you a copy as soon as it is ready within the next few days. If you wish to have the entire tapes reviewed, let me know and I will arrange a screening.

Copies of this letter are being sent to President Bush and President Hussein and the United Nations Ambassadors for the United States and Iraq.

Sincerely,

Ramsey Clark

[Text of Ramsey Clark's letter to Sen. Claiborne Pell, Chair, Senate Committee on Foreign Relations, on the fair application of international law and accusation of war crimes.]

April 13, 1991

Sen. Claiborne Pell
Committee on Foreign Relations
United States Senate
Suite SD-419
Dirksen Building
Washington, D.C.

Dear Senator Pell:

In its consideration of legislation concerning war crimes committed in the Persian Gulf conflict, the Committee on Foreign Relations must address the conduct of all the parties. Two important principles dictate this.

The first duty of every nation is accountability for its own conduct. Each nation and its citizens as well have the duty of insuring their own compliance with international law. Before you can credibly judge others, you must judge yourself by the same standard. Otherwise your foreign relations are based on power, not principle.

Second, nothing is more fundamental to the idea of government embodied in our Constitution than equal justice under law. Nothing is more corrupting of law than "victor's justice," an oxymoron. No nation, no person, is above the law.

The United States is primarily responsible for the systematic destruction of civilian water systems, power generation plants, telephone communications equipment, fuel oil pumping, refining, storage and distribution facilities, irrigation works, food production, storage and distribution centers, foodstuffs and residential, commercial and business structures. At least 25,000 civilians died from the bombings and many thousands more from its consequences, including deaths from polluted drinking water, lack of health care capacity and shortages of medicines. Commission staff members presently in Iraq have sent an alarming report of medical opinion that typhus, hepatitis, cholera and other illnesses that are a consequence of the destruction will rise sharply with the summer months. Of course, these casualties involve all the people of Iraq, Shiite and Sunni Moslems, Kurds, Chaldeans and others.

U.S. aircraft made civilians the object of attack, bombed indiscriminately, deliberately destroyed facilities and objects indispensable to the survival of the civilian population, failed to take precautions to spare the civilian population, used prohibited weapons and caused excessive and unnecessary suffering. The very ratio of more than 100,000 Iraqi military deaths to fewer than 200 U.S. military deaths evidences the excessive use of force by the U.S. against Iraq's army.

Among others, the conduct described violates provisions of the Hague Conventions of 1907, the Geneva Conventions of 1949 and Articles 51-57 of Protocol I, Additional to the Geneva Conventions of 1977, the Nuremberg Charter of 1945, and the several U.S. military service manuals addressing the laws of armed conflict.

Your Committee will fail in its duty to the American people if it does not hear independent evidence on issues of crimes against peace and war crimes committed by the Unites States and require executive branch witnesses to testify about U.S. military actions, including bombing targets.

The Commission of Inquiry for the International War Crimes Tribunal which is conducting its independent investigation requests the opportunity to present evidence in public hearings. I am available for discussion, testimony or other assistance.

I am enclosing a copy of a letter I sent to UN Secretary-General Javier Perez de Quellar and President Bush, dated February 12, 1991, after my visit to Iraq during the bombing and an announcement of the formation of a Commission of Inquiry for the International War Crimes Tribunal.

Sincerely,

Ramsey Clark

[It is important to remember while reading this report that Article 54 of Protocol 1 Additional to the Geneva Conventions, 1977 prohibits using civilians as a method of war or an object of war. So, too, is the destruction of the life sustaining infrastructure such as electricity, water, and sewer facilities a violation of the Geneva Conventions. The UN Genocide Convention makes clear that "Genocide means . . . deliberately inflicting on the group conditions of life calculated to bring about its physical destruction in whole or in part."]

Report to the Secretary-General on Humanitarian Needs in Kuwait and Iraq in the Immediate Post-Crisis Environment by a Mission to the Area Led by Mr. Martti Ahtisaari, Under-Secretary-General for Administration and Management

Introduction

1. You asked me to travel, as a matter of urgency, to Kuwait and Iraq to assess humanitarian needs there in the immediate post-crisis environment, and to bring with me a team comprising representatives of the appropriate United Nations agencies and programmes. Your decision was announced in a press statement of 1 March 1991. . . . I departed from New York on 7 March. The mission assembled at Geneva the following day. It comprised representatives not only of the Secretariat, but also of the United Nations Children's Fund (UNICEF), the United Nations Development Programme (UNDP), the Office of the United Nations Disaster Relief Coordinator (UNDRO), the Office of United Nations High Commissioner for Refugees (UNHCR), the Food and Agriculture Organization of the United Nations (FAO), and the World Health Organization (WHO). On my way to the Middle East, I consulted at Geneva with Mr. Claudio Caratsch, Vice-President of the International Committee of the Red Cross (ICRC). The mission travelled to Amman on 9 March and arrived at Baghdad on 10 March. At Amman, I was received by His Highness Crown Prince Hassan and by His Excellency Mr. Taher Al-Masri, Foreign Minister of Jordan. The mission remained in Iraq until 17 March. On that date I travelled to Bahrain while awaiting the outcome of consultations in New York and your further instructions. In Bahrain I met with the Foreign Minister, His Excellency Mr. Sheikh Mohamed bin Mubarak Al Khalifa. On 19 March you instructed me to return to New York. Leaving the remainder of the mission in Bahrain whilst awaiting the decision of the Kuwaiti Government, I departed that day and arrived in New York on 20 March. The Kuwaiti authorities have

now informed you that the mission is expected to depart Bahrain for Kuwait on or about 22 March.

I. Modus Operandi in Iraq

5. The mission began its work immediately upon arrival at Baghdad on 10 March, first linking up with the local UNDP and UNICEF representatives, and, later that day, meeting with His Excellency Mr. Mohamed Sa'eed al-Sahaf, minister of State for Foreign Affairs, and senior officials of the relevant government departments and of local authorities. . . . Field work was undertaken from 11 to 16 March at various locations in and around Baghdad. A longer field trip was made by a group from the mission, led by myself, to Mosul, 400 kilometres north-west of Baghdad, and I myself also inspected numerous locations in Greater Baghdad. . . .

6. The Iraqi authorities were fully cooperative in regard to the activities of the five specialist groups. These dealt with: food and agriculture; water, sanitation and health; transportation and communications; energy; and refugees and other vulnerable groups. Members were able to inspect all locations and facilities that they had requested to see in the Baghdad area and in several other governorates, and could also engage in independent field research in wholesale and retail markets and undertake household surveys. However, the Government was unable to accept to my request that we visit Souera, Moussayeb, Basra, Nasiriyah, and Kirkuk. In respect of some, the problems were said to be logistical; in regard to others, concern for security was conveyed. I expressed regret at our inability to cover the whole country, because it was important that the United Nations should be able to assess the humanitarian needs of the entire population of Iraq in all regions. The authorities also expressed their regret on this subject,and we agreed that locally based United Nations staff would travel to these areas as soon as conditions permitted. It has, however, been possible to infer from information available from various other sources that needs are unlikely to vary greatly from what we ourselves observed, but it is reported that conditions may be substantially worse in certain locations.

II. Summary of Findings and Recommendations in Regard to Iraq

A. General Remarks

8. I and the members of my mission were fully conversant with media reports regarding the situation in Iraq and, of course, with the recent WHO/UNICEF report on water, sanitary and health conditions in Greater Baghdad. It should be said at once, however, that nothing that we had seen

or read had quite prepared us for the particular form of devastation which has now befallen the country. The recent conflict has wrought near-apocalyptic results upon the economic infrastructure of what had been, until January 1991, a rather highly urbanized and mechanized society. Now most means of modern life support have been destroyed or rendered tenuous. Iraq has, for some time to come, been relegated to a pre-industrial age, but with all the disabilities of post-industrial dependency on an intensive use of energy and technology. . . .

9. My mandate was limited to assessing the need for urgent humanitarian assistance. It did not extend to the huge task of assessing the requirements for reconstructing Iraq's destroyed infrastructure, much less, to developmental matters. . . . Underlying each analysis [of urgent humanitarian needs] is the inexorable reality that, as a result of war, virtually all previously viable sources of fuel and power (apart from a limited number of mobile generators) and modern means of communication are now essentially defunct. The far-reaching implications of this energy and communications vacuum as regards urgent humanitarian support are of crucial significance for the nature and effectiveness of the international response.

10. These conditions, together with recent civil unrest in some parts of the country, mean that the authorities are as yet scarcely able even to measure the dimensions of the calamity, much less respond to its consequences, because they cannot obtain full and accurate data. Additionally, there is much less than the minimum fuel required to provide the energy needed for movement or transportation, irrigation, or generators for power to pump water and sewage. For instance, emergency medical supplies can be moved to health centers only with extreme difficulty and, usually, major delay. Information regarding local needs is slow and sparse. Most employees are simply unable to come to work. Both the authorities and the trade unions estimate that approximately 90 percent of industrial workers have been reduced to inactivity and will be deprived of incomes as of the end of March. Government departments have at present only marginal attendance. Prior to recent events, Iraq was importing about 70 per cent of its food needs. Now, owing to the fuel shortage, the inability to import and the virtual breakdown of the distribution system, the flow of food through the private sector has been reduced to a trickle with costs accelerating upwards. Many food prices are already beyond the purchasing reach of most Iraqi families. Agricultural production is highly mechanized, and much land depends upon pumped-water irrigation. Should the main harvest in June 1991 be seriously affected by a lack of energy to drive machines and pump water, then an already grave situation will be further aggravated. As shown below, prospects for the 1992 harvest could, for combined reasons be in at least as much jeopardy. Having regard to the nature of Iraq's society and economy, the energy vacuum is an omnipresent obstacle to the success of even a short-

term, massive effort to maintain life-sustaining conditions in each area of humanitarian needs.

B. Food and Agriculture

11. . . . Sanctions decided upon by the Security Council had already adversely affected the country's ability to feed its people. New measures relating to the rationing and enhanced production were introduced in September 1990. These were, however, in turn, negatively affected by the hostilities which impacted upon most areas of agriculture production and distribution.

12. Food is currently made available to the population both through government allocation and rations and through the market. The Ministry of Trade's monthly allocation to the population of staple food items fell from 343,000 tons in September 1990 to 182,000 tons, when rationing was introduced, and was further reduced to 135,000 tons in January 1991 (39 percent of the pre-sanctions level). While the mission was unable to gauge the precise quantities still held in government warehouses, all evidence indicates that flour is now at a critically low level, and that supplies of sugar, rice, tea, vegetable oil, powdered milk and pulses are currently at critically low levels or have been exhausted. Distribution of powdered milk, for instance, is now reserved exclusively for sick children on medical prescription.

13. Livestock farming has been seriously affected by sanctions because many feed products were imported. The sole laboratory producing veterinary vaccines was destroyed during the conflict as inspected by the mission. The authorities are no longer able to support livestock farmers in the combat of disease, as all stocks of vaccines were stated to have been destroyed in the same sequence of bombardments on this center which was an FAO regional project.

14. The country has had a particular dependence upon foreign vegetable seeds, and the mission was able to inspect destroyed seed warehouses. The relevant agricultural authorities informed the mission that all stocks of potatoes and vegetable seeds have been exhausted. Next season's planting will be jeopardized if seeds are not provided before October 1991.

15. This year's grain harvest in June is seriously compromised for a number of reasons, including failure to irrigation/drainage (no power for pumps, lack of spare parts); lack of pesticides and fertilizers (previously imported); and lack of fuel and spare parts for the highly-mechanized and duel-dependent harvesting machines. Should this harvest fail, or be far below average, as is very likely barring a radical change in the situation, widespread starvation conditions become a real possibility.

16. The official programme for the support of socially dependent groups

of the populations (the elderly, disabled, mothers and children, hospital patients, orphans, refugees, etc.) is affected by the overall grave deficiencies in the food situations.

17. . . . The government-initiated rationing system was designed to provide families with a fraction of their basic necessities at prices comparable to those prevailing before August. The system allows families either 5 kilograms per person, per month, of flour or 3 loaves of baked bread; 10 kilograms per family per month, of liquid cooking gas; 1 bar of soap per person, per month, etc. However, independent surveys conducted by the mission in several diverse areas of Baghdad showed that many families cannot draw their full rations, since the distribution centers are often depleted and they have great difficulty in traveling to other centres. The quality of food distributed has itself deteriorated to the point of causing health problems. Most families also reported that they could not meet their needs through the private markets. Despite official price controls . . . the price of most basic necessities has increased 1,000 percent or more. . . . In contrast to this hyper-inflation, many incomes have collapsed. Many employees cannot draw salaries, the banking system has in large measure closed down and withdrawals are limited to 100 dinars per month. . . . In short, most families lack access to adequate rations or the purchasing power to meet normal minimal standards.

18. The mission recommends that . . . sanctions in respect to food supplies should be immediately removed, as should those relating to the import of agricultural equipment and supplies. The urgent supply of basic commodities to safeguard vulnerable groups is strongly recommended, and the provision of major quantities of the following staples for the general population: milk, wheat flour, rice, sugar, vegetable oil and tea. . . . These are required to meet minimum general requirements until the next harvest. Safeguarding the harvest means the urgent importation of fertilizers, pesticides, spare parts, veterinary drugs, agricultural machinery and equipment, etc. . . .

19. The mission observes that, without a restoration of energy supplies to the agricultural production and distribution sectors, implementation of many of the above recommendations would be to little effect. Drastic international measures across the whole agricultural spectrum are most urgent.

C. Water, Sanitation and Health

20. As regards water, prior to the crisis Baghdad received about 450 litres per person supplied by seven treatment stations purifying water from the Tigris river. The rest of the country had about 200-250 litres per person per day, purified and supplied by 238 central water-treatment stations and

1,134 smaller water projects. All stations operated on electric power; about 75 per cent had standby diesel-powered generators. Sewage was treated to an acceptable standard before being returned to the rivers.

21. With the destruction of power plants, oil refineries, main oil storage facilities and water-related chemical plants, all electrically operated installations have ceased to function. Diesel-operated generators were reduced to operating on a limited basis, their functioning affected by lack of fuel, lack of maintenance, lack of spare parts and non-attendance of workers. The supply of water in Baghdad dropped to less than 10 litres per day but has now recovered to approximately 30-40 liters in about 70 percent of the area (less than 10 percent of the overall previous use). Standby generating capacity is out of order in several pumping stations and cessation of supplies will therefore ensue if current machinery goes out of order for any reason (spare parts are not available owing to sanctions). As regards the quality of water in Baghdad, untreated sewage has now to be dumped directly into the river—which is the source of the water supply—and all drinking water plants there and throughout the rest of the country are using river water with high sewage contamination. . . . Chemical tests are now being conducted at the stations but no bacteriological testing and control is possible because of the lack of electricity necessary for the functioning of laboratories, the shortage of necessary chemicals and reagents and the lack of fuel for the collection of samples. No chlorine tests are being conducted because of the lack of fuel for sampling. While the water authority has warned that water must be boiled, there is little fuel to do this, and what exists is diminishing. Cool winter conditions have prevailed until recently.

22. Only limited information is available to authorities regarding the situation in the remainder of the country because all modern communications systems have been destroyed and information is now transmitted and received by person-to-person contact. In those areas where there are no generators, or generators have broken down, or the fuel supply is exhausted, the population draws its water directly from polluted rivers and trenches. This is widely apparent in rural areas, where women and children can be seen washing and filling water receptacles. The quantity and quality of water produced by treatment centres is very variable and in many locations there are no chemicals available for purification. No quality control—chlorine testing, chemical testing or bacteriological testing—is conducted.

23. . . . Another major problem, now imminent, is the climate. Iraq has long and extremely hot summers, the temperature often reaching 50 degrees Celsius. This has two main implications: (a) the quantity of water must be increased and a minimum target of 50 liters per person per day has to be attained . . . and (b) the heat will accelerate the incubation of bacteria and thus the health risks ascribable to the water quality (already

at an unacceptable level) will be further exacerbated— especially viewed in the overall sanitary circumstances which have already led to a fourfold increase in diarrheal disease incidence among children under five years of age, and the impact of this on their precarious nutritional status.

24. As regards sanitation, the two main concerns relate to garbage disposal and sewage treatment. In both cases, rapidly rising temperatures will soon accentuate an existing crisis. Heaps of garbage are spread in the urban areas and collection is poor to non-existent. The work of collection vehicles is hampered by lack of fuel, lack of maintenance and spare parts, and lack of labor, because workers are unable to come to work. Incinerators are, in general, not working for these same reasons and for lack of electric power. Insecticides, much needed as the weather becomes more torrid, are virtually out of stock because of sanctions and a lack of chemical supplies. As previously stated, Iraqi rivers are heavily polluted by raw sewage, and water levels are unusually low. All sewage treatment and pumping plants have been brought to a virtual standstill by the lack of power supply and the lack of spare parts. Pools of sewage lie in the streets and villages. Health hazards will build in the weeks to come.

25. As regards health conditions, the mission reviewed the situation since the special joint WHO-UNICEF mission in February 1991 . . . the mission also identified any further immediate health problems that needed to be addressed. . . . It also identified constraints that hamper the implementation of the already-agreed recommendations of the joint mission. It found that health conditions in Baghdad and throughout the country remain precarious. . . . A major factor is the water and sanitation situation described above. Additionally, the total lack of telephone communication and drastically reduced transport capability pose other problems to the health system since basic information on communicable diseases cannot be collected and disseminated, and essential drugs, vaccines and medical supplies cannot be distributed efficiently. . . .

26. . . . The fourfold increase in incidence of diarrhoeal diseases amongst young children reported by the WHO/UNICEF mission has been reconfirmed by findings recently obtained in 11 sentinel sites in Baghdad. The water and sanitation situation contributes to this problem which must be expected to increase as the summer approaches. The mission concluded that a catastrophe could be faced at any time if conditions do not change. . . .

D. Refugees and Other Vulnerable Groups

28. Conditions described above affect the whole population of Iraq and, most especially, low-income groups. . . .

29. As regards the displaced and the homeless, the authorities themselves have not yet been able fully to assess the impact of the recent

hostilities. They have, however, calculated that approximately 9,000 homes were destroyed or damaged beyond repair during the hostilities, of which 2,500 were in Baghdad and 1,900 were in Basra. This has created a new homeless potential total of 72,000 persons. Official help is now hampered by the conditions described throughout this report and, especially, a virtual halt in the production of local building materials and the impossibility to import. The input of essential materials should be permitted.

E. Logistics, Transportation, Communications and Energy

33. . . . At present, Iraq's sole available surface transport link with the outside world is via Amman to Aqaba. (It has been reported that a bridge has recently been destroyed on the Iskenderun/Merian road to Iraq from Turkey, and the ports of Basrah and Umm Qasr are currently out of use, nor has there for some years been any direct cargo traffic to Iraq vis the Syrian Arab Republic.) Internal transportation by road is now severely affected by a lack of spare parts and tyres and, above all, by a lack of fuel. Some internal railway capability still exists on the Baghdad-Mosul line. The mission was informed that a total of 83 road bridges had been destroyed and a number were inspected.

34. As regards communications, the mission was informed that all internal and external telephone systems had been destroyed, with the exception of a limited local exchange in one town. It had the opportunity to inspect a number of war-damaged or destroyed facilities and experiences for itself the situation in the Greater Baghdad and other urban areas. Communication in Iraq is now on a person-to-person basis, as mail services have also disintegrated.

35. The role of energy in Iraq is especially important because of the level of its urbanization (approximately 72 per cent of the population lives in towns), its industrialization, and its prolonged, very hot, summers. Pre-war energy consumption consisted of oil and refined products (85 per cent), electricity (14.8 per cent) and other sources (0.2 per cent). About 30 per cent of electric power generation was hydro-power. Bombardment has paralyzed oil and electricity sectors almost entirely. Power output and refineries' production is negligible and will not be resumed until the first repair phase is complete. The limited and sporadic power supply in some residential areas and for health facilities is provided by mobile generators. There have, officially, been virtually no sales of gasoline to private users since February. . . . Minimal survival level to undertake humanitarian activities would require approximately 25 percent of pre-war civilian domestic fuel consumption. Its absence, given the proximate onset of hot weather conditions, may have calamitous consequences for food, water supply and for sanitation, and therefore for health conditions. It seems

inescapable that these fuel imports must take place urgently, and units and spare parts will also be required to enable Iraq to meet its own humanitarian needs as soon as possible. . . .

F. Observations

37. The account given above describes as accurately as the mission has been able, using all sources, including much independent observation, to ascertain the situation, which, within the time available and the travel limitations referred to earlier, was perceived to exist in regard to urgent humanitarian needs in Iraq during the week of 10-17 March. . . . It will be difficult, if not impossible, to remedy these immediate humanitarian needs without dealing with the underlying need for energy, on an equally urgent basis. The need for energy means, initially, emergency oil imports and the rapid patching up of a limited refining and electricity production capacity, with essential supplies from other countries. Otherwise, food that is imported cannot be preserved and distributed; water cannot be purified; sewage cannot be pumped away and cleansed; crops cannot be irrigated; medications cannot be conveyed where they are required; needs cannot even be effectively assessed. It is unmistakable that the Iraqi people may soon face a famine, if massive aid life-supporting needs are not rapidly met. Time is short.

H. Res. 86

Impeaching George Herbert Walker Bush, President of the United Sates, of high crimes and misdemeanors.

In the House of Representatives February 21, 1991

Mr. Henry B. Gonzalez (D.-Tex.) submitted the following resolution; which was referred to the Committee on the Judiciary

Resolution

Impeaching George Herbert Walker Bush, President of the United States, for high crimes and misdemeanors.

Resolved, That George Herbert Walker Bush, President of the United States is impeached for high crimes and misdemeanors, and that the following articles of impeachment be exhibited to the Senate:

Articles of impeachment exhibited by the House of Representatives of the United States of America in the name of itself and of all of the people of the United States of America, against George Herbert Walker Bush, President of the United States of America, in maintenance and support of its impeachment against him for high crimes and misdemeanors.

Article I

In the conduct of the office of President of the United States, George Herbert Walker Bush, in violation of his constitutional oath faithfully to execute the office of President of the United States and, to the best of his ability, preserve, protect, and defend the Constitution of the United States, and in violation of his constitutional duty to take care that the laws be faithfully executed, has violated the equal protection clause of the Constitution. U.S. soldiers in the Middle East are overwhelmingly poor white, black, and Mexican-American, and their military service is based on the coercion of a system that has denied viable economic opportunities to these classes of citizens. Under the Constitution, all classes of citizens are guaranteed equal protection, and calling on the poor and minorities to fight a war for oil to preserve the life-styles of the wealthy is a denial of the rights of these soldiers. In all of this, George Herbert Walker Bush has acted in a manner contrary to his trust as President and subversive of constitutional government, to the great prejudice of the cause of law and justice and to the manifest injury of the people of the United States.

Wherefore George Herbert Walker Bush, by such conduct, warrants impeachment and trial, and removal from office.

Article II

In the conduct of the office of President of the United States, George Herbert Walker Bush, in violation of his constitutional oath faithfully to execute the office of President of the United States and, to the best of his ability, preserve, protect, and defend the Constitution of the United States, and in violation of this constitutional duty to take care that the laws be faithfully execute, has violated the U.S. Constitution, federal law and the United Nations Charter by bribing, intimidating and threatening others including the members of the United Nations Security Council, to support belligerent acts against Iraq. In all of this George Herbert Walker Bush has acted in a manner contrary to his trust as President and subversive of constitutional government, to the great prejudice of the cause of law and justice and to the manifest injury of the people of the United States.

Wherefore George Herbert Walker Bush, by such conduct, warrants impeachment and trial, and removal from office.

Article III

In the conduct of the office of President of the United States, George Herbert Walker Bush, in violation of his constitutional oath faithfully to execute the office of President of the United States and, to the best of his ability, preserve, protect, and defend the Constitution of the United States, and in violation of this constitutional duty to take care that the laws be faithfully executed, has prepared, planned, and conspired to engage in a massive war against Iraq employing methods of mass destruction that will result in the killing of tens of thousands of civilians, many of whom will be children. This planning includes the placement and potential use of nuclear weapons, and the use of such indiscriminate weapons and massive killings by serial bombardment, or otherwise, of civilians violates the Hague Conventions of 1907 and 1923, the Geneva Conventions of 1949 and Protocol I thereto, the Nuremberg Charter, the Genocide Convention and the United Nations Declaration of Human Rights. In all of this George Bush has acted in a manner contrary to his trust as President and subversive of constitutional government, to the great prejudice of the cause of law and justice and to the manifest injury of the people of the United States.

Wherefore George Herbert Walker Bush, by such conduct, warrants impeachment and trial, and removal from office.

Article IV

In the conduct of the office of President of the United States, George Herbert Walker Bush, in violation of his constitutional oath faithfully to execute the office of President of the United States and, to the best of his ability, preserve, protect, and defend the Constitution of the United States, and in violation of his constitutional duty to take care that the laws be faithfully executed, has committed the United States to acts of war without congressional consent and contrary to the United Nations Charter and international law. From August 1990 through January 1991, the President embarked on a course of action that systematically eliminated every option for peaceful resolution of the Persian Gulf crisis. Once the President approached Congress for a declaration of war, 500,000 American soldiers' lives were in jeopardy—rendering any substantive debate by Congress meaningless. The President has not received a declaration of war by Congress, and in contravention of the written word, the spirit, and the intent of the United States Constitution has declared that he will go to war regardless of the views of Congress and the American people. In failing to seek a declaration of war, and in declaring his intent to violate the Constitution in disregarding the acts of Congress—including the War Powers Resolution—George Herbert Walker Bush has acted in a manner contrary to his trust as President and subversive of constitutional government, to the great prejudice of the cause of law and justice and to the manifest injury of the people of the United States.

Wherefore George Herbert Walker Bush, by such conduct, warrants impeachment and trial, and removal from office.

Article V

In the conduct of the office of President of the United States, George Herbert Walker Bush, in violation of his constitutional oath faithfully to execute the office of President of the United States and, to the best of his ability, preserve, protect, and defend the Constitution of the United States, and in violation of this constitutional duty to take care that the laws be faithfully executed, has planned, prepared, and conspired to commit crimes against the peace by leading the United States into aggressive war against Iraq in violation of Article 2(4) of the United Nations Charter, the Nuremberg Charter, other international instruments and treaties, and the Constitution of the United States. In all of this George Herbert Walker Bush has acted in a manner contrary to his trust as President and subversive of constitutional government, to the great prejudice of the cause of law and justice and to the manifest injury of the people of the United States.

Wherefore George Herbert Walker Bush, by such conduct, warrants impeachment and trial, and removal from office.

H. Res. 180

Resolution to Lift Economic Embargo on Iraq

The following resolution (HR 180) was introduced in the House of Representatives on June 24, 1991, by Congressman Henry B. Gonzalez (D.-Texas).

Expressing the sense of the House of Representatives that the United States should act on an emergency basis to lift the economic embargo of Iraq.

A Resolution

Whereas reports from the United Nations, the Physicians for Human Rights, the International Red Cross, a Harvard study team, other independent organizations, and private U.S. citizens have documented the fact that unless the economic sanctions imposed against Iraq are immediately lifted and Iraq is allowed to buy and import food, medicine and equipment, especially for power generation, tens of thousands if not hundreds of thousands of Iraqi civilians will die in the upcoming months;

Whereas a Harvard study team estimates that at least 170,000 Iraqi children under the age of five will die within the next year from the delayed effects of the war in the Persian Gulf if the imposition of the sanctions continues;

Whereas this is a conservative estimate and does not include tens of thousands of Iraqi civilians above the age of five who are expected to die from similar causes;

Whereas the Catholic Relief Service estimates that more than 100,000 Iraqi children will die from malnutrition and disease in the upcoming months due to the economic embargo and destruction of the war, and the United Nations Children's Fund estimates that 80,000 Iraqi children may die from these causes;

Whereas malnutrition has become severe and widespread in Iraq since imposition of the embargo and the war due to severe food shortages and the inflation of food prices of up to 1000%, which has effectively priced many Iraqis, especially the poor and disadvantaged, out of the food market;

Whereas cholera, typhoid, and gastroenteritis have become epidemic throughout Iraq since the war due to the critical scarcity of medicine and the inability of Iraq to process sewage and purify the water supply;

Whereas the system of medical care has broken down in Iraq, resulting in the closure of up to 50% of Iraq's medical facilities due to acute shortages of medicines, equipment, and staff;

Whereas the incapacitation of 18 of Iraq's 20 power plants during the war is a principal cause of the deterioration in the public health due to the resultant inability of Iraq to process sewage, purify its water supply, and supply electricity to health facilities;

Whereas the health care crisis cannot be addressed without the reconstruction of electrical facilities that enable the purification of water and treatment of sewage;

Whereas before the economic embargo of Iraq, three quarters of the total caloric intake in Iraq was imported and, moreover, 96% of Iraqi revenue to pay for imports, namely food and medicine, was derived from the exportation of oil now prohibited under the embargo;

Whereas the onset of the summer heat in Iraq will both accelerate the spread of disease and impede its treatment due to the lack of refrigeration facilities even in hospitals;

Whereas the acute shortages in food in Iraq, the inflation of up to 1000% in food prices caused by these shortages, the critical scarcity of medicine, and the essential need to reconstruct Iraq's capacity to generate electricity to enable sewage treatment and water purification, cannot be addressed or rectified without Iraq's re-entry into global commerce, at present effectively prohibited by the economic sanctions;

Whereas the immediate lifting of the sanctions would drastically reduce the number of Iraqi children who will die in the upcoming months from malnutrition and disease and would relieve the suffering of the innocent Iraqi population which is now bearing the burden of the embargo; Now therefore, be it

RESOLVED by the House of Representatives, That the United States should act on an emergency basis to lift the economic embargo of Iraq to save innocent Iraqi civilians, especially children, from death by disease and starvation.

The April Glaspie Connection

In the weeks before the Iraqi invasion of Kuwait, a time when negotiations between Iraq and Kuwait over the control of Rumaila oil fields, repayment of Iraqi war-debt, the use of the disputed islands Bubiyan and Warba, and the Kuwaiti violation of OPEC oil production guidelines were breaking down, President Saddam Hussein summoned U.S. Ambassador to Iraq, April C. Glaspie, to his office for what seems to have been a desperate attempt to get a final clarification of the U.S. position with regard to Kuwait. In the morning of July 25, 1991, Glaspie went to the Iraqi Foreign Ministry in Baghdad to deliver a message from the U.S. State Department about planned U.S.-United Arab Emirate military refueling exercises in the Persian Gulf. She also passed on the remarks of State Department spokeswoman Margaret Tutweiler who on the preceding day had told reporters that "We do not have any defense treaties with Kuwait and there are no special defense or security commitments to Kuwait." A half-hour after Glaspie's visit, Hussein called her back for a personal interview.

The conversation between Hussein and Glaspie shows clearly that the U.S. government was aware of the seriousness of the failing negotiations between Iraq and Kuwait and it shows also that the U.S. did not make even the slightest effort to suggest to Hussein that a massive war with the U.S. might be the result of any invasion of Kuwait—a statement which almost certainly would have prevented the entire war. The controversy over Glaspie's role in the invasion of Kuwait centers on the conciliatory signals she gave to Hussein about the position of the U.S. government with regard to the defense of Kuwait and Iraq's demands and rapidly growing hostile attitude. The transcripts of this meeting were released by Iraq on September 11, 1990, and they show that Glaspie only reassured Hussein's tough stand against Kuwait. At the time, the State Department conceded that the transcripts were essentially correct, but later in March of 1991 Glaspie said that the transcripts had been heavily edited by Iraqi officials who deleted the portions of Glaspie's remarks which made clear to Hussein that the U.S. would vigorously oppose any military solution to the dispute between Iraq and Kuwait.

In testimony before the Senate Foreign Relations Committee on March 20, 1991, Glaspie said that she repeatedly warned Hussein that the U.S. would not tolerate the use of violence to settle the dispute with Kuwait. She remarked that Hussein must have been "too stupid" to understand how the U.S. would react. Before the Senate, she gave her testimony without swearing an oath to tell the truth. She told the Committee, "I told him orally we would defend our vital interests, we would support our friends in the Gulf, we would defend their sovereignty and integrity."[1] Her description of the conversation differed so markedly from the transcripts, that several senators asked her to provide them with her own cabled report to the State Department written just after the meeting. Glaspie refused to supply this report, saying that she would not encourage such a violation of the tradition of diplomatic confidentially.

In July of 1991, Glaspie's cables to the State Department describing the meeting were finally released to the Senate Committee (the text is printed below). The cables showed that her March testimony before the Senate was largely a fabrication and that the original transcript released by Iraq was, in fact, accurate. On July 12, 1991, Committee Chairman, Claiborne Pell wrote an angry letter to James Baker demanding an explanation for the inconsistencies between Glaspie's testimony and the cabled summary which she sent to the State Department on July 25, 1990, after her meeting with Hussein. Senator Alan Cranston (D.-CA) charged that Glaspie had deliberately misled Congress about her role in the Persian Gulf tragedy. Her cables also revealed that on July 28, 1990, President Bush sent a secret cable to Saddam Hussein regarding the meeting.[2]

The April Glaspie affair is only the most visible in a pattern of diplomatic signals being transmitted between Iraq and the United State during the year leading up to the massive destruction of Iraq. These diplomatic connections are troubling because they show clearly that the U.S. was well aware of the increasing tension between Iraq and Kuwait, and they show just as clearly that the U.S. went out of its way to assure Saddam Hussein that it had no position on the mounting hostilities, that Arab nations were at liberty to resolve their disputes among themselves without U.S. interference. This was at precisely the time that Hussein was trying to suggest to the U.S. that in all probability his troops would invade Kuwait in the very near future. The U.S. was aware that Iraqi troops were massing on the border but the U.S. never warned Iraq or even suggested that the UN warn Iraq. Thus the invasion was not a surprise to top U.S. officials; rather they cultivated an attitude of complete indifference to the growing crisis—at least as far as they permitted Iraq to see of their actions and commitments. (It is well to recall that the U.S. Army under General Norman Schwarzkopf had been developing simulations of a war between Iraq and the U.S. for more than a year and that the U.S. government had been secretly encouraging Kuwait not to settle its disputes with Iraq.) The news briefing at which Tutweiler told reporters emphatically that the U.S. had no defense commitments to Kuwait was preceded by a visit of four Senators to Iraq. The Senators assured Hussein that the U.S. government supported him and that his only problem was with the U.S. press—which

Alan Simpson (R.-WY) called spoiled and conceited bastards who don't know
how to see things for themselves.[3]

On July 31, 1990, Assistant Secretary of State for Near Eastern and
South Asian Affairs John H. Kelly had the following dialog on the floor
of Congress with Lee Hamilton:

> *Hamilton:* Do we have a commitment to our friends in the Gulf in
> the event that they are engaged in oil or territorial disputes with their
> neighbors?
>
> *Kelly:* As I said, Mr. Chairman, we have no defense treaty relationships
> with any of the countries. We have historically avoided taking a
> position on border disputes or on internal OPEC deliberations, but
> we certainly, as have all administrations, resoundingly called for the
> peaceful settlement of disputes and differences in the area.
>
> *Hamilton:* If Iraq, for example, charged across the border into Kuwait,
> for whatever reason, what would be our position with regard to the
> use of U.S. forces?
>
> *Kelly:* That, Mr. Chairman, is a hypothetical or a contingency, the
> kind of which I can't get into. Suffice it to say, we would be extremely
> concerned, but I cannot get into the realm of 'what if' answers.
>
> *Hamilton:* In that circumstance, it is correct to say, however, that
> we do not have a treaty commitment which would obligate us to
> engage U.S. forces?
>
> *Kelly:* That is correct.[4]

Kelly's remarks were delivered as Iraqi leaders desperately searched every
clue for the U.S. position. Iraq's disputes with Kuwait were real and long-
standing. Most historians believe that the recent war must be traced back
to the British High Commissioner Sir Percy Cox who drew the boundary
between the two nations in such a way that the much larger Iraq would
have a coastline of only thirty miles while the tiny Kuwait would have
about three hundred and ten. To make matters worse, Iraqi access to the
Gulf was blocked by the Kuwaiti islands of Bubiyan and Warba. The border
between the two nations had never been agreed upon, but at least most
observers agreed that the Rumaila oil field was on Iraqi soil. Thus when
Kuwait began to pump and sell oil from this field, it used slant drilling
techniques so that oil could be extracted from the Kuwaiti side. Hussein
charged Kuwait with stealing Iraqi oil and then using that oil to depress
world oil prices. Iraq suffered twice from the theft of its oil. Hussein charged
that Iraq was losing about $14 billion a year because of Kuwait's over-
production and dumping. Iraq's desperate economic condition following
the eight-year war with Iran meant that it could not tolerate for very long
the economic aggression of Kuwait. On August 7, 1988, just two weeks
after the end of the Iran-Iraq war, Hussein sent his Minister of the Interior,
Samir Abdul Wahhab, to Kuwait to begin discussions aimed at resolving

the problems of the border, the islands, oil production, and debt repayment. He met with complete intransigence on Kuwait's part.

For two years, Kuwait quite inexplicably refused to negotiate on any of the issues which Hussein felt were destroying Iraq's economy. Kuwait had done nothing to develop the islands of Bubiyan and Warba, while Iraq had spent about a billion dollars to develop the ports of Umm Qasr and Khor Zubair, just across from the islands.[5] The U.S. diplomatic record shows a vigorus effort to exacerbate the problems by encouraging the intransigence of both sides. There is no record of the U.S. using its position or that of the UN to seek an accord between Iraq and Kuwait. Instead, as Glaspie's meeting with Hussein shows, the U.S. went out of its way to assure Iraq that it sought only better relations with Iraq. The criminal part of this assurance is that at the same time it was bolstering Kuwaiti hostilities; in short, forcing the day when Iraq would have to take matters beyond diplomacy to violence. Glaspie's focus on Saddam's phone call and the "nothing will happen" promise makes one wonder what she expected to happen when the Kuwaities backed out of the negotiations.

Text of April Glaspie's Cable to the U.S. State Department

Summary

Saddam told the ambassador July 25, 1990 that Egyptian President Hosni Mubarak has arranged for Kuwaiti and Iraqi delegations to meet in Riyadh, and then on July 28, 29 or 30, the Kuwaiti Crown Prince will come to Baghdad for serious negotiations. "Nothing will happen" before then, Saddam had promised Mubarak.

Saddam wished to convey an important message to President Bush: Iraq wants friendship, but does the U.S. Government? Iraq suffered 100,000's of casualties and is now so poor that war orphan pensions will soon be cut, yet rich Kuwait will not even accept OPEC discipline. Iraq is sick of war, but Kuwait has ignored diplomacy. U.S. maneuvers with the United Arab Emirates (U.A.E.) will encourage the U.A.E. and Kuwait to ignore conventional diplomacy. If Iraq is publicly humiliated by the U.S. Government, it will have no choice but to "respond," however illogical and self-destructive that would prove.

Excerpts from the Meeting

Ambassador was summoned by President Saddam Hussein at noon July 25, 1990. Also present were Fonmin Aziz, the President's office director, two note takers and the Iraqi interpreter. Saddam, whose manner was cordial, reasonable and even warm throughout the ensuing two hours, said he wished the Ambassador to convey a message to President Bush.

Picking his words with care, Saddam said that there are "some circles" in the U.S.G., including in the C.I.A. and the State Department, but emphatically excluding the President and Secretary Baker, who are not friendly toward Iraq-U.S. relations. He then listed what he seemed to regard as facts to support this conclusion: "Some circles are gathering information on who might be Saddam Hussein's successor"; they kept up contacts in the Gulf warning against Iraq; they worked to insure no help would go to Iraq from the Export-Import Bank and Commodity Credit Corporation.

Iraq, the President stressed, is in serious financial difficulties, with $40 billion debts. Iraq, whose victory in the war against Iran made an historic difference to the Arab world and the West, needs a Marshall plan. But "you want the oil price down," Saddam charged.

Resuming his list of grievances which he believed were all inspired by "some circles" in the U.S.G., he recalled the "U.S.I.A. campaign" against himself, and the general media assault on Iraq and its President.

Despite all these blows, Saddam said, and although "we were somewhat annoyed," we still hoped that we could develop a good relationship. But those who force oil prices down are engaging in economic warfare and Iraq cannot accept such a trespass on its dignity and prosperity.

The spearheads for the United States government have been Kuwait and the U.A.E., Saddam said. Saddam said carefully that just as Iraq will not threaten others, it will accept no threat against itself. Saddam said he fully believes the U.S.G. wants peace, and that is good. But do not, he asked, use methods which you say you do not like, methods like armtwisting.

Iraq will have to respond if the U.S. uses these methods. Iraq knows the U.S.G. can send planes and rockets and hurt Iraq deeply. Saddam asks that the U.S.G. not force Iraq to the point of humiliation at which logic must be disregarded.

The Ambassador thanked Saddam for the opportunity to discuss directly with him some of his and our concerns. President Bush, too, wants friendship, as he had written at the Eid and on the occasion of Iraq's national day. Saddam interrupted to say he had been touched by those messages.

The Ambassador resumed her theme, recalling that the President had instructed her to broaden and deepen our relations with Iraq. Saddam had referred to "some circles" antipathetic to that aim. Such circles certainly existed, but the U.S. administration is instructed by the President. On the other hand, the President does not control the American press; if he did, criticism of the administration would not exist. Saddam again interrupted to say he understood that.

The Ambassador said there were many issues he had raised she would like to comment on, but she wished to use her limited time with the President to stress, first, President Bush's desire for friendship and, second, his strong desire, shared we assume by Iraq, for peace and stability in the Mideast. Is it not reasonable for us to be concerned when the President and Foreign Minister both say publicly that Kuwaiti actions are the equivalent of military aggression, and then we learn that many units of the Republican Guard have been sent to the border? Is it not reasonable for us to ask, in the spirit of friendship, not confrontation, the simple question: What are your intentions?

Saddam said that was indeed a reasonable question. He acknowledged that we should be concerned for regional peace, in fact it is our duty as a superpower. "But how can we make them (Kuwait and U.A.E.) understand how deeply we are suffering." The financial situation is such that the pensions for widows and orphans will have to be cut. At this point, the interpreter and one of the note takers broke down and wept.

After a pause for recuperation, Saddam said, in effect, believe me, I have tried everything. We sent envoys, wrote messages, asked King Fahd of Saudi Arabia to arrange Quadripartite Summit (Iraq, Saudi Arabian Government, U.A.E., Kuwait). Fahd suggested oil ministers instead, and we agreed to the Jidda agreement although it was well below our hopes. Then, Saddam continued, two days later the Kuwaiti Oil Minister announced he would want to annul that agreement within two months. As for the U.A.E., Saddam said I begged Sheik Zayed (President of the U.A.E.) to understand our problems (when Saddam entertained him in Mosul after the Baghdad summit). And Zayed said just wait until I get back to Abu Dhabi. But then his Minister of Oil made "bad statements."

At this point, Saddam left the room to take an urgent call from Mubarak. After his return, the Ambassador asked if he could tell her if there was any progress in finding a peaceful way to diffuse the dispute. . . . Saddam said that he had just learned from Mubarak that the Kuwaitis have agreed to negotiate. The Kuwaiti Crown Prince/Prime Minister would meet in Riyadh with Saddam's No.2, Izzat Ibrahim, and then the Kuwaitis would come to Baghdad on Saturday, Sunday or, at the latest, Monday, July 30.

"I told Mubarak," Saddam said, that "nothing will happen until the meeting." And nothing will happen during or after the meeting if the Kuwaitis will at last "give us some hope."

The Ambassador said she was delighted to hear this good news.[6]

Notes

1. Thomas Friedman, "Envoy to Iraq, Faulted in Crisis, Says She Warned Hussein Sternly," *New York Times*, March 21, 1991.

2. Elaine Sciolino, "Envoy's Testimony on Iraq is Assailed," *New York Times*, July 13, 1991.

3. *Foreign Broadcast Information Service*, April 17, 1990.

4. *Developments in the Middle East, July 1990.* Report of the Subcommittee on Europe and the Middle East of the Committee on Foreign Affairs, House

of Representatives (Washington, DC: U.S. Government Printing Office, July 31, 1990), p. 14.

5. Elaine Sciolino, *The Outlaw State: Saddam Hussein's Quest for Power and the Gulf Crisis* (New York: John Wiley & Sons, 1991), p. 196.

6. Published by the *New York Times*, July 13, 1991.

Appendix C:

International Tribunals

The "Highway of Death." This massacre occurred after Saddam Hussein accepted a Soviet sponsored cease-fire plan and ordered his troops to leave Kuwait in accordance with UN Resolution 660. The Geneva Conventions of 1949 prohibit attacking soldiers who are out of combat. (Photo: Commission of Inquiry)

Report from Belgium:
Tribunal — June 13-15, 1991

The International Commission of Inquiry into war crimes committed by the United States at the time of the Gulf War conducted a hearing from Thursday, June 13, to Saturday, June 15, 1991, in the Palais des Congrès of Brussels, the most important and prestigious conference center in the capital of Europe. Some thirty witnesses, many of whom came from Arab countries, testified before the commission and a public audience with translations to Arabic, French, Dutch, Spanish and English.

The hearing concluded unanimously that there certainly were and are still war crimes being committed against the Iraqi people, including crimes against humanity, and that the struggle against intervention by the United States and the "coalition" countries must be carried out without slackening. The Commission has considered that it has received novel elements of proof concerning accusations 6, 8, 10, 12, 14, 16 and 18. The audience, some hundreds of people, was unanimously stunned by the horror reported and impressed with the seriousness of the witnesses.

Composing the Commission of Inquiry were Beji Khaled (lawyer, France), Husni Chiab (Jordanian parliamentarian and professor of international law), Jean Michot (president of the Institute of Islamic Philosophy, Catholic University of Louvain), Marc Vandepitte (Club of Antwerp), and presided over by Jean-Marie Dermagne (lawyer and researcher at Catholic University of Louvain).

Program of the Brussels Hearings of the International Commission of Inquiry

Introduction by Eddy Maes, chairperson of the Coordination of Support of the Peoples of the Third World.

I. Framework of the Gulf War
Ludo Martens, Co-author of the Declaration of Ouagadougou: "The Hundred Years War Against the Countries of the Third World."
Olga Mejia, President of the Human Rights Organization of Panama: "U.S.

Military Aggression Against Panama. What comparisons with Iraq."
Prof. Jean Philippe Peemans, Professor at Catholic University at Louvain: "Relations between the countries of the Third World and the countries of the West."
Camille Harb, Lebanese Jurist: "Petroleum and Colonial Frontiers in the Gulf: Direct Reasons for the Gulf War?"

II. The Embargo

Frans Wuytack, Member of the Bureau of the Coordination, participant of the Peace Camp in Iraq.
Oum Nasser, Organizer of the peace boat that was invaded by U.S. and British troops.

III. International Law

Mohammed Khair Horani, Jordanian Jurist: "The Efforts of Jordan for a Diplomatic Solution of the Crisis."
Dr. Miguel Di Estefano Pisani, Professor of International Law at the University of Havana, Cuba. "International Law and the Security Council."
Maitre Bouaita, Algerian jurist.
Camille Harb, Lebanese jurist: "International Law in Kuwait and Lebanon."

IV. Violation of Democratic Rights

M. Oussedik, French Jurist.
Anne Maesschalk, Jurist at the Free University of Brussels: "Report on the Violations of Democratic Rights in Belgium and in Europe."
Jacques Wattier, Vice President of the Coordination: "On the Organization of Protests Against the Gulf War."

V. The Role of the Media

George Kazolias, Radio France International.
Dominique Pradalie, Editor in chief at Antenna 2 (France).
Gerard de Selys, Journalist RTBF (Belgium).

VI. Medical and Social Consequences of the Embargo and the War

Jean-Jacques Peche, Journalist of the RTBF, recently returned from Iraq.
Dr. Julia Devis, International Commission on Medical Neutrality and member of the Harvard Study Team which had visited Iraq from April 28 to May 6, 1991.
Maitre Ben Abdallah Said, Vice president of the Algerian Red Crescent and President of the Peoples Rights Association.
Dr. Hassan Khreis, President and Dr. Moussa Abou Hmaid, Vice President of the Emergency Arab Health Committee, which coordinated support actions for Iraq.
Ross B. Mirkarami, Arms Control Research Center, USA: "Report on the Ecologic Effects.
Dr. Eric Hoskins, Physicians to Prevent Nuclear War.

Dr. Huub Dierick, Medicine for the Third World, Belgian Medical Mission in Iraq.

Taher Add Algabbar Abdalla, Palestinian in Kuwait.

Mike Ehrlich, American Psychologist Attached to the Military Counselling Network in Germany.

RITA Network. An Organization in France that Works with Soldiers.

Riad Malki, Professor at the University of Birzeit, occupied West Bank: "The Situation for Palestinians During the War."

Mohammed Khair Horani, Jordanian Jurist: "The Situation for the Jordanian People During the War."

Ramsey Clark, former U.S. Attorney General. Video Report on the Systematic Destruction of Iraq.

Rabah Hajlaoui, Journalist and President of Radio El Watan, who recently visited Iraq.

Mr. Kilkani, President of the Tunisian Association of Young Lawyers: "Reports on Inquiries into the Situation in Iraq."

Karim Jassen Altamimi, Iraqi, recently arrived from Iraq.

Jasmin Yavod, Iraqi woman.

The Murderous Embargo

The horror of the embargo was the object of upsetting testimony by a number of witnesses, including Frans Wuytack, member of the bureau of the Coordination Against the War in the Gulf (Belgium), who had participated in the Peace Camp in Iraq. Jean-Jacques Peche, director from the RTBF—Radio Television of the French Community in Belgium—showed interviews with two doctors made in Baghdad. Ben Abdallah Said, vice president of the Algerian Red Crescent, said that Arab Red Crescent and the International Red Cross showed themselves more than reticent to intervene in favor of the Iraqi population and that the ships transporting food and medicine had to pay substantial sums for rights of passage through Egypt to cross the Suez Canal.

Doctor Huub Dierick of Medicine for the Third World—Belgian medical mission in Iraq—who noted that Iraq had been bombed back to a pre-industrial era and that 90% of the workers in Iraq's industry are now jobless; the western bombing has destroyed all the stocks of food. Also, the Iraqis cannot preserve medication needing refrigeration, as 95% of electrical centers have been destroyed. In addition, the psychological effects of the bombing has affected all the Iraqi children.

Dr. Eric Hoskins of Physicians to Prevent Nuclear War, explained that the new bombs used by the Americans have the same effect as atomic bombs without having the "political inconveniences" of these weapons. He showed the horrifying photos of dead children in the hospitals following a shortage of medication. We can not cite all the testimony of those who were there, but all, without exception, confirmed that the maintenance of the embargo is another way of carrying on the war and causes an appalling number of deaths.

Flouting International Law

Miguel Di Estefano Pisani, professor of international law at the University of Havana, showed how the "coalition" countries ignored the United Nations Charter. This obliges nations to proceed by "peaceful means" to adjust or settle differences capable of leading to a rupture of peace, and that "the parties . . . shall, first of all, seek a solution by means of negotiation, inquiry, mediation, conciliation, arbitration, judicial settlement . . . or by other peaceful means of their choice."

Mohammed Khair Horani, Jordanian jurist, reminded the audience of all the attempts to negotiate peace tried by King Hussein of Jordan and Yasser Arafat. These attempts were systematically sabotaged by the U.S. during the entire period preceding the war. For example, the King of Jordan met Saddam Hussein on August 3, 1990. Saddam assured him he would remove the Iraqi troops from Kuwait and participate in an Arab summit with representatives of Kuwait. His condition was that Iraq not be condemned. Iraqi troops began to withdraw from Kuwait but, on Aug. 9, the United States succeeded in getting Iraq condemned.

For this witness as for the Cuban professor, the United States had therefore deliberately prepared its aggression against Iraq.

Finally, for those who still doubt the importance of the role of Israel in the war, the Lebanese jurist Camille Harb cited the statement of Norman Schwarzkopf on Israeli radio on May 22, 1991: "We made the war for you."

Violation of Democratic Rights

Mr. Oussedik, French jurist, testified on the blows to democratic rights in France during the Gulf War and crisis period. The most flagrant blow was to expel to Yemen twenty-two Iraqis residing in France, done in the framework of a giant police roundup called "Operation Vigipirate." He characterized these expulsions as a crime against humanity and, recalling that Goering had been hanged after having been found guilty of the same crime by the Nuremberg Tribunal, demanded the punishment of those who carry the same acts now.

Anne Maesschalk, a Belgian jurist, listed attacks on civil rights all over Europe. These included Great Britain's internment of ninety people of Iraqi origin, then the expulsion from this country of eighty-three people originally from Kuwait and Bahrain. Also the expulsion from Italy and Greece of people originally from the Middle East; administrative internments in Spain; the refusal of European governments to submit to or reveal to their parliaments their special plans for "maintaining order" or for surveillance. It included also the dismissal of certain North African workers from their places of work; threats against Arab radio stations in Belgium (in violation of article 14 and 18 of the Belgian constitution); and, still in Belgium, the systematic control or isolation of workers and other of Moroccan origin (in violation of the law of July 30, 1981, directed against racism and xenophobia). Also, the outlawing of demonstrations (in violation of Articles 6 to 14 of the Belgian Constitution), of which the Coordination Against the War in the Gulf had been a victim.

The Press's Complicity in the Crimes Against Humanity

Georges Kazolias, a journalist at Radio France International (RFI), gave numerous examples of self-censorship and of the systematic intoxication practiced by journalists of French radio. For example, his boss declared that it "would be better that the U.S. controlled the petroleum than the Iraqis," forbidding giving the number of demonstrators against the war. Also, the exclamation of a journalist regarding the exhumation of corpses of victims of an American bombardment in Baghdad: "Wow, toasted bread" . . . the same journalist almost broke down in tears when the television showed the (self)-beaten face of an American pilot captured by the Iraqi army.

Then there were the cries of victory by the journalists when the British fleet destroyed Iraqi "vessels" (the Zodiac inflatable boats); the refusal of journalists to speak of the ferocious repression of an attempt at an anti-war demonstration in Paris. Kazolias considered the journalists "covered with the blood of the Iraqi people," their attitude having helped to make aggression against Iraq by the Coalition Forces possible.

Gerard de Selys, journalist of the RTBF (Belgian Radio Television), quoted the Belgian penal code on authors of a crime and accomplices. De Selys considers that if the press had correctly played its role, the populations of the coalition countries would not have permitted the war against Iraq. He demanded thus that the tribunal should pronounce sentence on the crimes committed against the Iraqi population, as well as on the unarmed soldiers, retreating or surrendering, and condemn the press as an accomplice or author of these crimes.

Olga Mejia

Olga Mejia, chairperson of the Human Rights Organization in Panama, explained with the help of slides how the United State created more civilian victims in a few days at the end of 1989 at the time of their aggression against Panama, than Iraq created military victims in invading Kuwait. She explained also how the aggression against Panama was a preparation for the war waged by the West against Iraq.

The two aggressions present striking similarities: political preparation for the invasion; embargo; demonization of the leaders; massive bombardments; intervention of the 82nd Airborne Division; strict control of the media; total silence after the invasion; ruin of the economy and military occupation.

A New Colonial Order

Ludo Martens, chairperson of the Labor Party of Belgium, the only Belgium party to oppose the war and the blockade against Iraq, and signatory of the "Ouagadougou Declaration," established the general framework of the war against Iraq. Antagonist classes always have antagonistic conceptions of what a crime is, he explained. Any power opposing itself to the imperialist world is characterized, by the imperialists, as a "bloody dictatorship." But the Third World, even though it is subject to western propaganda, has understood that the Gulf War was imperialist aggression reviving colonial wars.

That is the reason why African intellectuals have written and signed the "Ouagadougou Declaration," which condemned the aggression against Iraq as being a North-South war. Colonial wars of the last century were justified by the imperialist powers the same way the United States and its allies did in the Gulf War. These were protection of international law, elimination of a "bloody dictator," "urgent necessity to contain aggressive expansionism [of Iraq]."

The advent of a "new world order," announced by Bush, is nothing but a return to the old "colonial order," but imposed with an even more relentless military and economic power. The conditions of surrender imposed on Iraq are a supplementary proof that the economic recolonialization of the Third World is now completed by military and political recolonialization. The "right to intervention" is the slogan under which imperialism rejects the sovereignty of Third World countries and dismantles international law to replace it by an arbitrary law of a colonial type.

Jean-Philippe Peemans

Jean-Philippe Peemans, professor at the Catholic University of Louvain, showed how the rich countries of the North, terrorized by the movement for democratization and economic independence of the South, first imposed on the countries of the Third World a new form of economic domination starting with the 1980s. This included indebtedness to first-world commercial banks, the World Bank, and re-structuring of third-world economies by the International Monetary Fund (IMF). Then this passed to a political offensive to break up the front these countries were looking to constitute. In the meantime the countries of the North reinforced themselves in organizations like the "G-7" where the West decides collectively its attitude with regard to the countries of the South. Being one of the last national-populist states to continue to exist, Iraq became an imperative target for the United States and its allies.

Crime Against Peace

In the course of a brilliant expose, former U.S. Attorney General Ramsey Clark pleaded that the notion of "crime against peace" be established in law. For this crime any country preparing war could be held in judgment. Such a procedure would avoid having to judge a country or its leadership for "war crimes" or "crimes against humanity," that is, after it is too late. Now, concerning the Gulf War, everything shows, explained Clark, that the U.S. prepared a military action against Iraq since 1988 at least. The former Attorney General called sharply for holding a tribunal to try the leaders of the war because "to accept such a massacre, is to have no vision, and a people without a vision will disappear."

Proofs for Eight Accusations

The Commission of Inquiry established by the Coordination for Support of the People of the Third World will still have to draw the conclusions from its work. But everything indicates that it will transmit an overwhelming report furnishing the elements of concrete proof concerning the guilt of the "coalition" countries, the United States at their head, regarding accusations 6, 8, 10, 12, 14, 16 and 18. The Commission of Inquiry will insist in addition that the tribunal which will pass judgment on these war crimes against humanity perpetrated during the Gulf crisis and the Gulf War, does not omit from responsibility those people physically directing the great organs of the western press.

Report from the Tribunals in Turkey – August 3 and 4, 1991

Defying threats from the pro-U.S. government and literally facing off against armed police, the Commission of Inquiry for an International War Crimes Tribunal in Turkey held hearings in Istanbul on August 3, 1991 and in Diyarbakir on August 4, 1991. Diyarbakir is a largely Kurdish city in southeastern Turkey. There were also meetings in Cizre and Silopi, two Kurdish towns near the Iraqi border, where people defied army and police terror to attend.

In Cizre, the meeting hall, the local office of the Socialist Party, was machine-gunned by police two days before the event. During the meeting police barricaded the town to prevent people from coming. Dozens of people stayed overnight in the hall to make sure they could attend.

These meetings documented crimes committed by the United States and Turkish governments during the Gulf War. The Commission investigated another aspect of the Middle East situation that has been completely hidden in the U.S. news media: the reign of terror being carried out against the Kurdish people by the U.S.-supported Turkish regime. The Commission of Inquiry's visit to the Iraq-Turkey border happened to coincide with a bloody attack on Kurdish villages in Iraq by the Turkish army. This operation was launched only two weeks after Bush visited Turkish prime minister Turgut Ozal to thank him for his role in the war against Iraq.

Former U.S. Attorney General Ramsey Clark and staff member Bill Doares from the Commission of Inquiry's main office in New York traveled to Turkey as guests of the Turkish Commission, whose members included journalist Abdurrahman Dilipak, Ali Reza Dizdar of the Istanbul Human Rights Association, Prof. Alpaslan Isikli, chairperson of the Graduates Society of the Faculty of Political Sciences, Dogu Perincek, chairperson of the Socialist Party, Prof. Haluk Gerger, Prof. Gencay Gursoy, Ercan Karadag, former chairperson of the Social Democratic People's Party, Celil Sener of the Kurdish magazine Free People and Bahri Zengin, vice-chairperson of the Welfare Party.

The Istanbul hearing was originally scheduled for a stadium that can hold 6,000 people, but it backed out under government pressure. The meeting went ahead in the 500-seat hall of the Journalists' Association, which was packed with a standing-room-only crowd.

In Diyarbakir, hundreds of people packed the town's largest movie theater for several hours in spite of daytime temperatures of over 100 degrees Fahrenheit to hear the Commission's report. Four weeks earlier Diyarbakir had been the site of the massacre by the Turkish police of mourners at the funeral of Vezad Aydin, a Kurdish leader who had been assassinated by a rightwing death squad. Sixty-three Kurdish activists were murdered by death squads in southeast Turkey in June and July.

In Cizre, the Commission visited the home and family of Hedaya Dilce, a 16-year-old Kurdish woman who the police murdered two days earlier. The police indiscriminately sprayed automatic weapons fire across the roof of her house. The Commission also took testimony from Kurdish villagers who had been tortured and terrorized by special police squads known as Rambos.

On the Iraqi border, just outside of Silopi, the Commission delegation saw the base of the U.S. and British "Poised Hammer" strike force allegedly stationed there to "protect the Kurds." Kurdish leaders in Turkey have charged that U.S. planes are flying reconnaissance and providing other logistical support for the Turkish army's war against the guerrillas of the National Liberation Front of Kurdistan.

In Ankara on August 7, 1991, Ramsey Clark and Dogu Perincek addressed a "U.S. Troops Out of Turkey" rally held by the Socialist Party.

The Turkish Commission concluded that "Turgut Ozal, members of the National Security Council, ministers in the cabinets of prime ministers Akbulut and Yilmaz, the Special War Department, the Motherland Party's group in the national assembly have been found guilty for committing crimes, in cooperation with the United States of America, against peace, humanity, the United Nations agreement, war legislation and the related international legal norms."

The Commission said the Gulf War was being used in Turkey to ban strikes, fire workers and freeze their wages.

As of August 1991, the translation from Turkish of the testimony presented at the hearings is unavailable. Below are excepts from the report of the Turkish Commission.

Introduction to the Report

The Commission for investigating the American government's war crimes has been visiting several related countries in order to determine the crimes and to gather evidence.

There is no doubt that the American government is the major war criminal. The present evidence is sufficient to condemn the U.S. in the common conscience of the peoples of the world. The U.S. government has committed the greatest war crimes not only by actually starting the war, but also by influencing the allies, including Turkey, through political, economic and even military pressure to participate in the war. Therefore, we agree with all of the accusations previously made by the investigation commission. We are also witnesses to the fact that the Turkish government has directly or indirectly participated in the significant portion of the war crimes committed by the American government—crimes already mentioned by the investigation commission.

We also believe that the government is responsible for additional crimes as well as violations of law. We also see that the Turkish government's crimes are at the same time those of the American government. Therefore, we have decided to meet in order to determine the crimes of the Turkish government and those who are primarily responsible for them, and to relate our findings to the Investigation Commission, and to present them through the Commission and the Court to Turkish and international public opinion.

[The Turkish Commission explains how they limited the boundaries of the investigation to the Turkish government's participation in American war crimes, and that they did not address many points of the historical background of the crisis and the Middle East, but they are aware of these points.]

At this point, we only call attention to the importance of the responsibilities of the United Nations and especially the Security Council, the relationships with the contemporary international system, and the required structural change in the region in order that the imperialist hegemony may be stopped and a just and peaceful world order that we dream of may be established.

Against those administrators who solely respect brute force and violent measures, the Investigation Commission and the International Court in which we participate do not have such a force. Yet we discover our enormous power in the depths of history, in the moral achievements of civilization, in human dignity and the laws of life on earth. We believe that, by displaying the truth beyond the image and the disgusting face of aggression and war, we are rendering an important service to the public opinion which has been harassed by the intensive and misleading attacks of various media channels. Hence, we once again emphasize that our aim is not to voice a particular political viewpoint or organization, but to reflect the common opinion of the public.

We inform our people to stimulate Turkish public opinion about those criminal acts committed by the minority government—acts already denounced by the overwhelming majority of Turkish citizens. We recognize the people of Turkey, who sincerely maintain the principles of solidarity and brotherhood among nations against the molestation of the imperialists and their collaborators, and who especially are the firm defenders of the national and democratic rights of the people in the Middle East as well as peace in the region, as the ultimate judge to our claims.

Claims

Our claims regarding the crimes of the Turkish government relating to the war in the Gulf have two aspects. First, we state the participation of the Turkish government in the crimes of the U.S. government against peace, humanity, countries and peoples in the region, United Nations Charter, Geneva Convention, and other international documents—crimes that have already been stated by the Investigation Commission. Second, we summarize the Turkish government's violations of law within the country.

However, we regard it our duty to summarize the American crimes against Turkey that directly involve the roles given to our country by America to be played in the Middle East. This has been neglected by the report of the commission.

Since WW II, the most fundamental aim of the strategy of the Western block countries led by America has been to use Turkey as an outpost for Western interests in the Middle East with predominantly military functions. It should be immediately remembered in this context that in the 1970s, when America was beginning to train forces against the Middle East and the Gulf in the deserts of Nevada, it was at the same time staging its classical destabilizing acts in the "outpost" Turkey where broad masses were demanding democracy, peace and independence. . . .

When the parliamentary regime, even in its limited form, was regarded a burden for the system and an obstacle to imperialist aims, people were made targets of oppression and violence; and these processes had been concluded by military coups. Today, America's dark role in these processes are patently evident. In Turkey, civilian or military, open or covert, U.S. presence has been materialized by military coups and through the leadership of American pacification and coup experts, Kommer and Abromowitz. And in the aftermaths of military coups, militarist governments have conducted their multifaceted activities against people, democracy, independence and basic human rights and freedoms with generous American support and aid.

In 1980, Jimmy Carter declared the Gulf an area of "vital interest" and made it a target for American military intervention; the same year Turkey, on whom important missions in the region were imposed, saw the greatest conspiracy against independence and human rights: the coup of September 12, 1980. The Junta which established its regime . . . upon the blood of thousands of people, was hailed with ardor by the American government; after it maintained the militarist "American stability" in the country, the Junta began to prepare for enacting its role in stabilizing the whole Middle East in the "peace" of imperialism, and it turned Turkey into a base for the "Rapid Deployment Force." Then this mission was taken over during the war in the Gulf by civilian administrators who acted in the social atmosphere created by the September 12th regime.

Another aim of the U.S. and its collaborator regimes has been to support pseudo-religious establishments by exploiting sacred values. This American approach is true not only for Muslims, but also for orthodox Christians. By taking the Orthodox Church under its protection, America wants to influence the developments in the Balkans and the Soviet Union.

American efforts to use religion as a Trojan Horse gained momentum under the oppressive regime of September 12. While America wanted to provoke the regime against religion by oppressing true religion and believers under the pretext of a war against terrorism and reactionism on the one hand, it also tried hard, using the press, to establish an American understanding of religion under the control of certain circles on the other. America has exploited religion, believers, society and human rights. It has made use of Turkey as a site of war for its plans.

We join in the examinations of the Commission for Investigating American War Crimes as claimants with a fundamental accusation: for several decades, and complying with its strategic aim to manipulate the country and its calculations to impose upon Turkey the functions of a military outpost, America has considered the Turkish people's right to sovereignty, as well as democracy, basic human rights and freedoms as greatest obstacles; America targeted and wanted to destroy these rights and freedoms. American governments have committed serious crimes against our country and our people. America attempted in act to use Turkey as a pawn, as an aggressor's base, and as a whip in its global strategy, wishing to make these roles the destiny of our people.

We accuse American governments in the name of our people. As unmediated witnesses to war crimes, we accuse American governments, before the social conscience of people, and in the name of human dignity and values of civilization.

The Turkish government has directly participated in American government's war crimes as a country in the region and as part of the international alliance for war led by the U.S.; it openly functioned as a collaborator. . . .

1. The U.S. provocations and attacks against Iraq prior to the occupation of Kuwait that the Investigation Commission mentions have been supported in act by the Turkish government. In parallel to the American conspiracy, an "Iraqi threat" against Turkey has been invented and Turkish public opinion was shaped according to this gross hyperbole; the Turkish regime has conducted systematic and well-coordinated campaigns for provocation.

2. After Iraq's occupation of Kuwait, the government led by Ozal exerted its full energy to sabotage peace efforts and provoked war. All avenues for peaceful solution and diplomacy have been concealed from the public, and

demands for peace and undertakings for dialogue have been calumniated as "Saddamism." And in foreign policy . . . the Turkish government conducted a misleading and provocative anti-peace campaign both internally and externally. It opted for urgent military intervention and acted as a war marketer.

The Turkish government has acted in violation of its membership in the U.N. and its rationale and founding principles which stand against war before exhausting all means of peaceful solution. With a mentality that regards the U.N. only as a legislating council for war, the Turkish government has defended the U.S.-led coalition declaration of war on Iraq.

Turgut Ozal wanted to deploy the Turkish Armed Forces early in the crisis; he hastily invited NATO's Rapid Deployment Force into the country; he permitted the widespread usage of Incirlik and other military bases in order that a northern front against Iraq may be opened and the dimensions and devastation of war may be enhanced.

3. From the very beginning, the Turkish government regarded war as a means of realizing imperialist ends in total disregard of the U.N. Security Council's objective of "ending the occupation of Kuwait." Ozal openly stated that the U.S. was going to establish a new world order upon the completion of war and that Turkey had to actively participate in war in order to join the victor's booty at the plunderers' feast. . . . For this reason, the Turkish government tried hard for the multi-dimensional militarization of the crisis. And because it opted for war rather than peace, it directly participated in the massacre in Iraq by allowing the military use of the bases in the country.

4. As a natural outcome of this policy, by opening the northern front against Iraq, by allowing the use of Incirlik and other bases, the bringing into the country of planes with nuclear capacity was accepted; thus Turkey approved and provided bases for air campaigns that directly targeted the civilian population and Iraq's future, as well as for the use of mass destruction weapons and the destruction of the environment. Hence, the Turkish regime has participated in the U.S. government's destructive crimes.

5. The end of the military campaign brought another operation of destruction onto the stage. During the massacre of the Kurdish people that deeply saddened humanity's conscience, and during the massive emigration that turned into a genocide in its own right, the Turkish regime heartlessly and calculatingly waited in order to gain political influence as an investment for the future. And when the great conspiracy left the Kurds hungry, naked, sick and helpless, the government shed hypocritical tears, while regarding this situation an occasion for occupation.

The government's policy of patronage that aims at keeping the Kurdish people and its political expression under surveillance went hand in hand with the depopulation of Kurdish villages, forced emigrations from the region and the terror of the "special war" imposed upon the Kurds. In order to gain control over them, the government played with the fate of the Kurds as a gambler. The Turkish government which is silent about the massacre at Halepche is one of the players at the gamblers' table, together with Bush, Saddam, and others, playing with the suffering and self-determination rights of the Kurdish people.

6. Imperialism continues its war and occupation in the Middle East. The bullying of brute force and occupation continues under the pretext of humanitarian cause, because the war's primary and fundamental aim of establishing a new order can only be forced upon the people of the region through violent means. . . . Now Turkey has become the base of the aggressive force in the region. It was previously announced that American weapons were to be stored in Turkey. In addition, the organization of a new NATO force that Turkey will also participate in and allow to settle within its borders is already on the agenda. . . .

All of these military operations violate the security of the people in the region, their democratic rights and demands; when one considers the dimensions of Turkish government's active involvement in all of these preparations, it becomes evident that the Turkish government is still an accomplice in the chaotic and critical scenarios freshly produced by imperialism. The Turkish government profoundly cooperates with imperialism in establishing the "new order" in order to divide and govern the peoples of the Middle East, to stabilize the imperialist plunder, to strengthen Israel, Zionism, and their collaborators, and to strangle democratic movements.

As an extension of its pro-war, pro-imperialist, and pro-aggression policies, the Turkish government has seriously violated the fundamental norms of democracy, basic human rights and freedoms, and present laws; it has committed serious crimes against people.

7. Throughout the war, the majority of the media, led by the government-controlled radio and TV, acted as war provocateurs. . . . The government's television applied censorship even to CNN, and the public was deprived of its right to receive accurate information from the media. Turkey was the last country on earth to get to know that Incirlik Air Base was being used by American war planes. It was not only lack of information the Turkish public suffered from; the public was also mislead by an inaccurate information campaign. Thus the Turkish public found itself as the target of a psychological warfare orchestrated by CNN's round-the-clock broadcasting and joined by other media. Hence, the declaration prepared by UNESCO and signed by Turkish government on November 28, 1978, concerning the regulation of mass media broadcasting, was also seriously violated.

8. The crisis has been used as a means of oppression and exploitation in domestic policy as well. An example of this is the government ban on strikes under the pretext of war and so-called security interests. During this period firings have increased, wages have been frozen, and working

conditions have grown to be worse, again under the pretext of the threat of war. The responsibilities of taking a side in the war have created an economic terror on the poor through price increases, paralyzed economy, commercial losses and military expenses. The so-called "aid" given to cover economic losses are spent for re-armament, and Turkish people became poorer as the monopolistic manufacturers of weaponry piled up their riches.

9. During the war it turned out to be a crime in Turkey to demand peace, to be for diplomatic and political solutions, and to be actively involved in such efforts. Peace meetings and demonstrations were banned, people were beaten, shot and even killed at the marches against the war. The Turkish government considered peace and peace-loving as crimes, and even youngsters have been detained on account of that.

10. Finally, the Turkish government has even violated its creator, the September 12th constitution, by inviting foreign armed forces to Turkey without any national or international legal basis whatsoever, and even without discussing the matter at the national assembly where it has the majority of the seats.

Conclusion

Turgut Ozal, members of the National Security Council, ministers in the cabinets of prime ministers Akbulut and Yilmaz, the Special War Department, and the Mainland Party's group in the national assembly have been found guilty for committing crimes, in cooperation with the USA, against peace, humanity, the United Nations agreement, war legislations and the related international legal norms.

Members of Commission of Inquiry (Turkey)

Atilla Coskun, Chairperson of Socialist Union Party in Istanbul
Abdurrahman Dilipak, Columnist in daily *Milli Gazete*
Ali Raza Dizdar, Istanbul Human Rights Association
Haluk Gerger, Associate Professor in International Relations
Gencay Gursoy, Professor in Medicine
Alpaslan Iqikli, Professor in the Faculty of Political Sciences, Chairman
of Graduates of Faculty of Political Sciences
Ercan Karakaq, Former Chairperson of Social Democratic Populist Party,
member of Executive Committee of SDPP
Dogu Perincek, Chairman of Socialist Party
Celil Sener, Representative of the magazine of *Free People*
Bahri Zengin, Vice-Chairman of Welfare Party

Report from East Asia: Tribunals in Hong Kong, Malaysia, Philippines, and Japan

An important series of hearings and mass meetings of the Commission of Inquiry on U.S. War Crimes in the Gulf were held in four countries in East Asia in early September 1991. In Hong Kong, Malaysia, Philippines and Japan, the U.S. War against Iraq was seen through the different perspectives of each struggle and was linked to the immediate issues in each country. The U.S. government built a huge international coalition of military and economic forces to gain control of the oil wealth of the Gulf. The opposition to the U.S. war in the Gulf was also international in scope. Each of these hearings were unique. They truly reflected the local issues and the way in which the U.S. war and the participation of the governments of each country in the war was opposed by millions of people on a local level. The hearings in East Asia were part of a series of international meetings on the U.S. war in the Gulf that were held in twenty countries and over thirty cities within the U.S.

Hong Kong

In Hong Kong, the Asia Student Association (ASA) organized on September 1 and 2, 1991, a press conference, a public forum on the work of the Commission, and a meeting with Non-Governmental Organizations of the United Nations based in Hong Kong. Steven Gan and Chow Wing Hang of the ASA Secretariat coordinated the meetings. ASA represents forty student organizations in twenty-eight countries in Asia. The ASA Journal had reprinted the Commission report and the Commission's 19-point indictment of U.S. government officials for war crimes.

A highlight of the visit was the opportunity to meet with students from many different struggles in Asia, including a student participant of the upheavals in Nepal, anti-dictatorship activists from Burma and a student just returning from major demonstrations in Seoul, South Korea. In Manila, at a meeting a week later of the ASA Secretariat, Ramsey Clark had an opportunity to meet with student leaders from twelve countries.

The ASA sent a student delegation to the Middle East in January. The delegation visited Iraq just a few days before the U.S. bombing began. This organization had been instrumental in organizing opposition to the war among student groups throughout Asia. An important issue in Hong Kong was the opposition of the Hong Kong government's contribution of $230 million to the Gulf War.

Malaysia

In Malaysia the hearings on September 4, 1991, drew over 1,000 people. The work of the Commission was prominently reported in the four daily papers; the coverage was in English, Chinese and Malay, representing the multi-ethnic composition of Malaysia. The 19-point indictment written by Ramsey Clark was reprinted in full in the *Aliran Journal* and in *Third World Resurgence Magazine*.

The work of the Commission in Malaysia was coordinated by Chandra Muzaffar and Fan Yew Teng, a former member of parliament. The Ad-hoc Committee on Gulf War Crimes had gathered hundreds of prominent endorsers and a wide diversity of ethnic, religious and cultural organizations to support the work of the Commission. Large meetings were held at the National University of Malaysia and at the University of Malaysia.

Despite official government support on the votes against Iraq in the Security Council of the UN, there was deep opposition to the U.S. war in the Gulf throughout the country. The proud struggle in Malaysia against British colonialism and the large Moslem population helped to create an identification with the embattled people of Iraq.

Philippines

In the Philippines, the hearings of Commission of Inquiry took place during the raging debate on the future of the U.S. base at Subic Bay. The mass meetings and press coverage focused on the connection between the new U.S. bases in eight oil producing countries of the Middle East and the legacy of poverty and militarism due to U.S. domination in the Philippines. Ramsey Clark's opposition to the continued U.S. occupation of Subic and the work of the Commission of Inquiry received front page coverage in the daily papers and on television and radio.

Activists in the Philippines constantly stressed similarities between the U.S. conduct in the war against Iraq and the Philippine-American War almost 100 years ago. By U.S. estimates, more than 200,000 Filipino people were killed and another 900,000 died of starvation as result of the five-year war for control of the Pacific.

The work of the Commission and the opposition to U.S. bases were also the focus of a dinner held at the home of Senator Wigberto Tanada with leaders of BAYAN and delegates to the International Peace Festival. Senator Tanada leads the opposition to U.S. bases in the Philippine Senate.

Commission members had an opportunity to meet with KAIBIGAN, an organization of overseas workers, who provided testimony to the Commission on the difficulties faced by tens of thousands of Filipino workers in the Gulf during the war. More than 20 percent of the Filipino workforce is forced to work abroad due to poverty and thirty percent unemployment in the Philippines.

The visit of the Commission was coordinated by Lidy Nacpil-Alejandro, the Secretary-General of BAYAN. The large meetings of the Commission were held at the University of the Philippines and the Polytechnic University of the Philippines on September 6, 1991 and were part of the preparation for the International Peace Festival held in Manila, September 4th to 17th.

Japan

In Japan there is a powerful movement against the rise of Japanese militarism. Japan now ranks third in military expenditures, after the U.S. and the Soviet Union. There is a growing awareness of the danger of increased rivalry between the U.S. and Japan.

The Commission hearing was timed to coincide with the court date for a suit against the Japanese government for the payment of $9 billion to the U.S.-led allied forces for the war against Iraq. Mass resistance had prevented the Japanese government from sending Japanese troops to the Gulf. The lawsuit involves twenty-six cases and 3,333 plaintiffs nationwide. It is a mass mobilization that challenges the government for violating Article 9 of the Japanese constitution. Article 9 declares that the Japanese people forever renounce war as a sovereign right of the nation and that land, sea and air forces will never be maintained for this purpose.

On September 10, 1991, the largest courtroom at Tokyo District court was packed for the first stages of the suit against the government. Later that same evening, over 1,000 people filled Yamanote Church for the hearings of the Commission on war crimes. Important new testimony on the use of U.S. military bases in Japan during the Gulf War was added to the growing public record. Kazumi Kenmochi and Yuriko Okawara coordinated the work of the Commission. Both events received prominent attention in the Japanese press.

Early the following morning there was a demonstration at Yokosuka Port against the arrival of the USS Independence. Ramsey Clark joined hundreds of demonstrators who went out on small boats to oppose the homeporting of this huge aircraft carrier at Yokosuka. Later the same day Clark addressed a special meeting of members of the Japanese Diet.

Index

Adams, Robert (Smithsonian),
146-154 *passim*
African people, 191-192
agriculture, 55, 64, 237-240
Ahtisaari, Martti (UN Report), 3,
45, 53, 56, 94, 236-244
Allen, Charles Eugene, 63
al-Amariyah Shelter, 48-49, 105-106,
120-122
Amnesty International, 144
anti-personnel bombs, 18, 86-87; *see
also* weapons
Arab-Americans, 22, 188-190
Arab League, 66
Arabian Peninsula, 10
archaeological destruction, 15, 45,
146-157, 213-214
Asian people, 191-192, 274-276
attacks, 211; *see also,* bombing,
military operation, infrastructure
automobile production, 112

babies, 99, 134-136; incubators, 54
Babylon, 102, 112-113
Baghdad, 2, 95, 103-108, 134-136
passim; bombing of, 48, 84,
120-123, 228-233 *passim,* 263
banks, 182
Basra; bombing of, 87-88, 163,
229-231
barbarism, 146
Bedouins, 16
Belgium, 4, 259-265
bombing 14-15; indiscriminate, 16,
36, 50, 53, 98, 104, 110, 112, 113,
123, 137-145, 227, 234; carpet,
87-88; cultural sites, 146-157

bombs, 45, 85-86; cluster, 17, 36,
92; super, 17; accuracy, 47-48, 57,
87, 88; smart, 47-48, 120; *see
also,* napalm, fuel air explosives,
weapons, anti-personnel
bribery of UN members, 13, 19, 42
bridge destruction, 8, 208
Brzezinski, Zbigniew, 63
Bubiyan and Warba, 250, 253
Bush administration, 3-4, 77, 102,
175, *passim*
Bush, Barbara, 24
Bush, George, 1, 13, 18-22, 33, 38,
47, 75-76, 88, 110, 173, 180;
impeachment 245-248

casualties, 3, 11, 15, 16, 34, 77, 173;
civilian, 14-15, 48-49, 96,
112-113, 119, 123, 137, 139-145,
234
Center for Strategic and
International Studies, 64-56
Cheney, Richard, 12, 33, 69, 120,
152
chemical/nuclear plants, 18, 214-215
children, 133-136, 180-183, 192; *see
also* hospitals, civilians
China, 173
CIA, 63, 65, 67-70, 78, 80, 185, 234
civilian population, 2, 8, 14-16, 34,
44-45, 47, 100, 101-111, 112,
164-169, 211-216, 227, 232
CNN, 23, 84; *see also,* press
climate, 241-242
coalition, 30, 48-52, 77, 84, 142, 180
colonialism (neo-), 23, 80, 81, 118,
122-124, 206-207, 264

Commission of Inquiry, vii-viii, 4, 9-10, 24-25, 29, 32-33, 39, 121, 178, 223-226, 235, 270

communications, 34, 53, 94-95, 97, 103, 229, 241, 243

Congress of U.S., 19-20

conscientious objector, 201-205

conspiracy, 11, 65-57, 74-81, 79-80, 247, 251-253

constitution of U.S., 19,-21, 36, 93, 234, 245-247

Cox, Sir Percy, 252

crimes against humanity, 9, 34, 140-141, 218

crimes against peace, 3, 9, 12, 13, 33-34, 40, 43, 218, 247, 265

Cuba, 174, 177-178

cultural sites, 146-157

death squads, 117

democratic rights, 262

demonization, 13, 30, 176-174

disarming the enemy, 52

disease, 95-98, 121, 164ff, 103-115, 132-136, 249

Dole, Robert, 65, 251

Duggan, Michael, 13, 43, 44

Dulles, John Foster, 205

economic capacity (of Iraq) 21-23, 53-56, 64-65; condition before war, 103, 132, 251-253; impact, 115-116

Egypt, 13

Egyptians, 139-145

electrical system, 21, 94-95, 97, 103-105, 135, 229, 243-244

embargo, 21, 115, 118, 140, 164-169, 248-149, 261-262

environment, 20, 45, 214

epidemic, see disease

everyday life conditions, 15, 108-109, 118, 164-169, 238-239; see also, economic capacity

executions, 22, 142, see also torture

expulsion of foreign workers, 191-194, 195-197

factories bombed, 14, 21, 112, 119; see also, infrastructure

Fahd, King, 75

FBI, 188-189

fires, 20, 86

Fitzwater, Marlin, 90, 91, 176

food supplies, 21, 56, 108-109, 158, 164-169, 223, 238-240, 248

force; excessive, 16, 36, 70; limits on, 43-45

free fire zones, 43-44, 87

fuel air explosives, 17-18, 20, 86

garbage, 242; see also, sanitation

gas (poison), 79-80

Geneva Convention, 2, 15, 16, 17, 20, 40, 43, 45, 49-50. 57, 91, 92, 211-216, 246

Genocide Convention, 236, 246

Glaspie, April, 12, 66, 250-256

Gonzalez, Henry, 41-42

Grenada, 24, 186

Gulf Peace Team, 99-100

Hague Convention, 15, 17, 20, 43, 95, 246

"Highway of Death," 17, 50-52, 88, 90-93

Hakim, Albert, 96

Hamilton, Lee, 66, 252

Harvard Report, 54, 248

health care system, 21, 54-58, 94-98, 164-167, 240-242

Heller, Jean, 76

high-tech warfare, 84-85; see also, bombing, surgical strikes, casualties, infrastructure

Hilla, 111, 102, 231

historical sites, see archaeological destruction

homes (destroyed), 15, 242-243

hospitals, 99-101, 106, 110-112, 132-136, 166, 227, 229-230; see also health care system

Hong Kong, 274

human rights, 22, 32, 158, 262-153

hunger, see malnutrition

Hussein, Saddam, 13, 24, 30, 63-69, 75, 153, 176-179, 186, 205, 250-256
Hussein, King (Jordan), 69
IMF (International Monetary Fund), 101
impeachment (Bush), 245-247
India, 191
indictment (charges), vii, 9-25, 259, 265
infrastructure (civilian), 8, 14-15, 44-45, 53-57, 77, 112, 212-213, 227
Intifada, 141
intervention (military) 269-270; *see also* Panama, Grenada, Iraq-Kuwait relations
investment foreign, 182
Iran, 10, 187-189
Iran-Iraq war, 63-64, 68, 78
Iraq; ancient history, 146-157
Iraq-Kuwait relations, 63-66, 74-75, 78-81
Iraq-U.S. relations, 12-13, 63-71, 74-74, 250-256; *see also*, provocations, negotiations
Islamic fundamentalism, 182
Israel, 141, 144, 198

Japan, 276
jingoism, 204-205
Jordan, 116
Jordanians, 17
justice; obstruction of, 19
Kellogg-Briand Pact, 40
Kelly, John, 66-67, 252
Kelly, Thomas, 17, 35, 49
Kerbala, 110-111, 102
Kirkuk, 154-155
Kissinger, Henry, 68
Khomeini, Ayatollah, 63
Klare, Michael, 70-71
Korea (North), 174
Kurds, 20, 68, 79, 168, 184-187, 267, 271-272; rebellion, 113-114
Kudistan, 184-187, 205

Kuwait, 10-11, 63-65, 102; oppression of Palestinians, 140-144; and U.S., 67; *see also*, Iraq-Kuwait relations
law, 36, 39-46, 48-49, 362
Lebanon, 144
Libya, 24, 173, 159, 177
life support systems, 21, 34-35, 88, 164-169, 237-239; *see also*, health care system, infrastructure
livestock bombed, 239

Malaysia, 275
malnutrition, 56-58, 106-107, 134, 248
massacres, 3, 4, 15, 17, 30, 50-53, 88, 246
Marines, 159-161
McBride, Sean, 37
McPeak, Merrill, 51-52, 84-85, 87
meat production, 105
media, *see* press
medical care, 21, 56, 95-98, 105-108; *see also*, health care system
medical supplies, 95, 100, 106-109, 132-136, 165, 248
Mesopotamia, 146-157 *passim*
milk, (infant formula), 21, 109, 115, 228
military; aid, 10; build-up 12, 70; presence, 11, 24, 114, 118; spending 70-71
military operations, 85-86, 211, 216; defensive/offensive, 13, 19-20, 75; planning, 75-76
Ministry of Defense (Iraq), 83
Mosques, 230
Mosul, 229

Najaf, 102, 110, 134, 231
napalm, 17-18, 20
National Coalition to Stop U.S. Intervention, 102
NATO, 186
natural resources, 70
Neal, Richard, 44, 87

negotiations, 3-4, 41-42, 220, 270-271
New World Order, 30, 31, 77, 81, 147, 173-175, 205-207
New York City, 174-175
Nicaragua, 11
Nixon administration, 10
North, Oliver, 68-69
al-Nouri, Abrahim, 100, 106, 248
Nuremberg Principles, 15, 17, 40, 52, 217-218, 246

Odeh, Alex, 188
office buildings (destroyed), 105
Oil, 14, 64, 80, 114; overproduction, 75, 252; politics, 10, 70, 186
Omdurman, Battle of, 30
OPEC, 12, 250
Ozal, Turgut, 266ff

Palestinians, 11, 17, 117, 125-131, 139-145, 198-200
Palestinian Aid Society, 102
Pan American Airlines, 189
Panama; invasion of, 11, 18-19, 24, 178-179, 186, 262
peace dividend, 70-71
peace proposals, 13, 70
Pell, Claiborne, 234
Pérez de Cuéllar, Javier, 227
Philippines, 4, 275
Physicians for Human Rights, 248
Pike Report, 68
Powell, Colin, 11-12, 16, 33, 38, 83, 89
poverty; feminization of, 181
pre-industrial age, 14-15, 113, 238
press, 5, 23, 30, 88, 93, 131, 197, 263, 272
prisoners, 140-141
provocations, 11, 63-71, 74-81, 245-46, 247

Qaddafi, Muammar, 173

racism, 176-179, 184
Red Crescent, 228

Red Cross, 130, 228, 248
Redman, Charles, 79
refugees, 20, 242-243, 271
relief agencies, 21, 167-168
religion, 270
reparations, 23
Republican Guards, 50-51
resisters (military), 22, 201-203
retreat (disorganized), 90-93
Roosevelt, Archie, 185
Russell, Bertrand, 39, 46

al-Sabah, 65
Sallal, Saad, 106-107, 132-133
sanctions, 95, 97, 115, 119, 164-169, 223
sanitation (sewage), 14, 53, 240-242
satellite photos, 76-77
Saudi Arabia, 10-11, 64, 69, 75, 182, 193-194
SAVAK, 10
Schwarzkopf, H. Norman, 11-12, 30, 33, 83, 92, 120, 185, 192; see also, military, massacres
Schwarzkopf, H. Norman (Sr.), 185
Senate Foreign Relations Committee, 251
Sikes-Picot Treaty, 1
Sitting Bull, 30
Shah of Iran (Resa Pavlevi), 10, 67-68, 78
Shatt-al-Arab, 63
Sheehan, Daniel, 71
Shiite Muslims, 20-21
Simpson, Alan, 65
Sloyan, Patrick, 3, 30
slant drilling (oil) 65, 74-75, 252
Soviet Union, 76, 78, 173
standard of living, see everyday life conditions
State Department (U.S.), 64, 79, 250-256
stealth bomber, 17, 84; see also, bombs, smart
Summit (Gulf Nations), 255
surgical strikes, 47, 83-89; see also, bombing, infrastructure

Talal, Talaat, 107-108
telephone exchanges, 231; *see also,*
    communications
television, 23, *see also,* press
temples, 152-1553
Third World, 70, 182, 191-192,
    195-197, 201
torture, 117, 125-131, 133-145
Tribunal, 37
transportation system, 14, 94, 97,
    123, 137, 231-244
troop movements, 70, 75-76
Turkey, 4, 185-186, 266-273
Tutweiler, Margaret, 66, 250

UNITA, 11
United Kingdom, 10
United Nations; corruption of, 19,
    36, 37, 42; Charter, 15, 23, 24,
    40-42, 219-220; UN Report, *see*
    Ahtisaari; Resolutions, 42, 91,
    164-169, 176, 233; Security
    Council, 1, 13, 29; Sanctions
    Committee, 95, 167-168;
    Children's Fund, 192; *see also,*
    bribery, sanctions
United States, *see* CIA, Bush, Iraq-
    U.S. relations, Kuwait-U.S.
    relations, military operations,
    State Department

urbanization, 243-244
USIA, 254

vaccines, 239
Vietnam, 68
video of war damage, 233
Voice of America (VOA), 66

war crimes, 2, 9, 24, 40-46, 93,
    217-218
War Crimes Tribunal, 9-10; *see also*
    Commission of Inquiry, tribunal
war simulations, 75; *see also,* Iraq-
    U.S. relations
water, 54, 55, 57, 95, 227; treatment
    of, 21, 95, 240-242
weapons; mass destruction, 17;
    prohibited, 35-36, 45; *see also,*
    bombs, napalm, fuel air
    explosives, anti-personnel
Williams, Pete, 3
Women's Peace Ship, 158-163
workers (foreign), 191-194, 195-197;
    see also, expulsion, Third World
World Bank, 181-182
World War I, 1, 118

Yemen, 13, 193-194

Ziggurat, 152-153, 156

WAR CRIMES

A REPORT ON UNITED STATES WAR CRIMES AGAINST IRAQ

Ramsey Clark and others
report to the Commission of Inquiry
for the International War Crimes Tribunal